Praise for *Transforming Nokia*

Nokia's turnaround is one of the most dramatic corporate transformations in modern history. In 2012, the once almighty market leader in mobile devices was rapidly running out of cash. Most investors had written it off altogether. Yet Nokia managed to defy the odds and, under Risto's chairmanship, is now at the forefront of network technology. This firsthand account reads like a thriller, with behind-the-scenes descriptions of the company's collapse, the courageous decision to shift direction, and Nokia's astonishing reinvention.

Along the way, Risto shares survival strategies and change-management methods he learned by leading through crisis. He explains how the power of paranoid optimism and the precepts of "Entrepreneurial Leadership" build sustainable success. His thoughtful reflections provide tangible lessons for any leader, and his leadership principles apply in both good and tough times.

— **Rich Lesser**, CEO, The Boston Consulting Group

Transforming Nokia is a must-read for business leaders as it serves as both a warning and a practical playbook on how to identify and act on threats and opportunities. Risto provides an honest and mesmerizing first-person view of the dramatic collapse and rebirth of an iconic company. Buy copies for your executives and board members to kick-start the discipline of being "paranoid optimists."

— **Charlene Li**, bestselling author of *Groundswell, Open Leadership*, and the forthcoming *The Disruptor's Agenda*

Transforming Nokia is a personal and powerful story of one of the most challenging and remarkable turnarounds in corporate history: the rebirth of Nokia. In times of continuous change the book is an inspiring reminder for leaders to constantly challenge assumptions, look for opportunities ahead, stay open-minded, and lead with an entrepreneurial mindset—no matter how successful the company is.

— **Jim Hagemann Snabe**, chairman of Siemens and Maersk, former co-CEO of SAP, author of *Dreams and Details*

Real leadership lessons aren't taught in class; they're learned under fire. In *Transforming Nokia*, Risto Siilasmaa vividly recounts how he and his team took an iconic company on the brink of collapse and brought it back to be a global leader in a new industry. It's a remarkable tale, rich with hard-won, practical insights on crisis management, restoring trust, the centrality of culture—and the power of "paranoid optimism."
—**Dominic Barton**, Global Managing Partner, McKinsey & Company

This is a captivating tale of how one of the world's most innovative companies transformed itself once again. Risto Siilasmaa's accomplishments at Nokia should inspire businesses everywhere that need to undergo dramatic change.
—**Adi Ignatius**, Editor-in-Chief, *Harvard Business Review*

Treating people with respect while having critical debates and exploring multiple options is the essence of good strategy making. This book shows in mind-blowing and engaging detail how Nokia's board lifted the company's strategizing to a totally new level.

Risto Siilasmaa is one of the greatest strategic thinkers of our time. He shows in a practical and appealing way how scenarios and data can be used to benefit strategy-making and negotiating. Highly valuable, actionable advice for any business leader. Even for a scholar who has studied Nokia for several years, this book provided new, textured detail of the behind-the-scenes dynamics that made all the difference. What's more, the book develops generalizable lessons from the detailed understanding that will benefit many organizations in the years to come. A must-read for executives, strategists, and scholars.
—CEO **Timo Ritakallio** and Professor **Timo O. Vuori**,
authors of *Living Strategy (Elävä strategia)*

TRANSFORMING
NOKIA

The Power of Paranoid Optimism to Lead Through Colossal Change

RISTO SIILASMAA

with

Catherine Fredman

New York   Chicago   San Francisco   Athens   London   Madrid
Mexico City   Milan   New Delhi   Singapore   Sydney   Toronto

1 2 3 4 5 6 7 8 9   QVS   23 22 21 20 19 18

ISBN   978-1-260-12872-7
MHID   1-260-12872-5

ISBN   978-1-260-12873-4
MHID   1-260-12873-3

Library of Congress Cataloging-in-Publication Data
Names: Siilasmaa, Risto, author.
Title: Transforming Nokia : the power of paranoid optimism to lead through
   colossal change / Risto Siilasmaa.
Description: New York : McGraw-Hill, [2019]
Identifiers: LCCN 2018027537| ISBN 9781260128727 (alk. paper) | ISBN
   1260128725
Subjects: LCSH: Nokia (Firm) | Cell phone equipment industry—Finland—History.
Classification: LCC HD9697.T454 N6566 2019 | DDC 338.7/62138456094897—dc23
LC record available at https://lccn.loc.gov/2018027537

All observations and views presented in the book are the author's personal views and observations, not those of Nokia.

CONTENTS

PART TWO: TRANSFORMING TO WIN AGAIN

(January 2012–April 2012)
*The concepts of entrepreneurial leadership are necessary for any
person and any organization to adapt successfully to today's
complex and dynamic world.*

(May 2012–June 2012)
*The eight rules laid out a framework for how we would operate
and the principles we would apply as we tried to control the chaos
confronting us.*

(June 2012–December 2012)
*Scenario mapping enables you to minimize the likelihood
that you might overlook something important and maximize
the likelihood that you are prepared for whatever scenario
eventually occurs.*

(January 2013–April 2013)
You can win or lose a lot depending on how you play the game.

(April 2013–June 2013)
We worked out a better way to negotiate: the 4 x 4 approach.

ACKNOWLEDGMENTS

THE IDEA FOR this book came from retelling the story of Nokia's transformation multiple times to audiences both in Finland and abroad. The story resonated with all sorts of audiences, from academic groups interested in case study material, to journalists keen on covering something both meaningful and entertaining, to current and former Nokians, to CEOs and chairmen interested in our lessons, and to many other groups. In almost all the events, at least one person would approach me to propose, "You should write a book."

A major reason for me to decide to go ahead was that Nokia's story deserves to be told. It pains me when I hear someone say, "Oh, Nokia is still around? I thought Microsoft acquired you guys."

I also learned so much during these years, and I hope I can share some of those lessons.

Learning is always associated with intellectual honesty, and honesty can sometimes be painful. Culturally, the opposite of a learning culture is a culture where bad news is suppressed, destructive behavior by leaders is tolerated, and experimentation doesn't happen because failure is a punishable offense.

It is not easy for me to admit that Nokia exhibited many of those behaviors. It would definitely be much easier for me personally not to talk about certain details of what happened. However, this is one glass ceiling that needs to be breached. We cannot learn from our past without being honest. We definitely cannot help others avoid our mistakes without being straightforward about our own experience. And we will never build a sustainable culture of competitiveness and constant renewal without being able to cast a critical eye on ourselves. Last, but not least, we cannot document corporate history by deliberately omitting key events and facts.

I have tried to find the best balance of honesty while minimizing references to individuals who were accountable for the deficiencies in our culture and decision making. If I hurt anyone's feelings, I apologize. While I realize some of the events I describe may be sensitive to the people involved, it was never my intention to cause pain.

However, if one company is saved because of the experiences shared on these pages, it was all worthwhile. If a few boards and management teams grow closer and work better together, this would be well worth the effort. If large corporations grow more entrepreneurial, it would be a dream come true. And if small start-ups learn to map out the future in a more systematic way, this book will have made a difference.

Everything I have written is solely based on my experiences. I take full responsibility for the content, and all the opinions are my own. Despite exhaustive fact-checking involving tens of people—thank you all so much—I am sure there are still some (my hope is they are small) mistakes in the book.

Before I try to give credit to people who have done all the hard work, I must make a grammatical comment that, funnily enough, is based on an aspect of my personal business philosophy. When we wrote the first draft for the book, I sometimes used "it" and sometimes "they" when talking about a company. This is obviously at best inconsistent and, at worst, confusing. When our copyeditor pointed this out, I realized that we had used "it" for companies that I did not know well and "they" for companies whose management teams I knew personally.

The reason I love business is that it is all about human interaction. Companies never do business, only people do business. (AI perhaps is starting to become an exception, but more about that later.)

It feels almost disrespectful to think of Microsoft as an "it" when one knows the people calling the shots. I just cannot write "It accepted our terms," when I know that Steve Ballmer and his team had done the thinking and made the decision. It has to be "They accepted our terms."

We tried using only one of the pronouns consistently, but the outcome just did not feel natural. In the end we reverted to the way we originally wrote it. I hope you can live with both "it" and "they" now that you know the logic behind the inconsistencies.

We always learn when we do something for the first time—and that includes preparing acknowledgments. I had always smiled when reading acknowledgments where the authors thank everyone, as if they had just won an Oscar. Now I understand better. There are so many people who deserve to be mentioned in this story about Nokia, but adding a lot of names would have made the book a harder read. The number of unsung heroes in this story is large. These people persevered year after year under the most difficult circumstances and still retained their capacity for humor and their ability to take risks and think outside the box. I cannot come close to naming all of you, and for those of you who are not mentioned by name, please know that it has been a true privilege to work with you.

Transforming Nokia relied on the efforts of many people. I did not do nearly as much as you might think after having read the story. There is an unfortunate tendency to personalize events and outcomes, both good and bad. In all things good, the people listed below deserve all the praise.

Therefore, thank you (in a semirandom order) Louise Pentland, Stephen Elop, Janne Laakso, Scott Simpson, Timo Toikkanen, Jo Harlow, Olli-Pekka Kallasvuo, Kai Öistämö, Timo Ihamuotila, Maija Taimi, Henry Tirri, Riikka Tieaho, Juha Äkräs, Tero Ojanperä, Juha Putkiranta, Marko Ahtisaari, Kristian Pullola, Janne Vestola, Jarmo Kurri, Marcus Boser, Gary Weiss, Rajeev Suri, Hans-Juergen Bill, Maria Varsellona, Marc Rouanne, Basil Alwan, Bhaskar Gorti, Federico Guillen, Marcus Weldon, Kathrin Buvac, Barry French, Ashish Chowdhary, Henri Tervonen, Minna Aila, Michael Daly, Jussi Koskinen, Elsi Hilari, Tuukka Seppä, Steve Ballmer, Brad Smith, Philippe Camus, Timo Lappi, Todd Schuster, Donya Dickerson, and numerous other wonderful people, whom I had the privilege to work with.

Thank you to my board colleagues (in an approximate order of seniority): Bengt Holmström, Marjorie Scardino, Keijo Suila, Georg Ehrnrooth, Henning Kagermann, Helge Lund, Kari Stadigh, Jouko Karvinen, Bruce Brown, Betsey Nelson, Jean Monty, Olivier Piou, Louis Hughes, Edward Kozel, Jeanette Horan, Sari Baldauf, and many others.

I also need to thank all the "Fellows" from F-Secure. You taught me what I know about entrepreneurship.

A special thanks to my assistant during these years, Irma Huotinen. I could not have done this without her.

I wrote this book together with Catherine Fredman. She claims I could have written the book without her, but it would have been a different book, and worse in all respects. Thank you, Catherine, for the partnership and all the laughs we have had during the journey.

And most important of all, thank you Kaisu, Nella, Mikko, and Jesse.

ON THE BRINK

. . . .

Our mobile phone revenues were almost in free fall.
Our investors were starting to categorize Nokia shares
as non-investable. The press was speculating about
the timing of the Nokia bankruptcy.

. . . .

I OFFICIALLY BECAME chairman of Nokia at the Annual General Meeting (AGM) on May 3, 2012. Over the course of my career, I had conducted lots of press conferences and been interviewed by the media hundreds of times. This press briefing was different. My head may have rationalized that I could handle things. My body thought otherwise. As I walked into the conference room, my head was surprised to find that my knees were shaking.

I couldn't help flashing back to my first Nokia AGM four years earlier. That one, too, was held at the Messukeskus Helsinki, Finland's largest convention center. Back then, board members arrived in a parade of individual chauffeured limousines. TV cameramen and photographers swarmed us, madly clicking away as if we had personally beaten the Russians in the Ice Hockey World Cup, then topped it off with a Nobel Prize. Thousands of people packed the auditorium.

Nokia in 2008 was on top of the world. In the late 1990s, Nokia had emerged from obscurity to become a powerhouse in the hottest new industry of the time: mobile phones. Its phones had cutting-edge technology and sexy designs, and people around the world were gobbling them up. By 2000, Nokia accounted for an astonishing 4 percent of the Finnish GDP, and it generated nearly a fifth of Finland's exports.[1] Nokia made as much money as *all* the other companies in Finland combined.[2]

Under the leadership of Jorma Ollila, the company's legendary CEO, Nokia had stronger global brand recognition than Toyota, Walt Disney, or McDonald's.[3] One analyst said, "Nokia was to mobile as Kleenex was to tissue."[4] "Not since the sauna have the Finns produced anything as popular as the Nokia mobile phone," gushed *Time* magazine in 2001.[5]

Year after year, newspaper and magazine articles routinely referred to Nokia as the "tech wunderkind"[6] powering the "Finnish miracle."[7] Business experts extolled "the Nokia Way."[8] The company seemed unstoppable. By the time of my first Nokia AGM in May 2008, Nokia owned just over half of the global smartphone market.[9]

Even more significant was Nokia's influence on Finland's global identity and how Finns viewed themselves. Nokia showed the world that we were smart and hip. When I was invited to join Nokia's board, I was thrilled to be part of this shining circle.

By 2012, though, the mood at Messukeskus had darkened.

Apple had introduced the iPhone in June 2007, and as successful as Nokia had become, it wasn't prepared to compete against Apple's touchscreen smartphone. It wasn't a question of technological prowess: Nokia's own smartphones had more features than the iPhone, and they were housed in a case sleek enough to slide into a shirt pocket and so tough that owners proudly boasted that even after accidentally backing their car over their beloved device, it still functioned just fine. Even as Apple improved its iPhones and Google launched its Android operating system in 2008 and Research in Motion (RIM) surged ahead with its BlackBerry, a technological challenge was something Nokia should have been able to answer easily.

But it hadn't. And as the months went by, one opportunity after another was missed. Nokia was still the dominant name in the industry, but it gradually became clear to me that something prevented us from reacting properly to the new competitive situation.

On the board, I was going through my own evolution. My initial starry-eyed admiration had given way to questions and confusion, then doubts. While Apple and Google were growing market share, attracting the brightest talent, and investing in the future, our market share was contracting, and we were laying off employees and reducing investments. Yet there was little concerted action in board meetings to systematically dig for the root causes of the constant failures to catch up. There was little discussion about finding new paths or leaders brave enough to take them. Concerns about our strategy were not taken seriously and alternatives not analyzed or even discussed, at least not in board meetings. My own attempts to start such discussions were brushed aside.

Was this how the board of directors of a best-in-class company worked? I didn't want to believe this was the best we could do.

But as the crisis deepened, as our faith in management forecasts became increasingly weak and our results got even grimmer, my doubts shifted to dismay and a growing dread.

Why wasn't Nokia able to react? Were its leaders incapable of accepting the mounting evidence that something fundamental was wrong? Were they unable to speak up or unable to listen?

As just one person—and the most junior member—on the board of directors, I felt an almost physical pain because I had neither the access nor the authority to instigate the kind of systematic, fact-finding deep dive that would have enabled me to understand *what* was happening and, more importantly, *why* it was happening. The board did not have visibility and therefore no real understanding. But it was also not doing anything to change that.

In the four years that I had been on the board, I had seen the company lose over 90 percent of its value. That spring of 2012, we issued two profit warnings over two quarters. Our operating loss was over €2 billion during the first half of 2012. Our mobile phone revenues were almost in free fall. Only a year after laying off 10,000 workers, we were planning another round of painful layoffs, the biggest in the company's history. Our share price was an agony to watch; it was barely €3, down from about €28 when I joined the board.[10]

The adulation at the 2008 AGM had turned into outright antagonism by the 2012 AGM. People at all levels of the company were frustrated, anxious, and scared. Our core investors were starting to categorize Nokia shares as non-investable. The press was speculating about the timing of the Nokia bankruptcy.[11]

As a member of the board of directors, I was seen to be at least partly culpable for Nokia's failure. Now as the newly elected chairman of the board, I was truly accountable for whatever happened next.

The enormity of the responsibility I had assumed suddenly hit me. From that day forward, I represented the Finnish face of Nokia—to everyone but especially to my fellow Finns. If things turned out badly, I would be blamed by my country forever.

How had I gotten into this mess? And how did we get out?

This book will reveal the story of Nokia's near death and its dramatic reinvention and revival. To all those people who assumed that Nokia would follow Motorola, BlackBerry, and other former shining tech stars into oblivion: You were wrong. Today we are among the top two players in the high-value global digital communications infrastructure market. Over the four years from 2012 to 2016, the value of our business increased more than 20 times, faster than many high-flying start-ups.

Our culture, too, has been transformed. Out of some 100,000 employees today, fewer than 1 percent held a Nokia badge in 2012. We're an almost entirely new Nokia.

I have been an entrepreneur all my life. I believe that the only way for any organization, large or small, to adapt successfully to today's complex and dynamic world is by adopting an entrepreneurial mindset. During my 18 years as CEO of F-Secure, before I joined the Nokia board of directors, I honed my ideas about what I call "entrepreneurial leadership": what it means to be an entrepreneurial leader and how to bring out those qualities in all people, whether they're in charge of a company of many or a company of one.

At Nokia, the precepts of entrepreneurial leadership served as our compass through chaos, helped us respond rationally when it would have been easy to panic, and continue to guide the company today. They kept me and the management team on course as we negotiated the deal that saved the company, and guided a badly beaten-down organization as we came up with a new vision for the future, constructed a strategy to implement the vision, chose the right organizational structure to drive the execution of the strategy, picked the best CEO and management team to lead the organization, and built the balance sheet we wanted to achieve.

At the same time, those precepts enabled us to stay flexible enough to adapt to constant change when the conventional way of doing things would have sunk us. Entrepreneurial leadership means assessing the resources available to you and using them in the best possible way to improve your company's performance and competitiveness. That's why even though I stepped in to serve as CEO for eight months during our massive reorganization—and could probably have continued in that position—I recognized that I was not the best CEO for the company we were becoming and willingly stepped away again. Our present CEO is much better than I would have been.

Entrepreneurial leadership is also about learning—about viewing every challenge, every problem, every piece of bad news as an opportunity to learn and improve. I learned a lot.

I learned to see through the sparkle of a hugely successful global corporation to spot the signs of trouble that could bring it down. I learned that being paranoid enough to always plan for the worst-case scenario actually enables you to be optimistic about opportunities. I learned that especially in complex circumstances, trust both greases the gears and is the glue that holds everything together. I learned that accountability, like trust, must be constantly reinforced. And I learned that once you have constructed a solid foundation based on these lessons of entrepreneurial leadership, you can become brave enough to dream big—maybe even bigger than you ever imagined.

I learned the pragmatic skills and tactics to implement these lessons.

I also learned about luck. We were hugely lucky and should always remember that. This was the only period in my life as a business leader when we undertook a sequence of big decisions and three massive transactions—including the sale of Nokia's core mobile phone business to Microsoft, the purchase of complete ownership of Nokia Siemens Networks (NSN), and the acquisition of Alcatel-Lucent—and even with the benefit of hindsight, I would not change any of those decisions in any meaningful way. It is rare to be able to say that, and I'm sure I will not experience this again.

That's why I am even more paranoid than before. The more paranoid we are, the harder we will continue to labor to shift the probability curve in our favor and the more optimistic we can afford to be.

Not every organization may face a situation as complex and life-threatening as the one that confronted Nokia, but I can guarantee that every leader will encounter plenty of challenges that are complicated and unpredictable. Whether you're managing a team or a corporate division, leading a small firm or a multinational corporation, heading up a start-up company or steering a solo practice, and whether you're running a business that is on the rocks or sailing along smoothly, the lessons I'll share will help you sharpen your foresight, expand your options, reinvent—if necessary—yourself and your organization, and enable you to thrive no matter what changes tomorrow brings.

· ·

A Word About the Lessons

This book is divided into two parts. Part One (Chapters 1–8) covers the period when I first became involved with Nokia as a software supplier and later joined the board of directors. In these chapters, I explain how both the board and management could have seen what was happening sooner, as well as what they could have done differently to prevent Nokia from going off course. Part Two (Chapters 9–18) covers the period after I became chairman. Those lessons are directly based on my experience of taking charge in a crisis, seeding resilience and renewal, and steering Nokia's transformation.

· ·

PART ONE

THE TOXICITY OF SUCCESS

1

THE NOKIA MAGIC

1988–2008

. . . .

Nokia was an industry titan that was leading the world
into the future. I needed to learn from their example.
I wanted to learn their secrets.

. . . .

WHEN I WAS growing up in the 1970s, Finland felt like the last place
you'd think of as a source of high-tech innovation. Our largest companies were in the wood and pulp business, and the fact that Finland
has a lot of trees and enough people to cut them down doesn't make
anyone a high-tech genius genius. So in 1988, when a fellow student at
the Helsinki University of Technology and I started an IT consulting
company, we weren't sure where the venture would take us.

I was just a 22-year-old student majoring in industrial economics. I
had chosen my specialization for the simple reason that it was the most
difficult to get accepted into and I liked the challenge. As it turned out,
it was a great preparation for an entrepreneurial career.

I was crazy about computers. I had bought my first computer—
a Commodore 64—when I was a teenager with the money I made
stuffing advertising leaflets into mailboxes in apartment buildings in
Helsinki. I was especially enamored with the early adventure games
and wanted to create a program that would beat Zork, the best adventure game at the time. When that didn't work—my program filled five

disks and it became obvious to me that my aspiration did not agree with my available hardware—I wrote an article explaining how to create an adventure game and sent it to a computer magazine. It turned into a multi-part series, and soon I was writing for Mac magazines, PC magazines, and magazines for computer games.

The company that became F-Secure started as an exercise in a short university course called "Founding a Company." In one exercise, students paired up to do the paperwork required to register a company. I still had the goal of writing a piece of software that would be used all over the world. My partner had also worked with computers for a number of years, including consulting for large firms. We thought it might be fun to start a real company. So we submitted the forms not just to the teacher but also to the Finnish trade registration office. We were in business! A couple of months later, my friend landed a permanent position in a company that enabled him to finish his thesis and stay on as an employee. I was alone and in charge.

Creating My Ideal Company

I had to learn everything the hard way. During the first five years, I took on pretty much every job in the company at one point or another. I did the bookkeeping, which was really useful later on, because you learn to understand the company's finances in a different way when you're the chief financial officer and chief accountant. I also did the hiring, paid the bills and salaries, wrote our distribution agreements, negotiated the distribution deals with our partners, was involved in coding applications, wrote some of our software manuals, translated them into English, and designed the first box we sold them in. I was the tech support person, so when our international partners had technical questions, they called my phone number. We couldn't afford a cleaning service, so I took turns to vacuum the floor and occasionally scrubbed the toilets. I don't think there was any task I did not do at some time and no part of the company I didn't know.

The early 1990s were a struggle for F-Secure and for Finland. When the Berlin Wall came down in 1989, my country was so dependent upon trade with the Soviet Union that its collapse sent Finland's economy into a tailspin. The resulting depression was one of the worst economic crises in our history, even worse than the Great Depression of the 1930s.

All my energy was focused on trying to keep F-Secure alive. I worked 16-hour days and only paid myself when there was money left after paying everyone else. As there were no venture capitalists in the country and banks were practically out of business, we had to finance all our investments from cash flow. To pay for our R&D, we wrote articles for computer magazines, trained people to use office software, did customized software development, and spoke at conferences. No customer was too exotic and no task too far from our core for us, as long as it brought in cash.

Talent was at the core of our hiring, and I believed that how we treated our people drove our growth. I considered all the people who worked at the company to be my colleagues, not my subordinates.

I wanted to create a very flexible, aspirational culture where people felt there was nothing we couldn't experiment with to make the environment even more attractive to top talent. Finnish companies at the time didn't offer free cappuccino to their employees; many did not offer free coffee. We were different. We had a pool table in the lobby, a full-time masseur, and a BMW convertible sports car that was lent to the employee of the week.

That period also defined my thinking about leadership and strategy. Without a boss, I had to teach myself the theory of what constitutes good leadership and the science behind what makes a good strategy. As my own boss, I got to experiment with putting those theories into practice. Somehow F-Secure survived, and grew rapidly. I learned valuable lessons about both leadership and strategy that would guide me—and Nokia—in the turbulent years ahead.

A Bug in the System

Finland didn't have many multinational companies in the early 1990s. When I started internationalizing F-Secure, now a cybersecurity product and services company, I tried to hide the fact that we were a Finnish company. Our corporate brochures were printed on paper back then, and I always listed our sales office in San Jose, California, as the first office location, so that people would think we were a U.S. company with headquarters in Silicon Valley. Our Finnish address showed up somewhere far down on the list.

But as the 1990s progressed, Nokia made us proud to be Finnish. At F-Secure, we now proclaimed that our headquarters were in Helsinki.

I was thrilled when in 2000, we convinced Nokia to contract with us to build an antivirus app for their proprietary Symbian Series 60 operating system for smartphones. Through our affiliation, my obscure company picked up some of Nokia's sparkle. It felt good. And as a young entrepreneur whose company had only recently gone public, I was eager to learn how a large, global corporation operated.

To get a sense of what was involved in building the app, I have to explain how a computer works. The apps that people use are programmed to operate on an underlying system that handles all the nitty-gritty details of dealing with the hardware. This platform is called the operating system (OS). How it is designed determines to a large extent how productive it is to write apps for that particular platform.

If you think about the lifetime of any complex piece of software as a living tree, a healthy system has a thick trunk and preferably no branches. That's because each branch in the code requires a specific group of developers to work on that separate version of the system, sapping energy and resources from the main code line. The trunk is the version that always serves as the basis for future releases; the branches are one-offs to serve a short-term purpose.

That's why it's preferable, for a device maker, to make the operating system the center of its universe. Developing and enhancing the software should take priority; work on hardware innovations should exist in parallel to the operating system, but not have automatic jurisdiction over the OS.

This is how Microsoft thinks about Windows, how Apple views iOS, and how the Linux community develops Linux, which became the basis for the Android platform. For those entities, the operating system was and is the center of their universe. To their way of thinking, the software comes first and the hardware—all the devices that run that operating system—comes second. You try to avoid customizing the basic operating system for one particular device model, especially if the customized changes won't work for any other devices. A branch in the code is a kind of dead end.

Oddly, though, Nokia didn't think about Symbian that way. Rather than pruning branches to strengthen the trunk, Nokia allowed the Symbian tree to sprout in different directions. That approach might have made sense back in the early 1990s, when Nokia was laying the groundwork for its industry dominance in mobile phones. Back then, the software portion was quite small for any device, and much of the competitiveness was built via the hardware. As the codebase was small, it was easily manageable and not a big effort to customize for a given device model.

But by 2006, Nokia was introducing a dozen different Symbian devices a year, and each new model was often customized with device-specific software. There was a maddening amount of duplication, obscure idiosyncrasies, and overall confusion. Instead of a well-defined tree, Symbian was an intricate—and, to many, impenetrable—hedge that caught and trapped everyone who came in contact with it, including F-Secure.

F-Secure also created security programs for Windows, Linux, some Unix variants, and Apple's Macintosh products, but working with them compared with Nokia was like day and night. And Symbian was just the tip of an iceberg of difficulties.

Nokia's legal processes were slow and bureaucratic (like those of many other global companies). Nokia's sourcing seemed to be interested only in squeezing out the lowest cost from the software providers, rather than creating an enduring partnership that could enhance the product's functionality. That struck me as the wrong way to act when an innovative product like software is such a crucial part of your end product.

I often reminded myself that Nokia employed thousands of Finland's—and the world's—best and brightest minds. Surely the company had a better understanding of the situation than I did. After all, I was only one entrepreneur of a small, relatively unknown company, and Nokia was an industry titan that was leading the world into the future. I needed to learn from their example. I wanted to learn their secrets.

The Second-Worst Partner for Start-ups

In 2005, Olli-Pekka Kallasvuo, Nokia's CFO who had also served as chairman of F-Secure from 2001 through 2004—I had asked him to join our board in order to bring more credibility to F-Secure for our initial public offering—invited me to speak at Panorama, Nokia's flagship internal training program for up-and-coming senior leaders. This was a tremendous honor, especially because among Finns, Nokia executives were regarded as above and beyond other businesspeople.

I decided to present my concerns and see how they would respond.

To bolster my credibility, with the help of a VC friend I asked a group of the top names in the global venture capital business to rate large technology companies—IBM, Hewlett-Packard, Microsoft, Sun, Nokia, and a few others—from the perspective of their portfolio companies. For instance, I asked, "If one of your start-ups is considering partnering with, say, IBM over Nokia, how does that affect your evaluation? If the start-up is determined to partner with Nokia, is that a positive or a negative?"

The findings reinforced my own experience: Overall, Nokia was the second worst of the large technology companies for a start-up to partner with—only Oracle ranked lower—and the delta was pretty big between Nokia and the others.

I feared I'd be shown the door, but to my surprise, my presentation got top ratings. These were smart, open-minded people who understood the importance of honest feedback. It was with a huge sense of relief that I returned to the F-Secure offices. These managers clearly understood that Nokia needed to change the way they dealt with their ecosystem partners, I reported to my colleagues. Our working relationship, I predicted, was sure to improve.

But nothing happened.

The Invitation

Over the next three years, as our collaboration continued, Nokia consolidated its leadership position in the mobile phone industry. No other company could come close to its market share. Its ability to pump out profits was the stuff myths are made of. Despite my frustrations, I was immensely proud to help a Finnish company achieve global dominance in such an unprecedented way.

When Jorma Ollila called late in 2007 to invite me to join the Nokia board of directors at the Annual General Meeting on May 8, 2008, I was thrilled. I was only 42 years old and I'd have the chance to be part of one of the world's top companies. I had stepped down from the F-Secure CEO position in 2006—after 18 years in the same role, I felt I wasn't learning anymore—and had more time to spend on my start-up investments and public company boards. I felt I could contribute something valuable and help Nokia better understand the software development community. Perhaps I could even help Nokia become a favored partner for software developers.

I was so excited that it was hard to wait for the first board meeting. A little voice kept interrupting my thoughts: I was going to be on the board of directors of Nokia!

. . . .

What Does a Board Really Do?

For those of you who are not very familiar with how corporate boards work, here is a short introduction. In Chapter 10, I will discuss how I would like to see a board function, but I will stick with a generic description here.

Each board is different, of course. The board is shaped by the current directors and the practices passed down from previous boards. However, there are certain universal tasks that boards undertake.

The board represents the shareholders of the company (with some exceptions in certain countries where the board represents other stakeholders, such as employees, as well). That is why board members are typically elected by the shareholders in a general meeting.

As representatives of the company's shareholders, the board's most important duty is typically considered to be the hiring and firing of the CEO. This is the biggest reason for an independent chairman. It is a little more challenging for the board to continually evaluate and, if necessary, fire the CEO if the CEO is also the chairman, although these companies usually appoint a lead director who has certain specific duties to minimize the downsides of a joint CEO-chairman role.

The second most commonly mentioned duty for the board is the approval of the company's strategy. Not the *creation* of the strategy, but the *approval*. Boards take various different approaches to this. Some are actively involved in designing the strategy together with the management team, and some only get involved when the time comes to approve it.

The third most important duty is ensuring that the company is well managed. This often relates to working with the auditor to ensure that the company's books are correct and that the processes related to the company's administrative functions, such as finance, legal, human resources, and accounting are of sufficient quality.

The fourth relates to setting the compensation practices for the company and, especially, for the executives of the company.

Boards usually do not meet more often than once a month, with the average being probably around six times a year. Individual meetings might take three hours each for small companies and two days for large ones. The amount of topics covered in a single meeting can be very high with hundreds of pages of pre-reading.

For new board members, it often takes eight to twelve months to start feeling they understand the company's business sufficiently.

Many of us have heard boards mentioned in a negative tone. (The boards of companies such as Enron, Tyco, or HP come to mind.) Or our impression may be based on movies in which a sleek bunch of cronies rubber-stamps the villainous proposal of a crooked CEO.

The truth is that the vast majority of boards are nothing like these. For every bad board, there are numerous good boards, working hard on behalf of their shareholders. There are great boards, too, who build tremendous shareholder value but rarely take any credit. Those boards happily give all the credit to the management team even if, sometimes, the successful ideas were generated in the board.

Board members are usually chosen for their deep knowledge in a certain area or their experience in running companies. Collectively, the board members should have expertise in all the areas relevant for the particular company and its business area. But despite their expertise, boards are composed of human beings, subject to human emotions and the full spectrum of human behavior.

. . . .

2

DAZZLED BY THE SPARKLE

2008

. . . .

This was like no agenda I had ever participated in.
But I was surprised by one item—or, rather, by its absence:
We spent only a few minutes talking about Apple.

. . . .

FROM THE FIRST Nokia board meeting I participated in—immediately after the Annual General Meeting (AGM) in May 2008—I felt I had entered a different world. It was a world that included some of the brightest stars in the corporate universe, and I was eager to absorb their leadership lessons.

Jorma Ollila was one of the primary reasons that I was so thrilled to be on the Nokia board of directors. Only 42 years old when he was appointed CEO in 1992, he bet that a bloated conglomerate staggering on the brink of bankruptcy could revive and reinvent itself by concentrating on the emerging industry of mobile communications. Now 58 and Nokia's chairman, Jorma was at the peak of his power and popularity. Some Finns encouraged him to run for the country's presidency.

Outside of Nokia House, the curved glass-and-steel headquarters overlooking the Gulf of Finland, he was the face of Nokia's success. The Nokia miracle was largely attributed to his leadership. Having read about him in scores of articles and interviews, I felt tremendous respect for his achievements and was eager to learn as much as possible from him. I hoped I could one day call him a friend.

Inside Nokia, he was an almost mythic character—equal parts revered and feared. Jorma cultivated a serious demeanor, usually wearing a conservative dark suit, a stylish but unremarkable tie, and professorial tortoiseshell glasses. He didn't laugh much and rarely joked. In the boardroom, he sat at the head of the polished wood table, his place embellished with a gavel and a silver name plate, an unquestioned ruler on his throne.

At the table at Jorma's left sat Marjorie Scardino, the vice-chairman, the CEO of the Pearson Group, and the first woman to head a FTSE 100 company. Dame Marjorie—she had been honored as a Dame Commander of the Order of the British Empire—matched a warm smile with a no-nonsense attitude and a sharp mind.

On Jorma's right was Bengt Holmström, one of the premier economists in the world. A professor at MIT, he had frequently been mentioned as a possible Nobel laureate (and would, in fact, win the Nobel Prize in Economics in 2016). Bengt combines a kind heart with a formidable intellect. There is not a bad bone in his body.

Another person I respected was Henning Kagermann, the former CEO of enterprise software giant SAP and the only other real tech person on the board in addition to me. Henning was a professor by background and a refreshing deviation from the standard CEO mold.

And so it went, in descending order of seniority, with each assigned seat identified by a name plate. Mine was at the foot of the table. I was the most junior board member and, at 42, the youngest by a good 10 years. I sat there with big round eyes, trying to take it all in.

When I joined the Nokia board, I was already the chairman of F-Secure, as well as Elisa Corporation, the largest Finnish teleoperator, and had served on a number of other boards during the past decade. I had grown F-Secure, taken it public in 1999, enjoyed the tech bubble's expansion and suffered its crash, been forced to lay off people I had hired, and crafted a new strategy that brought us back. I'd helped Elisa repel a hostile takeover attempt that involved deceptive board members, public knife fighting in the press, eleventh-hour brinksmanship, and a last-minute solution that, astonishingly, was honorable, acceptable, and enduring.

I'd seen a lot. But the Nokia board was different from anything I'd experienced.

Some differences were immediately noticeable. For instance, there was a dress code. In contrast to the sartorial sloppiness that was a point of pride in Silicon Valley, Nokia's male board members always showed up in well-pressed business suits and ties. I may have been the first man ever to attend a Nokia board meeting without a tie. That created some minor waves, and Jorma let me know that he noticed my deviation from the custom. (I persisted in dressing in a more relaxed way some of the time, although not because of trying to make a rebellious point or because it felt more comfortable; I actually believe that a more casual dress code encourages a more open and productive discussion environment as well.)

Then there was the way in which the board conducted business. I was accustomed to vigorous debate and detailed questioning. In contrast, the atmosphere in Nokia's boardroom reminded me of the genteel British gentlemen's clubs portrayed in old movies. There was a thick veneer of tranquility as topics were raised, briefly summarized, then calmly ticked off the list.

And what a list! At that May 2008 meeting, the day after the AGM, the agenda included, among other items: the fallout from Microsoft's $44.6 billion bid for Yahoo!; competing mobile phone manufacturer Motorola's decision to seek a buyer for its declining devices business; Sony Ericsson's difficulties with the joint venture that was supposed to boost *its* devices business; corporate responsibility and environmental strategy sessions; a quick review of Nokia's three-year strategy document with the encouraging prediction that Nokia's global devices business (which encompassed both conventional mobile phones and smartphones) would grow 22 percent from €40 billion to €49 billion in three years; a quick strategic overview of Nokia Siemens Networks (NSN), our joint venture with Siemens into the telecommunications equipment and services market; and Project Vineyard, a proposal to find a new investor for NSN.

The material was several hundred pages long. Some of those pages were so full of numbers that it took half an hour to fully understand a single page. For a new board member, this was like trying to drink from a fire hose.

(*A note about NSN*: Nokia Siemens Networks was created in 2007 in a merger between Siemens's networks business and Nokia Networks largely because the investments in 3G and 4G wireless mobile tele-communications technology were too expensive for either company to take on its own. The strategy aimed for NSN to be the most profitable infrastructure vendor by 2011; yet although NSN was only a year old, the profitability goal was starting to look extremely challenging if not downright impossible. In order to pull ahead of competitors Ericsson, Alcatel-Lucent, and Huawei, NSN would need to be able to acquire other companies and/or put massive amounts of money into R&D. Siemens was reluctant to pony up any more. A third investor willing to buy in for 20 percent—10 percent of Siemens's share and 10 percent of Nokia's—could break the impasse.)

This was like no agenda I had ever participated in. The numbers alone were mind-boggling. I sat there listening to talk about house-hold-name competitors and buying and selling portions of huge busi-nesses and getting new investors to cough up a billion-plus euros. It was all on a scale I had never dealt with before. I felt way out of my depth and just tried to float on the surface of the discussion.

But I was slightly surprised by one item—or, rather, by its absence: We spent only a few minutes talking about Apple.

A Fad or a Threat?

Apple had introduced the iPhone in June 2007 with its customary fanfare. Standing in front of the roaring crowd at MacWorld, founder Steve Jobs dismissed competing models that used a keyboard or a stylus, announcing, "We're going to get rid of all these buttons. We're going to use our fingers."[1] I watched that announcement remotely on a small screen. I felt that I had just seen the world's best product launch for the past, the present, and the future.

Nokia's board didn't appear to be worried. Mobile phone sales were booming; in some emerging markets, customers didn't even bother using the term "cell phone"—they just asked for a Nokia. Profits were steadily rising and revenues constantly growing. Nokia's earnings were so reliably consistent that when other tech companies' below-expectation quarterly numbers caused stock markets to waver, Nokia's announcements would calm investors and stabilize the market. So resonant was the impact of the Nokia effect, I later learned, that Olli-Pekka Kallasvuo, Nokia's CEO at the time, felt an actual responsibility for the stock market as a whole, not just for our performance in it.

The smartphone was a new world, but the people at Nokia felt it was already theirs. In fact, they felt they had even more of a claim because Nokia had invented the smartphone years earlier and quickly commanded more than half the global smartphone market.[2]

(*A quick explanation of the difference between smartphones and mobile phones:* Unlike mobile phones or feature phones, which are built from cheaper components and come with limited functionality, a smartphone runs on an operating system that allows third parties to provide software applications for it. In other words, its operating system is a platform for others to innovate on. Nokia had such a platform in its Symbian S60 operating system. A smartphone is basically a full-blown computer combined with wireless connectivity and delivered in a handy size.)

Nokia had smartphones with a QWERTY keyboard and a number keyboard; smartphones that could download and play music; smartphones that played audio and video and included an FM radio tuner; smartphones that could send and receive multimedia messaging and e-mail; and smartphones with cameras and video capability. The phones had organizer functions and other business crowd-pleasers, as well as a global positioning system with street-by-street navigation help from Nokia Maps.[3] When *Popular Science* and *Fortune* magazines compared the iPhone and Nokia's N95, launched two months earlier, both magazines proclaimed Nokia's model the hands-down winner.[4]

Consumers, investors, even the press all loved Nokia. In their eyes, Nokia was doing everything right and could do no wrong.

And that was the message at the May board meeting. Apple had the merest fraction of the overall market: In the first quarter of 2008, Apple had shipped 1.7 million devices versus Nokia's 115 million devices (which included both smartphones and feature phones). Nokia owned 40 percent of the global market volume share in mobile devices, followed by Samsung at barely 15 percent.[5] (Volume share is what most people think of when they see the term "market share." It measures the proportional share of total sales in a region, country, or the global market measured in number of units.) Motorola, once a giant, was fading fast. BlackBerry, although the darling of business buyers, was just a blip on the screen. Apple was lumped under "Others."

Nokia also ruled the smartphone space, commanding 44 percent of the global market. Blackberry, although the darling of business buyers, hovered around 15 percent.[6] Apple had barely 5 percent.[7]

In short, there were many reasons to label the iPhone a fad: The volumes were minuscule, the features subpar. Calls were dropped so frequently that the rumor was that many people carried two devices—an iPhone for e-mail and a conventional cell phone for voice calls. It didn't support copy/paste functions or MMS to shoot off photos. Unlike bombproof Nokia devices, the iPhone flunked Nokia's "drop test," in which a phone is dropped five feet onto concrete from a variety of angles. The iPhone rolled out a great launch, but the target group of customers didn't even seem as big as BlackBerry's, which had a very tight market among business users.

And yet: At that May meeting, Nokia's market capitalization was $111 billion. Apple's, due to the expectations of future growth, was $151 billion. Just five months earlier, the two companies' market caps had been just about equal at roughly $150 billion.[8] The markets were casting a vote against Nokia. Could it be that Apple was a bigger threat than Nokia's leadership believed?

Maybe the Nokia board members had talked about Apple in a previous meeting. Or maybe the chairman planned to dedicate a few hours to exploring the issue in a future meeting. Still, I was puzzled. I would have expected us to have spent more time on the topic.

The Symbian Trap

Our July board meeting took place in London, at the five-star Berkeley Hotel. The meeting proceeded in a manner that I later learned had been the routine since Jorma had become the chairman. Jorma opened the meeting with a summary of the current state of global economy. I was a little surprised that he was holding forth on the subject when one of the world's leading economists was sitting right next to him. But as far as I can remember, Jorma never asked Bengt to comment. And Bengt showed great restraint and pretty much never said a word.

The main topic on the agenda was Symbian.

When Nokia began developing smartphones, it partnered with Ericsson and Motorola to acquire an operating system developed by Psion and together form a company called Symbian. In order to make Symbian a standard platform with as wide a reach as possible, the Symbian partners wanted to attract many companies to that platform. So instead of owning the operating system, as Apple did with its iOS or Google did with Android, Nokia chose to make Symbian a joint indus-trial effort among all the main competitors in the mobile phone market. (Nokia repeated the successful GSM formula where competitors united behind a single standard to the benefit of all.)

Creating a global smartphone OS standard divided the pie among the players but allowed the pie to grow so fast that the individual slices were bigger than anyone dared to dream of in the first place. In addition, it made sense for Nokia specifically, by forcing all the Symbian partners to play by the same rules. As the companies were competitors and each company had its own idea about how the operating system should be developed, this naturally led to some splintering of the OS into distinct— and occasionally—rival sub-platforms and user interfaces. Still, as long as everybody played by the same rules, no one could disrupt the game.

By constraining competition to a box that Nokia knew really well, the competitive dynamics favored the biggest player in the box— and that was Nokia. Nokia was the first to introduce a true Symbian OS phone in 2000, then followed it up with a new user interface for the Symbian OS called the Series 60 (later renamed S60), which was licensed to other manufacturers to enable them to adopt the platform and further expand Nokia's reach.[9]

For the short term, the Symbian strategy was brilliant!

After a few years, though, Nokia was so dominant that it threatened the other partners in the joint venture. From their point of view, letting Nokia get what it wanted was dangerous, even when what it wanted made sense to all parties. From their point of view, preventing Nokia from taking big steps forward in Symbian's development was some-times prudent. From *their* point of view, hurting Nokia helped them competitively.

By July 2008, Nokia was by far the giant in the market. But now there were viable alternatives—Microsoft's Windows Mobile, Apple iOS, Android (to be launched that fall)—and each was owned by a sin-gle company that could push the technology forward as fast as it could.

Meanwhile, the Symbian OS was in such a sorry state that it sty-mied innovation instead of accelerating it. Symbian devices were noto-riously cumbersome to use with confusing menus, numerous options and settings, and a multitude of confirmations required by the user whenever something new was done with the device. Users were buying Nokia devices, but they were also complaining.

The partnership that had provided Nokia with a great solution against traditional competitors turned out to be a tremendous hin-drance in a disruptive situation when quick and dramatic actions were necessary. Furthermore, it actually invited disruptions: Years later, I read that Steve Jobs claimed that the delta between the current smart-phone usability and what was possible was so large that the temptation to enter the market was impossible to resist.

Nokia was trapped in a catch-22: Nokia needed to own all of Symbian in order to accelerate its development, but allowing Nokia to control 100 percent of Symbian would not be in the best interests of the other owners, because Nokia was their biggest competitor. To convince the others to give up control, Nokia came up with the idea of the Symbian Foundation. The Symbian code would be open-sourced, so everyone would be guaranteed similar access. Nokia would fund the foundation by buying out the other parties and donating what it just bought to the foundation. The goal of the foundation was to provide royalty-free software and accelerate innovation.

It was an improvement but not ideal. Too much time had been already lost, and more would be lost before the foundation would be functional. The damage had been done when the joint venture was established. Speed was everything, and a committee of competing companies did not easily agree to anything one of the parties proposed. Furthermore, Nokia still thought of the operating system as the slave of devices, rather than the master of the mobile universe.

It wasn't that Nokia didn't do the right thing; it was that it did the right thing for too long. Putting the hardware over the software had been the right approach for simple mobile phones. In the smartphone era, though, things had changed. Software, and especially the operating system, i.e., the platform, now defined competitiveness.

Shifting to Software

In fact, Nokia had already begun to shift its point of view. At the meeting, a presentation showed a growth in R&D investments from €2.9 billion in 2007 to €3.5 billion in 2009, and much of that growth went to software development. A new smartphone operating system based on Linux was in the works. This would be Nokia's most advanced operating system and was expected to replace Symbian over the next decade. The PowerPoint slide promised that the combination of software specifically optimized for a robust user experience and Nokia's acknowledged expertise in hardware would put us smack in the market sweet spot.

To achieve that would require focused commitment from top management and flawless execution. But that's what Nokia was famous for.

Competition in the smartphone market was heating up. Apple had just launched a 3G iPhone.[10] 3G phones had been in the market for quite some time, so Apple was late. Moreover, so much was still missing from its device: There was only one backward-facing camera, and it was of poor quality; there was no video-recording capability, no memory card slot, no changeable battery; and—the greatest flaw, to Nokia's thinking—there was no keypad model available. Nokia still believed that touch was just one form factor among many and that to win in the market, one had to support all major form factors.

As well, the first Android phone was expected to hit the market in the fourth quarter. T-Mobile's G1 would combine full touchscreen functionality with a QWERTY keyboard.[11] How seriously should we take Android?

An Eye-Opener in Beijing

On September 15, 2008, Lehman Brothers declared bankruptcy. The United States immediately plunged into financial crisis. In Europe and Asia, however, it was still pretty much business as usual; European politicians and central bankers were confident the turmoil would stay on the other side of the Atlantic. Yet there was a weird sense of breathlessness as we waited for the economic repercussions to hit.

It was a Nokia custom to hold one board meeting a year in a topical market and invite the spouses of board members to join. For the October 2008 meeting, Jorma chose to take the board to China.

I was looking forward to it. New board members, I had discovered, actually had a very limited opportunity to learn about the company. Between the daylong board meeting in May, the July meeting in London, which lasted five and a half hours, and an hour-long conference call in September, we had spent a grand total of two working days together as a board over a five-month period. I was eager to spend several days with my colleagues. And as a bonus, I would get to learn more about China, one of Nokia's most important markets.

While I understood that Nokia was a big deal in Finland, the board meeting held in Beijing really opened my eyes to Nokia's global stature. When Nokia started investing in China in the early 1980s, most Western high-tech companies used China solely as a base for low-cost manufacturing and did their advanced R&D work elsewhere to prevent the theft of valuable intellectual property. Nokia took a different approach and made complete product lines in China, with our complex in Beijing encompassing manufacturing, R&D, and everything in between. Nokia became the biggest exporter in the Beijing region, the flagship for a high-tech foreign company in China.

China was already the world's biggest internet market, with more internet users than the United States,[12] and Nokia was surfing that wave. Nokia had a huge market share in China—over 40 percent of mobile phones and a jaw-dropping 70 percent of smartphones[13]—and the Chinese market was growing so fast that our factories could barely keep up with demand. Nokia wasn't just the leading mobile device brand; it was crushing the competition with over 50 percent of consumers preferring to buy a Nokia compared with barely 10 percent who wanted a Samsung or Motorola, the runners-up.

We board members felt as if we were honored guests of the state. Whenever we moved from our base at the Ritz-Carlton Beijing—suites for all board members and their spouses—a fleet of sleek black Audi A8s, *the* status car in China,[14] was lined up in front of the hotel, white-gloved chauffeurs smartly standing at attention. We weren't just driven to the factory—we swept through the broad avenues of Beijing in a motorcade. The only thing missing was little Nokia flags fluttering from the hoods, but, in fact, those would have been almost redundant. I saw Nokia signs everywhere—on billboards, in storefront windows, on street kiosks. I couldn't look in any direction without spotting the familiar dark-blue logo.

After our visit, a police car escorted our motorcade to the airport, where the panoply of power continued all the way back to Finland. Jorma had booked a private jet and invited all of us to hitch a ride. Jorma's Gulfstream was another sign that I was now part of a new world, the world of a corporation that literally had money to burn on aviation fuel. The whole trip—the private jet, the police escort, the fleet of Audis, our spouses accompanying us, the Ritz-Carlton suites, the universal respect and attention—was a dazzling display of Nokia's wealth and influence.

I was definitely dazzled.

A Question of How and Why

There was just one niggling doubt that wouldn't go away.

When I joined the Nokia board, there were many things I was excited about learning from the world's best businesspeople. At the top of my list was how to do strategy. Nobody has perfected the way to create a winning strategy: It's as much an art as a science. I expected that the board would spend a lot of time on strategy. Nokia was so successful that I assumed there must be a clear, almost causal, process to explain *how* we would win and *why* we would win in some areas, and *why* we would not even try to win in others. For me, this was the holy grail, and I couldn't wait for it to be revealed.

Five months in, I was still waiting.

Nokia's three-year strategic objectives had been outlined at the May board meeting. Its vision of the future was a world in which everybody and everything is connected. To maintain a leading role in this world rested on three elements, with seven strategic objectives:

- Make the best mobile devices to:
  - Take market share and drive value
  - Enhance and capture market growth in emerging markets— which we were already doing
- Emphasize context-enriched services to:
  - Differentiate by enhancing everything to do with people and places, such as mapping and content
  - Deliver a winning user experience
  - Take a larger share of the business mobile market, the lion's share of which belonged to BlackBerry
  - Maximize monetization potential through advertising
- Strengthen the trusted consumer relationship by:
  - Maximizing the consumer lifetime value to Nokia

It made sense, but it seemed superficial and pretty vague: more of a list of objectives than a clear explanation of how we would achieve them and why that approach would not just work but would win. "Deliver a winning user experience": Without an explanation of why we hadn't been able to do that so far, how we could change course, and why we would be able to do things differently in the future, this was just an item on a wish list.

When people say, "We want to do this," that's the *what*. When they say, "We will take these three steps to do this," that's the *how*. But then we need to ask, "*Why* will that be enough? *Why* haven't we done it before? *Why* will we be able to do it this time?" The *why* forces us to face a deeper level of logic. It demands a more pointed discussion. In my book, *why* trumps *what* and *how* every time.

As the months progressed and the board meetings proceeded in their atmosphere of almost otherworldly calm, the *why* continued to be absent.

I would have loved to have spent more time digging deeper into the reasoning behind the decisions. But the meeting agendas were already full, there was a ton of material for each board meeting, and, I reminded myself, the best professionals in the world were creating the agendas and managing the business. Maybe my point of view was too entrepreneurial and too invasive. I was still a complete rookie. I would learn.

"Things Were Very Different"

By the time of the board conference call on November 26, 2008, it was clear that the financial crisis had spread across the globe and the world was teetering on the edge. The market for mobile phones had dropped a sickening 11 percent, and everyone was suffering: Sony Ericsson reported its first quarterly loss in five years; once-mighty Motorola, suffering from massive losses, abandoned the Symbian platform and made a desperate jump to Android; and Nokia's market cap slumped from $67 billion to $53 billion in just a matter of weeks.

There was no ignoring the fact that things were very different from when I had joined the board just six months ago. In addition to the uncertainty of the financial crisis, the competitors were changing. As OPK (which was what Olli-Pekka Kallasvuo was often called) wrote in his monthly letter in September, "It seems that just yesterday Motorola was our greatest concern. Then RIM emerged, and then Apple, and now Google."

At the end of the third quarter, Nokia still boasted over 40 percent of the global smartphone volume market share, followed by RIM at nearly 16 percent. However, Apple had tripled its market share over the previous year and was now nudging 13 percent,[15] and was aggressively rolling out the iPhone in country after country. Would the future winner be a touchscreen or a QWERTY keyboard or some combination of the two? Nothing was certain.

Nokia was well positioned to weather both storms—the financial crisis and the new competitors. The company was extremely profitable, with huge economies of scale, a distribution channel reaching to all corners of the globe and far surpassing anything the competitors had, a research arm that was bigger than anyone else had or could afford, and a management team that had continued to increase profits year after year. Even if the iPhone was a new kind of a competitor, it still lacked a lot of key features. It could be beaten. The first Android phone was just about to ship, and it could well be a flop. Nokia just needed to execute well and it should continue to do fine.

Among the board members, there was a "don't rock the boat" feeling. With the financial crisis putting everything in jeopardy, the management team had so much to do just to navigate through the turbulent waters. From the board's point of view, the only question was how to best support the management in the crisis.

. . . .

Learning to Lead with Paranoid Optimism

I never had a boss. So I didn't have the luxury of working for a great leader or the experience of working for a really bad leader. I had to teach myself what is good leadership and how to implement it, and what is good strategy and how to create it. Over time, as I observed what worked, what didn't work, what seemed right, and what felt comfortable, I formed a holistic framework for the way I wanted to implement leadership.

At some point, I had a "eureka!" moment, when I understood that there was something very fundamental in what I found to be working. That crystallized into the concept of paranoid optimism.

Paranoid optimism combines vigilance and a healthy dose of realistic fear with a positive, forward-looking outlook expressed via scenario-based thinking (something I'll describe in more detail in Chapter 11). Being paranoid is a good way to hone your antenna and those of the people you lead, but a steady diet of paranoia is demoralizing and unhealthy unless it's balanced by the optimism inherent in identifying and exploring alternative scenarios.

Paradoxically, optimism is a direct consequence of paranoia. Because you are paranoid, you're more likely to have foreseen all the worst-case outcomes and thought of how to prevent them. Because the people around you know you'll be asking them to think about those scary scenarios, they are not shaken by bad tidings because they've already thought through what they will do to mitigate the new situation.

From a leadership point of view, if you're not an optimist, you can't energize people. But if you don't also help them preempt downside scenarios, the company will not build true resilience.

In essence, because you are paranoid, you can afford to be optimistic. And optimism grounded in reality is something people look for in a leader, especially during a crisis.

In 2008, few people would have forecast a crisis for Nokia. But I often think that in business, we all drive cars where the front windshield is a giant rearview mirror. There's a small opening in that mirror through which we can look forward, but in general, we are so focused on the historical metrics that we have little ability or inclination to search for direct information on what lies ahead; we are satisfied with indirect information gained by extrapolating from past data. And when everything you see in this giant financial rearview mirror is great, how can you begin to understand that, actually, your fundamental competitiveness has already dramatically decreased over the last several years?

In your right mind, you would never want to drive such a car. But we run huge businesses with exactly that approach.

All companies should be focused on forward-looking indicators. They should look for past data that best correlates with what will happen in the future. Financials, however, are one of the worst indicators. Customer satisfaction, for instance, is much better. Customer perception of the difference in velocity between improvements in your competitiveness and improvements in your competitors' competitiveness might have even more predictive power.

Paranoid optimism leads directly into scenario-based thinking. It can be daunting to collect the huge amount of real-time information required to constantly test and validate your scenarios. However, artificial intelligence (AI) offers a powerful tool to automate and deepen this analysis. With the power of today's data analytics, you can gather all the possible historical data and automatically identify the metrics that have historically best predicted future market share. With machine learning, you can create a self-learning system that continuously predicts your future market share based on the latest data. In some cases, you can use data science to create or identify new scenarios. There is no reason not to try to do this.

The point is, you have to find a way to break through the mirror to get a true view of reality. And the more successful you currently are, the more you should strive to do this. Success is toxic and tempts you to be satisfied with using past metrics.

You need to do this over and over and over so that you can spot the road signs pointing out potential disasters ahead before they show up in your rearview mirror. Paranoid optimism is how you do it.

At Nokia at that time, the view was only optimistic. Many people knew of some of the problems, but because bad news was collectively suppressed, no one was able to connect all the dots. Very few signs of paranoia penetrated the windshield. We were driving blind.

. . . .

3

MIXED SIGNALS

JANUARY 2009–JULY 2009

. . . .

In a crisis, companies may fail to identify separate events and
mistake all as a single causal dynamic. One easily ends up
treating leukemia by applying a cast to the left leg.

. . . .

ONCE APPLE'S TOUCHSCREEN smartphone was recognized as a
serious competitor, Nokia launched a high-priority program to introduce its own first touchscreen device as soon as possible. The Nokia
5800 went on sale in January 2009. The press hyperbolically called it
the "iPhone killer."[1]

The 5800 was a mid-range device. It was much cheaper than the
iPhone, and its resistive screen technology forced users to press down
pretty hard for the device to sense their touch, as opposed to noncha-
lantly swiping Apple's capacitive touchscreen. Except for the display, it
was the best the company could do, but it wasn't designed to beat the
iPhone. And customers soon knew it.

Early in 2009, I was visiting New York and made a point to visit
Nokia's flagship store on Fifth Avenue. The product displays were
attractive and the sales staff were knowledgeable and helpful, but I had
the place almost all to myself. My next stop was the Apple store just
up the street. I could barely maneuver through the crowds thronging

the aisles. The alarm bells that had been tingling in my head for many months started to toll louder.

The news was not good at the Nokia board meeting held at the end of January 2009. Sales of Devices & Services (D&S) in the fourth quarter of 2008, which included the all-important holiday bump, were 29 percent below forecast, a huge miss. The year-over-year decline was an equally gut-wrenching 27 percent. The term "D&S" encompassed all our devices—from cheap cell phones to high-end smartphones—and the accompanying services, such as messaging, e-mail, music, navigation, and so on, so these double-digit declines punched right into Nokia's core business.

The Q4 decline paled compared with how 2009 started. Years later, Olli-Pekka Kallasvuo still remembered how the Nokia CFO called him in early 2009 and said, "I have got a sobering number for you." Our January D&S revenues had declined by 53 percent from January 2008.[2]

On one hand, it was easy to explain away some of our poor performance because of the financial crisis. Every industry got burned. Less easy to explain was why some competitors, especially the new ones, did better than we did. Was that somehow related to their smaller market share? Did the crisis treat the market leader more brutally than a smaller fast-growing new entrant?

Regardless of the interpretation, we were facing a very uncomfortable situation. It is bad enough to decline year-over-year, but it is devastating when you are completely surprised by the magnitude of the drop and have not been able to prepare. The impact resonated all the way up the distribution channel. Our factories had churned out devices according to what we thought the demand would be and shipped them out anticipating that they would be gobbled up by hungry consumers. When those sales didn't materialize, the channel was clogged from the stock rooms of retail shops to the warehouses of local distributors to the master distributors' massive shipping centers. The product surplus meant that no one would order new devices until the old ones started to move, so manufacturing ground to a halt. Worse, because Nokia booked revenues when we shipped devices to the channels that had no right to return unsold devices, no shipments meant a drop in revenues for the first half of 2009—a double whammy.

"The outlook is now clearly more negative than only a couple of weeks ago," OPK wrote to the board members. "It is obvious we need to accelerate our opex cuts, both short and long term."

Cutting opex—operating expenses—entailed killing projects and shutting down eight factories. A lot of people worked in those factories and on those projects, so this was a big move affecting many people and causing turmoil throughout the organization.

And while it would save money, it wouldn't address the key issue: Consumers were buying, but they weren't buying enough *Nokia* devices.

Chasing the Horizon

Nokia's annual planning cycle started early in the fall. In September 2008, Nokia still expected sales volumes to grow moderately in the first half of 2009. When the November sales data came in, the expectations for the first half of 2009 were pruned to 8 percent growth—a very modest amount. The December sales data caused expectations to be slashed to a 15 percent decline from the previous year. With each month's disappointing results, management responded by proposing deeper cuts.

We were doing what I would call "chasing the horizon." When the market changes, it is typical to underestimate the change. You end up reacting in several steps, each one more severe than the previous. But it still feels that nothing is enough. No matter how fast you run, the horizon always remains far away, tantalizingly out of reach.

From my place on the board at the time, though, it was like being blasted by a tornado. There was so much debris swirling around that it was hard to see clearly enough to assess whether the steps taken by management were sufficient. So many issues demanded attention, all at the same time. Apple's app store had hit 10,000 apps, twice as many as Nokia's—could we catch up? The Symbian Foundation was scheduled to launch on March 1, nine months after the decision to set it up. Nine months is an eternity in this business. The cost of the Symbian joint venture for Nokia's competitiveness just kept piling up. To top it all off, Nokia D&S was undergoing a major reorganization into five business lines, but no one was sure how the planned opex cuts would affect whose budget and things ground to a halt.

Those were just some of the big items; there were plenty of smaller ones, too.

What's the right course of action? Under these circumstances, people tend to panic and instinctively try to protect themselves by reacting to the most obvious problem—in this case, by cutting expenses to appease the shareholders and analysts. I am not saying there is necessarily anything wrong in cutting costs. Often, cost cutting is absolutely needed. But if management reacts by cutting costs because it does not know what else to do and wants to be perceived to be active and on top of things, the prognosis for the company is not good.

I've since learned that when you're trapped in a tornado, the worst thing to do is think *only* about the crisis at hand. No matter how difficult it is to see beyond the immediate maelstrom, you have to force a focus on understanding the root cause behind the crisis. Even when the root cause (financial crisis) seems obvious and completely external, a deeper analysis may reveal weaknesses and mistakes on your own turf (Symbian challenge, customers having alternatives with real differentiation, cultural weaknesses, etc.). In a crisis, companies may also fail to identify a number of separate chains of events and mistake all as a single causal dynamic. If that happens, one easily ends up treating leukemia by applying a cast to the left leg. And the problem is not that the leg might not be broken—it is—but no one looked for more serious long-term illnesses once the obvious ailment had been identified. (I'll provide some ideas on how to achieve this broader perspective in Chapter 9.)

At Nokia, we should have been considering the possible scenarios: How likely was it that the touch phone would become the dominant smartphone platform? What would we need to do right now to compete in that reshaped landscape? Were we investing in the right products and technology platforms that would enable us to succeed in the future? What was the real status of those development programs?

If Nokia hadn't been profitable, the way forward would have been clear: Make whatever cuts were necessary to stay alive. But we entered the crisis while we were still bringing in a lot of cash.

We weren't the only company suffering in the wake of the financial meltdown—Samsung, RIM, LG, and Palm all issued profit warnings—but we were in better shape than our competition: We were still expecting a healthy €2.2 billion in operating profit for the first half of 2009 even while forecasting a 12 percent drop in revenues year-over-year and expected to beat the market consensus. We had the time and resources to explore alternative scenarios and invest in different pathways.

But that wasn't the agenda at the January board meeting. Instead, the focus was on the short term—as people often do when in the middle of a crisis.

A Guest at the Wrong Party

At the Consumer Electronics Show (CES), the enormous industry show-and-tell held each January in Las Vegas, Symbian was still powering LG, Samsung, and Sony Ericsson devices. Apple was there, of course. Very few Android devices were on display.

At the January board meeting a few weeks later, the Markets unit, which was in charge of sales, marketing, manufacturing, and logistics, presented its strategy for 2009 and 2010. The snazzy-looking slides with rah-rah slogans proclaimed, "We *must win* in these areas," and touted "ultimate convergence offering" and "community services." I struggled to understand what they were talking about in practice, what we had to do, and what steps we had to take to achieve it.

What *was* clear was that our lead devices were still largely based on physical keyboards.

At CES, all the highlighted product announcements from our competitors had celebrated their full-touch products. Even with the 5800, we weren't part of the party.

At the board meeting on March 19, 2009, we learned that Nokia forecast a further 25 percent decline in revenue for D&S year-over-year. We had lost 70 percent of our market cap over the last 12 months.

We could find consolation in reports from the field which, citing a drop in Apple's market share in the fourth quarter of 2008 and the first quarter of 2009,[3] claimed "Apple is running out of steam." Nokia's smartphone value share—the amount of revenue from Nokia smartphones compared with its competitors' sales of similar products—was down to 27 percent, but it was almost twice that of Samsung, the closest competitor at 17 percent, and much, much higher than Apple's. We were still the undisputed king of the mobile devices market.

Into the Symbian Tunnel

Soon enough, Nokia came out with devices that were mechanically equal to the iPhone. But while the physical design of Nokia's smartphones was streamlined, its Symbian operating system was anything but.

There were many aspects of Symbian that our users did not like. One of the most irritating was the series of repetitive approvals asked of users when they tried to get basic things done. For instance, when you installed a Symbian application, it often forced you into a multi-step, yes-no dialogue about whether you really wanted to install the application, were you aware it could cause data charges, did you know this might generate some extra costs, were you sure you still wanted it, and so on. These irritating software prompts were forced on Nokia partially because of its operator customers, such as AT&T and Verizon and Telefonica. The operators were paranoid about end users complaining about extra billing, so they insisted they—which meant Nokia—needed to ask permission from the user. But most users didn't give a hoot about the reason. All they cared about was that a clunky operating system asked for permission every time you connected and sometimes you had to click "yes" nine times to make the application load and start.

Apple didn't ask those questions. It didn't have to. As the newcomer with no preexisting relationships with operators, Apple could dictate the rules, and rule number one was ease of use for customers. If one operator didn't agree to the terms, tough luck—Apple would find another that did. Once the iPhone started to sell so well, Apple could say to any operator, "This is our contract template. If you don't sign it, your competitor will. Take it or leave it." Eventually, they all took it. Consequently, Apple users could do many things on their phones much quicker and easier than what had previously been possible.

Nokia didn't feel it could easily stand up to the operators, nor did it feel it needed to, so the company was stuck playing by *their* rules.

This is the traditional catch-22: When you are doing well, you can rationalize not fixing irrational aspects of relationships with your partners or customers because clearly, you are doing quite well even without everything really making sense. Also, you are scared your customers will vote with their feet, ruining the short-term results and everybody's bonuses. When things turn south and the things that used to be merely irritating become destructive, you may feel that in your weakened state, you cannot afford to pick the fight required to straighten things out.

At F-Secure, I had long known about and struggled to resolve Symbian's complications. Now, it seemed, everyone knew that Symbian was a beast. But now consumers had another option—and they were choosing it.

"Challenged from Many Directions"

A slide that was presented at our March board meeting encapsulated our situation: "We are challenged from many directions," the headline read. It listed the key areas of weakness: "Service satisfaction is below that of competitors" in games, photos, maps, downloaded apps, and, especially, music, where only 34 percent of Nokia users were satisfied compared with 78 percent of the competitors' customers; "we are losing share in the low end" in both volume and value share of cheap mobile phones; "and we are losing share in smartphones"—again in both volume and value share. The dismal conclusion: "While competition takes profits, ours are declining." And the gaps were getting bigger.

The contrast between us and the new competition was stark.

Apple and Google were starting from scratch in the smartphone universe. They could use the latest technology and forge new alliances. We were weighed down by a load of bad legacy: old code, out-of-date architectures, compromising contracts, and development teams spread around the world using different tools and speaking different languages, all held together by rubber bands and chewing gum.

Apple made simplicity a core strength. It initially released one device per year with one form factor and one environment. It could marshal its resources behind a unified user experience: All the application developers could focus on one uniform device family, and the same app would work on the previous year's model. Nokia had multiple operating systems and several versions of each, all rife with incompatibilities. We had QWERTY keyboards, full-touch screens, and slider screens, not to mention a boatload of different screen sizes. Just changing the screen resolution may force the application developer to do some customization; customizing all the applications for each of these form factors was a horrendous experience for the developers. All those separate devices spawned confusion among our marketing and management teams. And because of the fragmented architecture, we were investing far less for each of these domains than Apple spent for its one domain, even though our overall investment was significantly higher.

Apple and Google were able to create a new business model in which they weren't held hostage by preexisting relationships with operator customers. Nokia was in thrall to the carriers. If we planned to do something they didn't like, such as improve the user experience by reducing the number of prompts, at least some of them threatened to cut us off.

If Nokia had announced that the smartphone was a new game with new rules, some operators might have penalized Nokia, but the majority, despite initial complaints, would eventually have fallen into line. But Nokia didn't push the change, so the operators saw no reason to change, and Nokia ended up trapped in a software dead end.

This translated to the real strength of the Apple franchise: the developer ecosystem. Providing a good user experience meant increasing numbers of users. More users meant more buyers for third-party software, which meant strong revenues for the developers, making it attractive for more and more developers. More developers meant more apps, and more apps made the devices more attractive for users, leading to further growth in the ecosystem for all participants. Once the virtuous circle starts, it is very difficult for competitors to get it to turn in the other direction.

Nokia could not compete.

Culturally, we were locked into the old way of working, with hardware taking center stage and the operating system in a supporting role. And emotionally, Apple and Google were growing, recruiting, and investing. They were bursting with positive energy. Nokia was declining, laying people off, and constantly thinking about which project could be killed in order to tighten the belt another notch. Short-term profits trumped long-term survival.

The bell was tolling for a generational shift. It was no consolation that our traditional competitors were much worse off than we were. Sony Ericsson and Motorola were getting killed. New competitors like Apple and RIM were rising; RIM's quarterly results ending in February 2009 showed a jaw-dropping growth rate of 84 percent and gross margins of 40 percent.

The upstarts were driving the old kings to extinction. And this was before Android had truly gotten traction.

How Bad Can It Be?

The board of directors wasn't blind. But there was no general sense of urgency. Despite the circling competition in smartphones, there was plenty of good news. Nokia still held the incumbent's advantage in conventional handsets. We sold roughly 15 phones *every second* 24/7.[4]

As board members, we were constantly being told in multiple ways in every management presentation that nothing was irrecoverably wrong. A plan that would fix the issue was already being executed. There was no reason to take a deep dive into the situation, because it would soon be fixed. In any case, a culture of taking deep dives into topics of concern did not exist, so the board remained blissfully ignorant of the state of the true competitiveness of the company. (And there always truly was a plan, and it was truly being executed. What we failed to do was find out what the root causes of the challenges were and, once that was understood, whether the plan addressed those root causes.)

We took our cues from Jorma. He often explained to us how much time he spent focused on Nokia's affairs, so the board naturally believed that he was very much aware of all the details. He did not implement any changes in how the board worked. Therefore, it seemed obvious that, in his expert opinion, management had things under control and the board was already doing everything necessary.

The agenda for the board meeting on April 23 listed 15 topics to be covered in 4 hours, a brain-numbing romp that allocated barely 15 minutes per topic on average. Only one had anything to do with long-term competitiveness, and that focused on the Navteq mapping unit. It was ninth on the agenda, a signal that it wasn't really very important.

The next day, we gathered for the annual strategy meeting. The presentations looked and sounded highly professional: lots of flashy terms like "irresistible solutions" and "vibrant ecosystems" were being thrown around, and promises that "we will create an attractive business case for developers" were made without explanations of how to achieve this. There was a climactic proclamation: "We have started one of the most important transformations of Nokia: to become a consumer-led solutions company."

I had little idea what that meant in practice.

The sort of thing I *did* understand wasn't happening. There was no real, let alone rigorous, competitive analysis. What were we doing differently or not as well compared with what Apple, RIM, or Google was doing? If necessary, we should have allocated a day to focus on each company, bringing in people who had worked for those companies and who understood technology to describe the different approaches to product design, marketing, and management models.

The new market demanded a new type of talent, so we should have explored the differences in leadership and technology capabilities. Nokia had lots of hardware experts, but that really wasn't the game anymore. The question was whether we had the necessary expertise in the world of apps and software.

We should have given our engineers and design people iPhones and BlackBerries and Androids, and encouraged them to let their own fingertips reveal the difference in the user experience. But as I would discover a year later, employees in general were not given a choice: They all got Nokia devices, and the use of iPhones was frowned on even if people paid for the phones themselves. How could they know how good the iPhone user experience was if they were not allowed to experience it themselves?

I'd been on the board for a little over a year now. That might sound like a long time, but it was just seven meetings—not that many to understand a complex company in a complicated industry going through a rapid transformation and coinciding with a crisis threatening the existence of the global financial system. During that time, more and more cracks had shivered across my mental picture of Nokia's omniscience. More and more often, I found myself surprised and confused by what I was seeing and hearing at board meetings.

Until this time, I had been struggling to understand the conflicting signals I was receiving. On the one hand, our new competitors were marching rapidly forward and fighting with weapons we could not match. On the other hand, we had huge strengths of our own and our management was constantly executing plans to bring us back to the top. If I had to describe my thoughts in one word, I would use "confused."

During the spring and summer of 2009, I moved from being confused to concerned.

Issues that struck me as critical—such as the fact that our product launches regularly fell behind schedule and we constantly missed sales targets—weren't treated in the board with the seriousness I thought they deserved. Don't misunderstand: The chairman, and the rest of us, clearly criticized the misses. Everyone was feeling the pain. But we were not even trying to break out of the cycle of bad news coming in, the board demanding fixes, management explaining the recovery plan that it was already executing, and the board moving on to the next topic on the agenda.

The next meeting followed the same pattern, and the next one, and the one after that.

Reorganization Whiplash

My concerns mounted at our July 22 board meeting.

The fact that Nokia had been named the most environmentally conscious company for a record-breaking six times in a row was highlighted by the management as a sign of our strength. But while green values are important to people, they clearly didn't influence their buying preferences.

We heard that Samsung and Apple had good second quarters. The iPhone 3GS had launched at the end of June and sold more than a million units in just three days after its release—a stunning figure back then. Revenues for Nokia's Devices & Services unit were down 28 percent year-over-year.

Symbian troubles continued to sabotage our ship dates. But there was another culprit for our declining results. In an attempt to boost profitability, Nokia chose to use older, i.e., cheaper, components to increase its gross margins. Our components were outmoded by the time the devices were scheduled to hit the street; the shipping delays meant they were practically ready for the dust bin as soon as they came out of the box.

The double whammy couldn't have come at a worse time. While many of Nokia's latest devices ran on 600-MHz processors, advertising from competitors hit us where it hurt most. Samsung was touting an 800-MHz processor—33 percent higher than ours. HTC topped Samsung at 1 GHz. Apple's marketing slogan was "Two times faster and more responsive" than the previous iPhone model.[5]

Reorganization whiplash was a constant companion. In large companies, when a decision is made to change direction and reorganize, it takes time for the orders to filter down to the people on the ground and turn into action plans, and even more time for change to take effect. Whiplash occurs when people have just started to move in the new direction and have barely got up to speed, then they're told that a new decision has been made to shift in a yet another direction. It's like what happens when you crack a whip: When you snap the handle down, the tip of the whip goes up; when you snap it up, the tip goes down. But snap it back and forth quickly and the tip will flip around uncontrollably. In organizations, people don't know which direction to go in or which instructions to follow. Everything gets scrambled, often at exactly the time when clarity and concerted action are called for.

The board presentation slide read, "Active preparation for selecting the D&S operational mode continued and high-level decisions were made." In plain English, that meant chaos.

While the reorg matrix charts looked good, they failed to explain how the company would be managed in practice. If the board couldn't figure it out, I could only imagine how incomprehensible the charts would seem to employees.

The forecast for the second half of 2009 was once again upbeat. Although our market share was down year-over-year, our product portfolio—led by the 5800 "iPhone killer" and the Eseries smartphones—had recovered from its slump. There was positive momentum to support the prediction that our value share would start growing again.

But from which area? We had devices selling well in many different parts of the portfolio: the 5800 touch device; the N97—a true mobile computer with a touchscreen that slid up to reveal a QWERTY keyboard; the 6700 traditional mobile phone; and the E71, a BlackBerry-type QWERTY device. Three out of our four bestsellers were keyboard devices. At the same time, after two years, we were catching up from the surprise of the iPhone. We had seven different touch devices coming out in 2009, although their price points—and margins—were much below the iPhone's. And, of course, their user experience was hamstrung by the Symbian platform.

The final presentation was by Henry Tirri, Nokia's chief technology officer, who ran the Nokia Research Center. Nokia employed more than 500 researchers in six labs in a dozen locations around the world, from China to India to the United States to Cambridge, England, to Helsinki. Henry's report sparkled with the fairy dust of imagination becoming reality: We were investing in nanotechnology, software radio, data analytics, new battery technologies, even a phone that could be wrapped around your wrist.

Among the board, this display was oddly reassuring. We thought, "Nobody else can afford to invest as much in future-oriented research." It validated our faith in the Nokia Way and the economies of scale we had achieved. We had wallowed in the waves of the financial crisis, but we were a huge company, and once we regained our momentum, our size would enable us to surge forward and succeed where others struggled.

Lunch with Jorma

Once or twice a year, Jorma invited me to lunch in his private meeting room in Nokia House. The large airy room on the eighth floor had all the trappings of power: warm wood paneling, a fireplace, and picture windows framing gorgeous views of the Gulf. There was a small adjoining kitchen where the meal was prepared; it was served by a waiter, who presented us with a menu and then the dishes.

I did not know Jorma well, so it was with some trepidation that I walked into these meetings. It was common knowledge that Jorma assiduously cultivated his public image. During our 2009 meetings, Jorma typically complained that the press unfairly criticized him for Nokia's lack of progress, while the CEO was given a soft ride. Mostly, though, I got the impression that he wanted me to validate his own point of view. If I said something critical about the wrong topic, he would snap, "Risto, you come from a small software company. You just don't understand how a global company the size of Nokia works."

How could I argue without sounding arrogant? There were very few tech companies the size of Nokia in the whole world. So I just swallowed and he'd move on to the next topic on his agenda.

I was not as interested in how we were perceived externally. I was worried about the meanings hidden in our internal data: *why* Nokia's financials were falling. You can't fix disappointing numbers by focusing only on the numbers; you can only fix them by figuring out the reasons for the slump. I felt I had to raise my concerns.

"Something doesn't seem right," I said at our lunch. "I know the management team is hard at work on fixing our issues, but we're constantly late in shipping products, we typically drop several key features from each launch, and we cannot seem to be able to forecast our sales even for the ongoing quarter."

He didn't disagree, which gave me the courage to continue.

"I probably don't understand," I said, trying to sound respectful. "But it seems to me that we may be missing the big picture of what is happening. We're not having the deep discussions with management and among ourselves that would give us a clear understanding not just of what's happening but of how we might be able to fix it. We have failed to invest sufficient time analyzing technology and competitors."

Jorma visibly stiffened. Perhaps taking my comment as a personal rebuke of his skills as chairman, he snapped, "Risto, you need to remember that you come from a small software company. You just don't understand how a global company the size of Nokia works. The board cannot become operational."

Perhaps that's true, I thought. But I began to wonder if our unwillingness to truly find out what ailed us was the right approach. We were accountable to what would happen to the company. We could not remain half-blind spectators.

. . . .

Three Questions That Reveal the Right Facts

Nokia was heading toward disaster; we know that now. However, it is often very difficult to see that in the boardroom. The higher you ascend in the hierarchy, the more removed you are from the action. The farther you are from the front lines, the more filters the information will go through before it reaches you, and the more likely it is that you will be the last to know what's really happening.

The big challenge for any board member is to learn what's really going on in the company and the industry. A board member is almost entirely dependent on the information provided by the management team. If certain topics are not addressed, the board will not learn about them. The board may not even realize that the topics exist.

Many of these dynamics apply to all teams and, especially, to new team members or a new team leader.

In today's fast-moving business world, you may not have the time to do the in-depth research to answer these questions. You may not have the authority to demand it. However, if the culture allows, you can propose that your colleagues think through the following questions:

- **Are we discussing the right things?**
  This is a major challenge for any team. How do you separate what is of utmost long-term importance from what is interesting from a tactical point of view but has very little strategic importance? How much of the team's time is diluted by secondary topics? How do you distinguish the forest from the trees?

  For example, the typical Nokia board agenda during my first year as a member included reviewing past financials, reporting to the stock exchange, overseeing the auditors, following compliance topics, worrying about corporate social responsibility, analyzing the company's balance sheet, discussing shareholder distributions and share buybacks, tracking lawsuits against the company and by the company against other companies, examining compensation issues, hearing about cybersecurity preparedness, and a hundred other topics. These were important topics, but they did not help the board understand the competitive status of the company.

  We didn't dedicate enough time to the topics that *really* affected the company's health and well-being: its sources of competitiveness, how its core technologies and products compared with the competition's, and other subjects that explained the company's present performance and dictated how the company would perform in the future.

  To be honest, this is never easy. There are always too many subtopics to cover them all. Just imagine you have five categories of products, each of which addresses the evolving needs of a particular customer group, each group targeted by different competitors and their solutions, with different approaches in different geographies . . . You could easily ramp up to many tens of topics related only to competition. And when all those topics must be covered in a busy board meeting, you'll perhaps have only 10 minutes to devote to the company that will be morphing into your fiercest and most powerful competitor.

How do you prevent the agenda from being a mile wide and an inch deep? Minimize time spent on topics of secondary importance and maximize time for topics that really matter. Consider how to delegate topics to committees of the board or to subgroups of the management team to create more time for the essential topics. Constantly reevaluate your priorities and adjust how time is allocated.

Which raises the question, how do you recognize what is essential? When you feel you are in the eye of the tornado, it may be extremely difficult to separate the essential topics from the trivial ones. As I suggest in Chapter 9, taking a step back to determine what is truly essential with the board and management team will inevitably take you closer to the right focus. You always benefit by stopping to think about this. And if you won't try, you will definitely miss something.

• **Are we discussing the right topics the right way?**
Even if you have the right agenda and are dedicating a thoughtful amount of time to the factors that will decide the company's success or failure, if you're not able to have deep and candid discussions, then the time spent will not produce useful results.

During my first few months on the board, we were lulled into complacency by good financial results. No one openly questioned if this state of affairs might not continue. I've since come to regard the reporting of good financial results without a hefty dose of doubt as a smoke screen that will blind you to the dangers lurking in front of you. P&L isn't even a historical fact; it's a historical opinion and consequently a poor indication of future success.

It's very difficult to realize if smoke is being blown in your eyes and very time-consuming to gain confidence about exactly what is hiding behind the smoke screen. Questions must be encouraged and welcomed, not just on a superficial level, but as far down as it takes to divulge a realistic response.

- **Are we comfortable challenging the leaders' opinions?**
Many boards find it difficult to challenge the CEO or the chairman. Similarly, many teams fall silent at the thought of questioning or contradicting a senior manager. To be able to do that requires immense trust between both parties, something that can only be achieved through careful cultivation of the relationship.

The fundamental fact is, no leader can be above criticism or questions. In a good team, the team leader enjoys being challenged intellectually. No one aims to embarrass, but everybody strives to thoroughly understand what might threaten the company's future success and how the threats could be mitigated.

· ·

4

PLACING OUR BETS

SEPTEMBER 2009–DECEMBER 2009

· ·

Maemo showed that Nokia still had the magic touch.
Now we needed to translate that magic into product sales.
From a business point of view, we urgently needed a win.

· ·

EVEN WHILE MEANT as a prototype, the N900 (a forerunner of great future Maemo devices) was the first mobile device I had ever used that felt like a real PC. It had a full browser, where the browser on most smartphones typically had limited functionality and modified the web pages to fit the smaller screen. Despite a resistive touchscreen (why on earth?), N900 allowed you to do true multitasking with zippy performance and a three-row full QWERTY keyboard.

We demonstrated it that September at Nokia World 2009, the huge event where we announced the biggest launches of the year. The reception was everything we could have wished for. "The Nokia N900 is truly outstanding," the CNET reviewer gushed. "With multitasking and lightning-fast performance, the N900 is pushing smartphones to genius levels."[1]

What really made the N900 so exciting was what was inside its boxy exterior. Rather than trying yet another tweak to the trouble-plagued Symbian, the N900 inaugurated an early version of a new operating system. Maemo was based on Linux, just like Android.

As a new smartphone software base, Maemo didn't have the large bank of apps to download that Apple did. But Nokia was confident that would soon change—this was Nokia, after all!—and developers would create newer and better apps than those available for iPhones and Android devices. One example being rolled out at Nokia World was Nokia Money, a way to transform your smartphone into a personal bank that you could stash in your back pocket and access from anywhere. With Maemo, it seemed that any application that you could imagine could be made real.

Maemo showed that Nokia still had the magic touch. Now we needed to translate that magic into product sales. From a business point of view, we urgently needed a win.

While the N900 was a shining ray of hope, news about the N97 was dismaying. When it was announced in December 2008, this high-end Symbian-based smartphone was supposed to storm the market. Instead, by the time it limped into its June launch—having repeatedly missed its shipping dates—what was supposed to be Nokia's flagship had been overtaken by a fleet of some of the hottest devices yet produced: the Palm Pre, the iPhone 3GS, and the Google Ion/HTC Magic.[2] Features that were drool-worthy in December were now considered ordinary. One reviewer wrote, "Don't get us wrong; the Nokia N97 is absolutely filled to the brim with functionality. However, it's not enough to match a competitor feature for feature anymore. You have to provide quality hardware and a good user experience, and sadly, the N97 falls a bit short in those departments with an inferior resistive touch screen and clunky user interface."[3]

Making matters worse, the N97 suffered from poor quality. The return rates were very high, and we knew that lots of disappointed customers would turn their backs on Nokia after their bad experience and migrate to other brands.

Overall competitiveness and profitability depended on doing well in the high end. Nokia was already struggling in that area. Apple sold 5 percent of Nokia's volume and brought in one-third of its revenues, but its operating margin was twice that of Nokia's because it was developing only a single platform, and therefore its development costs were much lower. The average selling price (ASP) of Apple's devices was €449 ($646) against €64 ($92) for Nokia's. Samsung was somewhere in the middle: It had half of Nokia's volume, two-thirds of its revenues, and an ASP that was 50 percent higher. Its profit margins were low, but it could afford to sacrifice profits for volume.

With the N97 flunking out, Nokia basically was sitting on the sidelines until the N900 was released. Meanwhile, our already weak position in the important North American market was rapidly being eclipsed altogether by the Apple-Android-RIM triumvirate. My premonitions when I'd visited Nokia's almost-empty Fifth Avenue store earlier in the year were bearing out: RIM and Apple held 51 percent and 29.5 percent of the North American smartphone market, respectively, compared with Nokia's "barely visible 3.9 percent."[4] In December 2009, Nokia announced it would shutter its stores in New York and Chicago.

But there was a palpable sense that the acute phase of the 2008 financial crisis was over. Global GDP growth was expected to start again, and Nokia was improving its forecast for the devices market in 2010. There was strong overall demand for both touch and QWERTY devices, which seemed to endorse Nokia's decision to continue to straddle the fence.

At the same time, though, we were receiving strong signals that Android was catching on in a big way with new manufacturers signing up and blockbuster apps, like Facebook, starting to support its platform. HTC offered four Android-based devices, Huawei offered two, and LG had just announced it would be launching one. Motorola had barely survived the smartphone onslaught; now it was reinventing itself by releasing its Droid model with a full Android 2.0. Samsung had three different models, and reports said it was aiming to make 100 million touch devices in 2010. And in November, Sony Ericsson, one of the oldest supporters of Symbian, announced that it, too, was jumping on the Android bandwagon and would ship its first Android-based smartphone, the Xperia X10, in the first quarter of 2010.[5]

Nokia had always based its devices on its own operating platforms. It was unthinkable to consider anything else. But I started feeling that we should at least hedge our bets and come up with an Android prototype, if only to learn more about it. We could easily afford to experiment, but we couldn't waste much time.

The clock was ticking.

NSN's Punch in the Gut

A mirror image of the Nokia-Apple handset fight was also playing out in the infrastructure industry. Our joint venture with Siemens, NSN, was in big, big trouble: Sales were down 21 percent year-over-year, while Huawei's revenues ballooned 46 percent.

Two months earlier, the board had received a memo from the bankers who had been asked to analyze whether NSN could make money for its investors. In a fairly forthright manner, they described a bleak situation: "As you are aware, the telecommunications infrastructure industry is much challenged today. There is no reason to expect industry growth beyond GDP growth, and it is fully possible that the future trend is worse than that. In addition, competition has continued to intensify. Incumbents, including NSN, are struggling to preserve market share against each other, but also and more importantly, against the Chinese new entrants. The Chinese players are leveraging not only their innovation and operational efficiencies, but also the power and support of a well-aligned government to rapidly gain share, especially through aggressive pricing.

"NSN's customers are keen to see NSN survive this climate in order to ensure a healthy, competitive supplier set for the future. But despite NSN's aggressive and successful efficiency measures, it simply does not have the cost structure to profitably compete against what are effectively subsidized competitors in the case of the Chinese."

The options were limited. The bankers didn't believe selling NSN would be feasible—no one would be willing to buy it at a decent price. The other possibility was to continue cost cuts with the idea of doing an initial public offering later on. An IPO was not likely to succeed, the bankers warned us—NSN was light-years away from being in good financial shape—but they thought the discipline of at least starting to behave like a public company would be helpful. If that didn't work, they recommended a third option: distribute the shares to Nokia and Siemens shareholders and offload the problem onto *their* shoulders.

It was clear that the integration of Nokia Networks and Siemens Networks had been bungled.

I don't think anyone on the board had realized that things were this bad. The board only saw what was on the agenda, and we had spent very little time discussing NSN. The company urgently needed a cash infusion to avoid breaching the covenants of its syndicated loan. The parent companies each agreed to contribute €250 million. It was another financial punch in the gut at a time when Nokia was increasingly less able to take it.

Wherever we looked, trouble loomed.

Shifting Strategy—Again

At the final board meeting of 2009, in November, Niklas Savander, the head of Services & Software, announced that Nokia was placing a big bet on a new services strategy. The idea was to develop services according to an integrated model with people in the center. By opening one name on the user's contact list, the user would immediately see any meetings, e-mails, text messages, calls, and other data linked to that name.

I thought it made a lot of sense. People matter to people, and this approach made it very easy to connect the different dots related to all the people in your universe. Another attraction was that it was very different from Apple. The lack of integration was the major weakness in Apple's model, so this was a chance for Nokia to offer a more sophisticated, more intuitive, and all-round better user experience. (It is simply amazing that as of the middle of 2018, Apple still has not made meaningful changes to its basic app-centric user interface or created stronger integration around the core data.)

Niklas's presentation aimed to prove that the company had changed a lot. He recapped the recent acquisitions, mostly on the software side, aimed at boosting our ability to execute. He emphasized that many of the senior people in the services organization had been recently hired and that they came from the best companies in the software and internet industries. He talked about the achievements and the 2010 goals for Nokia's different services. The Services business had posted 123 percent year-over-year growth. Niklas now listed eight reasons that would propel even loftier aims in the coming year. By 2011, according to his presentation, business would be tracing the happy hockey stick pattern of exponential growth.

It was difficult to say how the objectives and choices made could have been improved. And with Maemo off to a good start with the N900 and the promise of a pipeline bursting with many more Maemo-based devices, we were all hopeful that something great was coming.

I was intrigued by the unspoken message of Niklas's presentation: It indicated that the leadership team acknowledged that things had been mismanaged earlier. But the recent acquisitions and shift to focus on services implied that this time, it would be different.

I also thought it was noteworthy that the most advanced improvements were targeted for the Maemo platform, with less and less attention being paid to Symbian. It validated my own concerns with Symbian and implied that Symbian was on the way out.

But it also reinforced the need to ensure that Maemo would succeed.

The challenge, as always, was execution. This was getting to be a familiar playbook. Whenever the board had a serious discussion about the company's issues with management, management would say that the actions it had just taken in previous weeks would improve the situation in the coming months. And, of course, even though the numbers were slipping downward, the actions were so recent that they had yet to make an impact.

There was still an ingrained belief among the board that it wasn't appropriate to truly challenge the management team. At my lunch with Jorma, when I tentatively raised the question of doing a deep dive into the reasons behind our constant launch slippages and poor quality of products, he made it clear to me that it wasn't the board's place to be operational.

The fear of becoming "operational" is also a weapon to use against any board that might start to "interfere." Just blame the board for being too operational. As always, it is very hard to prove the nonexistence of something. Therefore, the board will typically take a step back. When the chairman is the one blaming board members for being operational in asking too many questions, it is truly difficult to change the status quo.

Once again, we had to wait to see if the management's actions would be enough. But the sand was running out of the hourglass. It was no longer so easy to accept being silenced.

. . . .

The Toxicity of Success

From the moment I joined Nokia's board, it was clear that huge changes were reshaping the industry. Thanks to the cheap chipsets being pumped into the market by Asian manufacturers, anyone who could design a small PC could design a mobile phone. There was no need to invest in radio research and development; you could buy a chipset from MediaTek, an emerging Taiwanese manufacturer, build your device; and immediately connect to a mobile network. MediaTek had shipped 150 million chipsets in 2007, and it expected to ship more than 300 million in 2009.[6] MediaTek's customers alone were shipping 70 new models per month, about 1,000 per year. That's *a lot* of new products to try to keep up with and fierce competition between the myriad players. That level of competitive pressure also meant lots of innovation and experimentation.

The numbers were cause for concern; the implications were even more worrisome. The most complicated part of a mobile device has always been the radio. When I joined the board, I remember being told by Anssi Vanjoki, the head of Nokia's Markets unit, that 3G was so complicated and the R&D investment so prohibitive that the game was over; no new players could ever enter the market. But companies like MediaTek and Qualcomm did not want to create phones; they just sold chipsets to mobile phone manufacturers. Freed from the cost of developing their own chipsets, those manufacturers, in turn, could focus on the computer part of the device. The result was that the radio R&D costs were spread over the combined volumes of multiple mobile phone manufacturers.

Suddenly, our strongest competitive advantages were crumbling. But we didn't seem to realize it. The subconscious assumption was that our past success guaranteed our future success. The unspoken message I heard was: We are Nokia. We invented this industry. Let's keep doing what we do so well. Nobody does it better.

It's easy in hindsight to see that Nokia was heading into lethal trouble, but it didn't seem that way when our closest competitor could barely scratch out half our market share. Nokia's strategic goals made sense, and the company was trying to do the right thing. To be sure, the signs were there. But out of the multitude of data points, it's so easy to focus on the 90 percent that are good and ignore the other 10 percent.

All companies make mistakes, but companies suffering from their own huge success may become unable to admit or even see those mistakes and therefore become culturally unable to recover. One of the most valuable lessons from this experience was learning to recognize four toxic symptoms of success:

• **Bad news doesn't reach you or your team.** People may be afraid to air negative news for fear of being criticized. Or if they insist on bringing bad news to you anyway and subsequently *are* fired or reprimanded, that sends a message for everyone else to clam up.

In the board meetings, we discussed bad news all the time, but the "news" was typically historical facts that could not be avoided. We did not discuss data points that indicated significant weaknesses in our future plans. Most importantly, we did not insist on understanding the root cause. We didn't put real pressure on the management team to explain the why of the failures. Every time we allowed disappointments to remain not fully understood, we strengthened the behavior of the people on the management team and gave them a role model to repeat with their own teams as well.

- **Your team doesn't dig for negative news or hard facts.** This is a two-way street. Bad news needs to reach you, but you also need to go hunting for it. You may justify in your own mind that while you are not investigating the root causes of the company's problems, the people reporting to you certainly are. And if they had found anything significant, certainly they would have told you.

  But that may not be true.

  There was a leadership team running one of the strategic platform projects in Nokia, where each of the R&D leaders knew that his sub-project was late, but misled the leadership team to believe things were fine. Each did this believing he was the only one who was late and could catch up. Unbeknown to everyone, they were all failing. The leader of the team completely relied upon the information given to him by his subordinates and never took the trouble of deep-diving into the topics with the people who actually did the work lower down. The leader, and his boss on the Nokia group leadership team, only found out the true state of affairs after it was too late. The whole project was scrapped, and one more opportunity for Nokia to regain competitiveness was lost for good.

- **Decisions are constantly postponed and watered down.** Meetings throughout the company are routinely held without decision-making power. There might be 10 people present, each convinced he or she has a right to veto any decision, but none feeling that they have the right to force a decision. When working smoothly, a matrix organization has many advantages, primarily by forcing teams to work with each other with no one team controlling all the necessary resources. Making cooperation mandatory can get a large company much closer to a groupwide optimum in resource and capital allocation compared with independent business units all trying to sub-optimize for their own benefit. But the intrinsic complexity of this model makes it easy to fall into the trap of—and dangerous to become a victim of—postponed and diluted decisions. Such a company is practically paralyzed.

- **There is often just a single plan with no alternatives.** To see alternatives and present them to others requires trust, the ability to discuss possible bad outcomes, and an open communication culture. And vice versa; a generic lack of alternatives in planning speaks of potential cultural problems. Any major decision taken without considering alternatives is a warning sign.

Years after I became chairman, I asked one of the leadership team members from 2009 about the lack of alternatives. He told me that it was not possible to discuss alternatives with the board. Any signs of uncertainty were frowned upon by the chairman and deemed unprofessional.

These symptoms aren't immediately apparent; you will only find out who is wearing a swimsuit when the tide ebbs. Today's success can obscure tomorrow's possible failures. You must remain constantly on alert for indicators that suggest an organizational culture ill-prepared to cope with change. Every time you start believing that your advantage is so strong that new entrants can't compete, you should slap yourself in the face and say, "I'm wrong even if I don't yet know how."

Good times are the best times to become a paranoid optimist. You can look for danger signals precisely *because* you still have the resources to make the changes that will steer you back to safety. Being paranoid also gives you the courage to endure the pain of taking action early, preempting competitors' future actions, and mitigating negative market dynamics. If you are just an optimist, you will not make the hard calls; you do not feel they are truly necessary.

When signs of trouble do emerge, taking visible action helps turn paranoia into optimism. Making changes to agendas, adding more time for the meetings, adding new meetings to the schedule, establishing a board committee to focus on the issues, using external consultants to help the management team, or even having the board hire a consulting team to answer the questions the management could not answer (difficult, of course, as this communicates mistrust)—all these are actions that convey that the situation is serious but that you are taking steps to address it.

Everyone takes cues from the leader. Everything that the top leaders do—or don't do—sends a message. Actions not taken, questions not asked, communicate loudly.

Conversely, by instilling a culture that is characterized by data-driven analysis, regular deep dives to understand root causes, and constant paranoia regarding competitors and markets, a culture that encourages communicating bad news quickly and an imperative for always being presented with alternatives, you can combat the toxicity of success and better prepare to withstand the storm.

. . . .

5

REALITY BITES

JANUARY 2010–AUGUST 2010

. . . .

In a flash, I saw the root cause of what had unnerved
and confused and worried me for the past two years.

. . . .

THERE WAS PLENTY of positive news to report at the first board
meeting of 2010.

December had been a good month for us. Sales in Nokia's Devices
& Services unit were so strong—a 40 percent hike over the previous
year—that they hoisted the entire fourth quarter out of the red. First-
quarter estimates predicted continued growth and decent profitability.

The Services group had ended the year above target with some
90 million active users, a number we expected to skyrocket with the
imminent launch of Project Highway. Project Highway would bundle
the rich mapping data we had acquired when Nokia bought Navteq
in 2008 with free turn-by-turn navigation in all our S60 handsets.
Offering it for free was an industry disrupter, especially against Apple.

Things were progressing with Maemo, too. Nokia had signed a deal
with Intel, which had also been working on a Linux-based operating
system, to merge its Moblin platform with our Maemo.[1] The engineers
had nicknamed the common platform "M2" for Moblin and Maemo,
but no one wanted to call our software savior "me, too." It was officially

named "MeeGo" and would be announced next month at the annual Mobile World Congress. It was felt to be a positive move that would expand the ecosystem and attract more app developers. In the short term, of course, it slowed everything down. There was a need to coordinate between the development teams in Nokia and Intel, and it took time to agree on who would do what and when.

Even NSN had experienced a good fourth quarter. That wasn't surprising; companies like to use up all the money in their budget by the end of the year. Of course, there's usually a boomerang effect, and the first quarter, consequently, is seasonally the weakest quarter. We knew that the risks remained high. Still, at least NSN had retreated from the brink of breaching its financing covenants.

We could all exhale. The crisis had been averted. Maybe we were back on the right track.

A Provocative Memo

Still, I couldn't dismiss my fundamental concerns. With the Christmas break providing ample time for reflection, I decided to clarify my thoughts by writing my own strategy document for Nokia.

I outlined what I thought were the main external threats to Nokia's continued success in mobile phones and smartphones: the challenge to our high-end smartphones from Apple's iPhones, especially in the vital North American market; the threat to our low-end mobile handsets from China; and the possibility of being outgunned in the mid-tier by Android.

I warned that the battleground was shifting from hardware competence to software competence, from operating system platforms (Symbian, MeeGo, iPhone OS, etc.) to ecosystem platforms (iTunes, Ovi Store, iAd, etc.) and from internal capabilities to ecosystem capabilities. I explained in the document, "A key source of sustainable competitive advantage in this industry has moved from the 'who has the best device' towards 'which device is most suitable to consume digital content' and 'which device has access to the largest selection of most desirable content.'"

I added, "This poses a huge challenge to Nokia as we have moved beyond the time when the creation of a hero device would have been a quick fix to Nokia's dilemma." Nokia's brand had suffered among smart-phone customers, with repercussions in the developer communities that made it unlikely that Nokia could win back meaningful loyalty from the North American developer community in the short or medium term. Worse, I wrote, "This challenge is rapidly spreading to the rest of the world as iPhone and Android devices gain market share and mindshare."

I suggested scenarios and alternatives to think about: Maybe we should admit that we were not ready to attack in the United States and instead concentrate our forces in the huge Chinese and Indian markets and try to win over the developer communities there. Maybe we should institute a change in our culture to better serve the developer community.

And what if we failed to launch hero devices with high demand or failed in building good developer relationships and accumulating key apps that Apple and the Android community had already? If we failed, it would be relatively meaningless whether we shipped great hardware and provided a wonderful user experience.

Maybe we should consider a Plan B.

Maybe, I wrote—although this verged on treason—we should con-sider embracing Android to hedge our risks. Starting an Android pro-gram would give Nokia better insight into the future competitiveness and direction of Android. It would give Nokia a portion of the Android market and put pressure on competitors in the Android camp. And—again approaching disloyalty—it would provide Nokia with a quicker alternative in case the MeeGo ecosystem did not develop favorably. (Remember that, at the time of writing the memo, Android was still very young and its success was still not guaranteed.)

I also wrote about the need to renew our culture. In its glory days, Nokia had been applauded for a straight-shooting culture that encour-aged people to question the status quo and tell the truth as they saw it.

Had that ever been true? I really did not know, but I certainly hoped so. I wanted—no, I needed—to believe that Nokia could never have risen to the position it had without having had such a culture with low hierarchy and a strong focus on products and customers. Could this culture be revived? I fervently hoped so. If not, I had real doubts about the company's future.

The time for flowery and vague goals like "irresistible solutions and vibrant ecosystems," "best devices," and "smart services" was past. I concluded my memo by writing, "The current circumstances require a strategic plan of brutal honesty and stripped of all marketing-oriented statements."

I realized that what I was doing by writing and submitting my provocative memo was probably completely unprecedented in the Nokia board. Jorma would certainly interpret it as an attack, and I could only imagine how he would react. Still, I thought that after an initial explosion, Jorma would not just appreciate my insights; he would actually see the sense in my proposals. If we were to discuss the lines of analysis that I laid out, we would have nothing to lose and everything to win. If the ideas were found to be lacking, nothing would change. If they were to be found sensible, we would benefit.

In my study at night, the curtains drawn and the house quiet, I went through several drafts, sweating to find the right words to convey my meaning. I didn't want to lose the content of my concern and proposals, but I agonized over how I could avoid a major confrontation with my chairman.

When I felt I couldn't change another comma, I e-mailed the document to Jorma.

Of course, when you send something like this to the chairman of an enormous corporation, you can't expect an immediate response. At least, that's what I told myself—often—even as several days passed. But there was no reply.

After three or four days, on the off chance that my e-mail had gotten lost, I sent the memo again. But the result was the same—nothing.

I then sent the document to the CEO. I'd known Olli-Pekka Kallasvuo for years. I considered him a good friend and valued his insights, both as a well-respected and liked leader and from years earlier, in the early 2000s, as F-Secure's chairman and my boss. Never completely comfortable before an audience, OPK often appeared stiff and self-conscious in public. One journalist described him as having stepped off the set of an Ingmar Bergman movie.[2] In private, though, he was a caring man with a gregarious and self-deprecating personality and a great sense of humor.

OPK was the first to admit that he wasn't a tech nerd. He had spent most of his career at Nokia drawing on his background in law and banking to move up the ranks in the legal department, before jumping over to the finance department, where he eventually became chief financial officer. But he had successfully run the mobile phones business for a few years and was no slouch when it came to strategic thinking. He was one of the "Dream Team," the legendary group of four leaders whose no-BS approach to getting things done had been the engine of Nokia's success.

I couldn't imagine that OPK would brush aside my memo.

To my relief, he responded immediately—OPK was always ready to talk—and promised to take the memo forward. However, he did not return to the topic. When I saw him a few weeks later and asked about the memo, he seemed evasive and noncommittal. The creeping feeling that I might never get a response coalesced into the certainty that I was being deliberately ignored.

I decided to wait for my next meeting with Jorma to bring up the memo and the proposals therein. Face-to-face, I could probably best communicate my good intentions in a credible way and avoid things escalating.

"Android Is Everywhere"

In the meantime, I had asked for and was granted permission to attend the Mobile World Congress. (Nokia board members typically did not attend industry shows.) Held in Barcelona every February, it's the biggest show of the telecommunications industry and *the* place to spot trends in the business.

This year's trend was as obvious as a billboard. "MWC 2010: The Year of the Android" blared *Wired* magazine's headline on its feature covering the event.[3] The article proclaimed, "Android is everywhere, on handsets from HTC, Motorola, Sony Ericsson, and even Garmin-Asus. Pretty much every manufacturer puts it on its machines."[4]

I didn't need any further confirmation that my memo made sense. If anything, the need to develop competence in Android was more urgent than ever. We were late already, as it takes considerable time from making a decision to getting a product ready to launch.

It was also significant that there were competitive offerings of Android devices in the sub-$150 segment. Nokia pretty much owned the market for cheap handsets. But what if Android devices could crack the $100 barrier? Would they replace us as the entry-level "smartphone"? If Nokia's S40 platform and Android competed in the same category, our "sort-of-smart" feature phone would lose hands down to a real smartphone stripped of resources to make it as cheap as possible.

Android had other advantages as well, the *Wired* article continued. "The real customer for Android? It's the handset manufacturers. They have been given a customizable, powerful and actively developed OS, and they get it free. . . . This is what Microsoft is up against with its fussy new Windows Mobile 7."[5]

Microsoft's Windows Phone 7 operating system, which was announced at the event, offered a brand-new design concept of home screen tiles instead of icons. The user experience was built around people—pretty much exactly as Nokia was planning to do in MeeGo's Direct User Interface.

The MeeGo announcement had been well received by all parties: Nokia and Intel partnering together gave the impression of two real powerhouses creating an almost irresistible force. But if the pundits predicted that Android was sounding the death knell for the Windows Mobile operating system, where did that leave MeeGo? Windows Mobile had already been on the market for quite some time, and it had the might of Microsoft behind it. MeeGo was still an unknown quantity and was starting from zero.

"You Are Not My Competitor"

The market continued to recover, and at the board meeting on March 11 at London's Connaught Hotel, the mood was cautiously optimistic. The fourth quarter had been strong for Nokia. Our share price had moved up sharply.[6] The word on the street was, "Nokia's machine is not broken."

The leadership team once again raised its estimates for overall market growth. The growth was largely driven by smartphones. Nokia expected smartphones to account for more than half of the market for mobile devices in 2011. Even our profit share—Nokia's slice of the total profits of the entire industry—had jumped from 26 percent to 31 percent. We had pulled even with Apple. In fact, Apple and Nokia together accounted for approximately two-thirds of all profits in the industry.

However, Apple also had a stellar fourth quarter, and so did Samsung. Both anticipated solid growth as they expanded into new markets. Other manufacturers did poorly, with many abandoning Symbian and, as I had seen in Barcelona, jumping on the Android bandwagon.

Looking ahead, Nokia's position in smartphones seemed especially vulnerable. The company did not have any major launches of new high-end devices scheduled for the first half of 2010. While the portfolio looked to improve in the second half with Dali, MeeGo's flagship smartphone, its August introduction felt a long way off.

(Had I known that Dali would be soon postponed by a full year, the outlook would have seemed much dimmer. And this was not all. I might have felt even more perturbed if I had known about a conversation OPK had with Steve Jobs a few weeks earlier. Apple's founder bluntly told OPK, "You are not my competitor. Apple is a platform, and there is only one other platform company—Microsoft. Of course, there's Android, but they are stealing my IPR. [Jobs apparently believed that Eric Schmidt had taken Apple's IPR, or intellectual property rights, with him when he resigned from Apple's board of directors and became Google's chairman.] I have been building my platform for decades. You are just beginning." When OPK told me about this, years later, he said that what shocked him the most was that in Jobs's opinion, Nokia was already a has-been.)

A Silent Message from the Chairman

In the next board meeting, the leadership team once again announced a new strategy and a new organization. As I understood it, the company was shifting to a "solutions-driven strategy": Under the three-cornered umbrella of Solutions, Devices & Services, certain services would target different types of users and be coupled with the devices those users would want to buy. The usual names showed up on the org chart, just in unfamiliar boxes. I'm sure other people found it confusing; I certainly did.

There was no mention of my memo or the topics I proposed.

I met with Jorma in mid-spring 2010 and once again brought up the topic of confronting Nokia's difficulties. Jorma confirmed that he had received my memo but didn't say anything further. It was as if a door had silently slammed shut.

I left our meeting deeply disturbed. What was driving the reluctance to discuss alternatives? Why was it so difficult for us to at least try to find out why we were constantly failing to meet our objectives? What was stopping us from doing a real analysis of our own capabilities versus those of our competitors? I did not understand why Jorma was preventing the contents of my memo from being discussed.

For the first time, I seriously considered resigning from the board. But I hated the idea of giving up and of watching a company I was affiliated with continue its downward spiral. I believe an entrepreneur should never give up. I mentally gritted my teeth and resolved to, at least, wait for our spring strategy meeting. Surely, we would address the issues then. They were too important to ignore.

I tried to console myself by reminding myself of something that Steve Jobs often did when someone suggested something new. Jobs would first vocally demonstrate how bad the new ideas were, then wait a few weeks and present the same ideas as his own. Maybe Jorma would do the same in the strategy meeting.

For the future of Nokia, I very much hoped so.

Helsinki, We Have a Problem

When I received the package of information customarily sent to board members in advance of the Annual General Meeting on May 6 and the strategy meeting on May 7, I eagerly scanned the material to see if my suggestions had been incorporated. There were the usual topics for strategy discussions, ticking off Nokia's core businesses as well as a long-range plan for the next three years. There was no mention of the main issues I had raised nor the actions I had proposed.

I did not expect there to be a proposal to invest in Android, but I had expected a scheduled discussion to analyze the pros and cons of participating in this rapidly growing competing ecosystem. Instead, there was no indication that my document had ever existed.

To have it completely ignored left me stunned.

The business updates at the meeting just before our AGM didn't make me feel any better. Apple, Samsung, and RIM all did well in the first quarter. Nokia did not.

With hundreds of small new Chinese mobile phone manufacturers springing up like mushrooms after an autumn rain, we had underestimated the size of the 2009 market—adjusting the volumes for the previous year dropped our share of it by roughly 3 percentage points to below 30 percent in the fourth quarter. Our value share dropped, too, to just 25 percent. Samsung was biting at our heels with 20 percent, and Apple, despite its low-volume share compared with that of Nokia, had climbed to 15 percent.

At the end of the first quarter, Nokia's market capitalization was down to $31 billion.[7] Apple's had climbed to $215 billion.[8]

OPK delivered more grim news in his CEO update. Symbian^3 was delayed once more.

This was a disaster both because of the direct pain a further delay caused to our competitiveness, but even more because it meant we definitely had not turned a corner yet in our Symbian development. We were consistently several months behind schedule with our device programs. Not only did this wreck our credibility with operators, the distribution channel, and end users, but it was a problem that kept cascading. The same people in Nokia's R&D departments who were supposed to work on the next-generation devices were held up working on the previous device, so future devices were inevitably late as well. And when we did manage to ship something, it had been thrown together under so much pressure that the quality was below par.

The delays in getting devices into market also meant that we were shipping devices with outdated components. In the handset business, when you build a road map and say, "Let's introduce this device next April," in order to launch a high-quality device, you commit to buying the latest camera components, chips, sensors, and other parts that will be available from the suppliers for a device shipping at that time. But if you are six months late, you'll be stuck with components that are now at least six months old. Your high-end device will no longer be state of the art, and in this business, where models have the shelf life of lettuce, that's really bad. Meanwhile, your suppliers have moved on to next-generation components, which they're busily selling to your competitors, so *their* products are fresh and exciting.

Nokia's situation was even more depressing, as the company often chose to use older components to improve margins. When a device using previous-generation components was badly delayed, our latest products were sometimes two generations behind.

The Symbian news was more than disappointing, though. It was dangerous. Our user experience was way below par, and we were counting on the new Symbian^3 user interface to help fix the worst drawbacks of our solutions.

It was no secret how desperately we needed Symbian^3. It had already been delayed twice, for a total of six months. Committing to the latest timetable had been so vital that all the teams working on the OS had put their hands on their hearts and promised OPK, "It WILL ship on May 10."

Then, as OPK told us, Kai Öistämö, who oversaw the Devices group, called him at the end of April and told him, "It will not ship." The teams needed another three months, Kai said.

It was like being hit with a one-two punch. The Symbian^3 delay condemned Nokia's customers to a prolonged purgatory of lousy user experience, and we had little to preserve their faith. Our product portfolio had *nothing* that would be competitive at the high end for the first half of the year. The high end was where the big margins were made, and we might as well be invisible.

Under the circumstances, the announcement that the board of directors also had a bit of a shake-up didn't make much of an impression. Due to the previous Audit Committee chairman resigning from the board, we needed to select a replacement. I was appointed to be chairman of the Audit Committee as well as a member of the Corporate Governance and Nomination Committee. The CGNC prepared some of the key decisions, such as proposals for appointments to the board and other crucial actions. I'd been admitted to the inner circle.

Or so I thought.

Surprise at the Strategy Meeting

The May 7 meeting was held at the Nokia training center in Båtvik, located on a peninsula stretching into the Gulf of Finland. Outside the picture windows, it was a beautiful spring day, the blue water of the sea sparkling in the sun.

The meeting started off in its customary deliberate fashion. Jorma occupied his usual place at the head of the table; I was almost down at the end. The entire management team was there.

At his turn, Kai Öistämö stood up to discuss our smartphone strategy. Kai had written his PhD thesis on mobile protocols,[9] and Nokia had snatched him up with the ink barely dry on his diploma. In his mid-forties, Kai was one of the world's leading experts on mobile radio technologies.

As with all the strategy presentations, Kai opened with an overview of where we were before talking about what we were going to do. "I'd like to acknowledge the delays we have experienced in releasing our devices on time. The delays with Symbian^3 really hurt us," he said a bit nervously, adding, "But we have taken measures to counteract them."

Kai was moving on when I stopped him. "Excuse me, Kai. We've fallen behind schedule over and over. Why hasn't the situation improved?"

Kai's response followed the usual practice of emphasizing the solution over the problem. "It is true that this has been a consistent problem, but I believe we have now started to truly fix the issue," he reassured us.

I bore down. "Can you tell us more about the root causes and what's being done to improve the situation?"

Kai hesitated, then said, "Well, there are several issues, but just as an example, it used to take us 48 hours to compile the whole Symbian platform. But now it's only 24 hours, and we have a plan to make it even quicker."

If you didn't know about application development, like most of the board, this wouldn't sound so bad. To a software guy like me, though, it was a formula for disaster.

Compilation is the process in which the higher-level language in which programmers write code is translated into the machine language that microprocessors understand. The programmers run their files through a software tool called a compiler, which produces machine-language versions, which are then linked with certain toolbox files. The result is an executable program that you can run. Basically, Kai's words meant that making any change in the Symbian code and recompiling the whole platform (you can often also only compile the modified parts) took a minimum of 48 hours—in addition to the time spent getting everything prepared for compilation. It was the equivalent of a movie director on a set having to wait 48 hours to view the latest take before deciding whether it needed to be redone. Even a 24-hour compilation time was appalling. Waiting 48 hours to test how well a program works is an eternity.

Worse, the fragmented nature of Nokia's Symbian software organization hobbled it at every step. Apple had only one device to create software for; Nokia had *dozens*, each requiring its own software specifications and development process.

With growing dread, I realized that if this kind of inefficiency in such a crucial area had been the reality for a long time, the whole development organization had learned to perceive it as acceptable. This, in turn, meant that a lot of other unacceptable things had become acceptable as well. The reasons for the frustrating delays began to fall into place.

For example, the employees in Symbian-related research and development all *must* have known about the long compilation time. They had seen that the leadership hadn't reacted with alarm and urgency, so, they logically concluded, this was nothing truly dangerous. If their leaders weren't raising the alarm about something that should be so vital, it was only natural for the employees to conclude that they could take their time on a lot of other things. Or for employees who were concerned that this type of inefficiency was unacceptable, leadership not reacting in any way must have been hugely demotivating.

What other things are equally broken? The thought pierced me like a white-hot wire.

I couldn't believe this hadn't been brought to the attention of the board before now: After all, the delays had been our constant companion for years. I blew a fuse. "I don't appreciate you hiding bad news and only telling the board after the problem has been fixed," I told Kai. "You need to have the courage to tell us about the problem *before* you have a fix."

Kai agreed. He's a genuinely good guy and understood why I was upset. He just said, "You're right. It's really bad. I don't know what to say. I only learned about this recently."

Now I felt as though someone had hit me in the head with a sledgehammer. "Are you serious?" I sputtered. There were fundamental flaws in how we developed the platform that most of our profitability and all of our potential near-term growth depended on, and yet the person directly in charge of getting winning devices to the market hadn't known there was a problem of this magnitude. I was so flabbergasted that I didn't know what to say.

My mind flipped through the implications like a doomsday scenario Q&A. Why didn't the head of the Devices group know something this fundamental? Why hadn't he been told? The only answer could be that the middle management obviously had been afraid to bring the news to the top team. What did that say about the culture that must exist in the company for managers to prefer to watch the house burning down rather than alert the leadership team that there was a fire? Hundreds or perhaps even thousands of software developers must have known about the inefficiencies we were now discussing. Why hadn't they said anything? How was it possible that no one in the top leadership had known? Why hadn't these leaders tried to find out what was going on? Didn't they *care?*

In a flash, I saw the root cause of what had unnerved and confused and worried me for the past two years. A virus had been spreading throughout the culture and the company, shielded by our past success, feeding on fear of failure, rebuffing bad news, and suppressing a sense of accountability.[10]

(If I had known the whole truth, I would have been even more shocked. I flipped out over the 48-hour compilation time. As I later learned, the overall build time—which covers not just the compilation, but also the process of gathering the code to be compiled from the different teams working on the various components and preparing it for compilation—was *two weeks*. When the build was tested and bugs were found, the teams had already moved on to coding new stuff and the findings from the testing were two weeks out of date. This was a recipe for catastrophe, and a catastrophe was exactly what we had staring straight into our eyes.)

I drew in a breath to speak. Jorma interrupted me. "Risto, let's keep our tempers under control. We need to move on," he said. He adjusted his glasses with a gesture as final as if he had slammed down his gavel.

I shut my mouth and tried to calm down. *Breathe*, I told myself. *I can bring this up again at a later time.* But I felt as though I'd just learned that a dear friend had been diagnosed with advanced cancer. I needed time to think things through.

I had printed several copies of my strategy paper before the meeting, although I was still uncertain about whether to pass them out. Now, alarmed by what we had heard, I crawled out on a limb and distributed copies to the board members during a break. I knew I would get an earful from Jorma for taking matters into my own hands, but I had to do something.

Several board members commented positively on the paper during the meeting breaks. Some others got in touch with me about it over the next weeks. But the topics were never discussed in an official meeting.

Changing the CEO

The May 2010 board meeting was a wake-up call for me that things were bad in a more profound way than I had ever feared. Nokia's problem wasn't just a technology issue or a leadership issue. It was a cultural issue that pervaded the entire organization. Bad news wasn't percolating up from the bottom, and the top-down process of fact-finding and problem-spotting didn't work either. This indicated a lack of courage in the former and a complete misunderstanding of a critical aspect of good leadership by the latter.

I had supported Olli-Pekka in discussions with Jorma earlier and meant it. He had an open mind and listened to feedback. But no matter how good a human being he was, as the CEO he had to take the blame for creating or, at least, not changing an existing management culture that didn't emphasize accountability and responsibility, that didn't focus on the right things and didn't care enough to follow through.

When no one cares, the only resort is to change the people at the top—starting with the CEO.

Changing the CEO is not the same as demonizing him. OPK might have been a good CEO under different circumstances. I personally thought that the toxic culture had started long before OPK became CEO. But as CEO he should have resisted and changed that. (In hindsight, I can see that OPK was unable to do that.)

Now we had the opportunity to bring in someone new who would be able to start fresh—to face facts and not fear speaking out. I don't know whether my fellow board members saw the same nightmare scenario that I did, but the news that Symbian^3 was once more delayed galvanized everyone: The gist of the conversations in the coffee breaks was that we needed to replace the CEO.

Over the next couple weeks, Jorma called each of the board members one by one. He opened our conversation by asking what I thought about OPK. I told him that I had lost faith in OPK as Nokia's CEO and believed we needed a change. "That's exactly the discussion I have already had with most of the other board members," he said.

In late spring of 2010, the board agreed to launch a search for a new CEO. Jorma convinced the board that we shouldn't tell Olli-Pekka. I didn't understand why this should be a secret. I knew OPK's values and was sure he would stay on as long as necessary while working as diligently as ever. But Jorma felt that secrecy was prudent. I reluctantly convinced myself that it was Jorma's responsibility as chairman to oversee this transition and that, as OPK's colleague of over 20 years, he knew best.

As a member of the nomination committee, I assumed I would be on the search committee for the next CEO. I found out that Jorma had already formed a search committee, one that was identical to the nomination committee with one exception—me.

The board didn't hear much of anything for a month or so. Then, in July, the vice-chairman Marjorie Scardino called me.

"Risto, I'm calling all the board members to inform them that we have a candidate who looks very strong. But there's one thing you ought to know," she said. "This candidate has requested total confidentiality, so we can't tell you who it is."

That didn't make sense to me. "Marjorie, the board's central duty is to select the CEO. How can we do that if we don't know who the candidate is?"

"I understand how you feel," she replied. "We might have to approve the new CEO without the majority of the board knowing who it is. You'll just have to trust us."

The more I thought about it, the more it didn't seem right. It was the weekend, and I was driving across the Finnish countryside, so on impulse I called Jorma from the car. I assumed he would be equally shocked at this deviation from normal corporate governance. Instead, he exploded. "Risto, why the f*ck do you have to put your nose into the most minute details? You're always criticizing!" His expletive-filled screaming went on for a few endless minutes. I did not say much. I realized I had been naïve; had I stopped to think about it, I would have understood that Jorma was very much behind the request. He had just delegated the duty to call the board members to Marjorie.

Jorma never referred to the conversation again, and I saw no point in bringing it up.

Later, the board was told that this candidate was no longer an option. I never learned for sure who it was. (The press later speculated that it might have been Tim Cook, then COO of Apple, something Jorma later indirectly hinted at in his book by describing the candidate as being in his fifties and the number two man in a large U.S. technology company. I still do not know whether Tim Cook was the candidate.)

Another sour note echoed through the whole business. Jorma had not informed Olli-Pekka before the news leaked that he was a dead man walking. On July 20, the *Wall Street Journal* published a short item headlined "Nokia Conducting Search for New CEO."[11] According to the reporter's sources, the board was "supposed to make a decision by the end of the month."

Olli-Pekka called me the same day to ask what I knew about it. My heart sank. I said, "You have to talk to Jorma." I was following protocol, but I felt rotten. Olli-Pekka sounded gutted. "I know it is completely unfair asking you, but why wasn't I trusted with this information? Did I fail Jorma in some way that he wouldn't tell me? What do I do now?" He was clearly deeply hurt by what was, from his point of view, a betrayal by his closest colleague of 20 years and a man he thought was his friend. Why he wasn't allowed a gracious exit is a question that still goes unanswered.

I did not want to blame Jorma, so I just said, "You will be remembered as much for your behavior over the next few weeks as for what happened leading up to this." I continued, "I know the person you are. You will work 100 percent for the company until your last day on the job, and then you will walk out with your head held high, because you will have done the best you can until the very end."

That's exactly what he did. That is the man he is.

In August, Marjorie called again with news of another good prospect. This time she shared a name: Stephen Elop, the head of Microsoft's business division, which oversaw the Microsoft Office line of products, and a member of the company's senior leadership team.

The full board met with him for 90 minutes. I was okay with that; compared with approving the previous month's mystery man sight unseen, 90 minutes face-to-face seemed generous.

(In the middle of the meeting, something happened that I had forgotten but Stephen remembered years later. One of our older board members' mobile phone started to ring, and it seemed he did not know how to turn it off. This was one of Stephen's first impressions of Nokia's board; he later told me that he felt the board was not technologically competent. He also thought that the level of formality was beyond anything he had ever experienced.)

We also looked at three internal candidates. Stephen easily outshone them. His understanding of software, the cloud, customers, sales, and the vital American market clearly made him the best choice. Jorma had met Stephen several times, and the search committee members had talked with him a number of times. Jorma and the committee recommended him strongly. The board unanimously voted to select him.

· ·

Refuse to Be Defined by Your Role

When I joined the board of Nokia, I was joining a company and a team that I had huge respect for. I expected everything the company did to be as close to perfect as possible. I took my cues from the board members, and especially my idol, Jorma Ollila. Even after my eyes finally started to open, I wasn't confident enough to forcefully challenge the status quo. I tried several times to convince Jorma that we needed to try a new approach, but without success. (And I did not have any magic bullets. I just knew that what we were doing was not working.)

Since Jorma was not ready to make changes, one solution might have been to change the chairman. In fact, Jorma was supposed to step down in the spring of 2010. This was what our vice-chairman

Marjorie Scardino had told the rest of the board a year earlier. The next I heard about this was in late 2009, when Jorma called to let me know that due to receiving strong requests from several board members, he had agreed to stay on.

In many ways, we were all captives of our perception of our roles. I was imitating the behavior of the board members in the belief it was the best practice. The other board members were likely doing the same. We all trusted our chairman, the man behind the success of the company. We believed that he understood the market, the technology, and the competitors. We believed that, no matter how bad things looked, he was intimately involved with the management team and fixing the problems. Similarly, when Nokia was still doing relatively well, we had full trust in the management team to the extent that little was questioned and everything was taken at face value.

In a crisis like the one in which Nokia found itself, the board's role changes.

Because the board is ultimately responsible for the company, the board needs to adopt a different approach during different times. In the end, the board must define its own role and the role of the management team, not the other way around.

Interestingly, my conditions for the need of a Plan B all came true. Nokia failed to create or otherwise become part of a winning ecosystem. We never had a competitive app offering, not for Symbian or for Windows Phone and definitely not for MeeGo. We did have competitive hardware such as Lumia 920 and 1020, but as I predicted, it was meaningless without the ecosystem. I regret that we never discussed the proposals in my paper. A Plan B might have dramatically changed Nokia's course.

As a result of this experience, I believe even more strongly that you must always question your role and refuse to be bound by it. Act based on facts and current circumstances, not based on tradition. Use common sense and be pragmatic. As the public service announcement in New York City's subways and buses frequently enjoins riders, "If you see something, say something."

In hindsight, as a board member, I was accountable. I should have acted sooner and more strongly. I should have tried to convince others to join me. I was too timid.

. . . .

6

A NEW HAND ON THE WHEEL

SEPTEMBER 2010–JANUARY 2011

. . . .

Symbian was no longer competitive. MeeGo was in its infancy.
Given the advantage Apple and Android had,
could Nokia catch up?

. . . .

NOKIA'S FIRST NON-FINNISH, non-Nokia-bred CEO started work on September 21, 2010. From the outset, Stephen Elop brought a new sense of direction to Nokia and an outsider's way of doing things.

As the head of Microsoft's $19 billion Office business, Stephen had run one of the world's largest, most profitable software businesses. Now 46, a stocky man with a shock of short blond hair, he was known for embracing challenges and resolving internal conflicts. With a keen interest in technology—he always carries a bag bulging with the latest gadgets—he had a good overall understanding of both software and hardware.

I liked Stephen from our first meeting onward and thought he was a competent leader with important ideas and the right intentions. But I couldn't help wondering how he would fit into the Finnish community.

On his first day, Stephen sent an e-mail to every employee through-out Nokia—some 60,000 of them.[1] The purpose of his e-mail blitz: to ask what they thought he should change, what they thought should be left alone, and what they feared he wouldn't understand. People were initially startled; this wasn't the sort of thing that was usually done at Nokia. But more than 2,000 responses flooded in.[2] Stephen answered every single one, summarized the feedback, and got a good start in understanding what was working in the company and what wasn't.

(Throughout his time at Nokia, Stephen maintained the practice of direct dialogues with employees on SharePoint, so others could see the conversation as well. It was quite a statement that the CEO was engaging with everyone.)

Another break with convention: As part of his contract, Stephen negotiated a personal security detail. Microsoft executives typically travel with bodyguards, but this was almost completely unknown in Finland. People couldn't help noticing: Stephen would speak at an all-hands meeting, and there was a bodyguard standing at the side of the room; Stephen would come to the office accompanied by a bodyguard. The security shadows were a constant reminder that a foreigner was at the helm.

(The sad thing was that Stephen needed extra security. It is hard for non-Finns to understand, and probably hard even for Finns to remember, how much attention Nokia commanded in Finland. The Finnish press went way overboard in their attempts to report on Stephen. Journalists tried to enter Stephen's house outside Seattle when his family was in residence, and Finnish tabloids offered cash to any citizen who spotted Stephen and called a number to alert the paparazzi. Partially fueled by the press, normally sedate Finns started behaving uncharacteristically. Stephen was once attacked on a Finnair flight by a man crawling over seats on the plane to get his hands on Stephen. It was not uncommon for groups of drunk Finns to confront him at airport gates. Stephen did not make a big issue out of any of this and did not even share any of the details with the board members. I am not proud of what some of my countrymen did.)

Amid the heightened attention, even little things loomed large. My mother, who is now 85, saw a news clip of Stephen giving a public speech. As is typical of speakers in the United States, Stephen was striding back and forth on the stage as he spoke. In Finland, however, people tend to be less mobile while making a presentation. My mother declared to me, "I do not trust that man. An honest man would not need to walk like that." I tried multiple times but failed to convince her that just walking while speaking was not proof of dishonesty. I wondered how many other Finns might react like my mother.

(I shared my mother's comment with Stephen and advised him to reduce his motions by 50 percent when speaking to a Finnish audience. He was surprised but good-natured enough to take it seriously and tried unsuccessfully to stand still.)

More than the expected cultural collisions, I was concerned about Stephen's leadership style and effectiveness. Would Stephen be able to restore a sense of urgency and accountability? Would he be able to knit together Nokia's disparate and divided programs? Could he shift Nokia from its hardware-grounded history in which it was an undisputed leader to a software-centered ecosystem in which it was still a nonstarter? Could he somehow transform the company to compete against Apple, Android, and BlackBerry, to survive in an app-based future defined by data, not voice? And, of course, what kind of relationship would form between him and the chairman?

In the wake of the latest reorganization that past spring, the company that Stephen took over was divided into three businesses: Devices & Services, comprising smartphones and mass-market mobile phones, which supplied the lion's share of the company's revenues, more than double the sales of the other two businesses;[3] Location & Commerce, which focused on the development of location-based services such as Navteq (soon to be renamed "HERE"), acquired three years earlier; and the consistently money-losing NSN.[4] In addition, there was Nokia Technologies, our storehouse of revenue-generating patents.

Stephen didn't waste any time uncovering the challenges facing the company. He promptly launched "Project Sea Eagle," a sweeping internal review of Nokia's capabilities and competitiveness. In addition to enhancing Stephen's understanding of the company's ability to implement the current strategic plan, it was meant to map available alternatives. At the same time, Stephen commissioned McKinsey, the noted management consulting firm, to provide an outsider's perspective to Project Sea Eagle.

The most urgent challenges were what was happening with Symbian and with MeeGo. Nokia's hopes of the future depended on these two operating systems. But it was difficult to tell whether they—and their teams—were working in tandem or competing against each other.

Symbian's Development Debt

Through the responses to his e-mail, town hall meetings, and individual interviews, Stephen soon uncovered the sad state of the Symbian platform and the poor competitiveness of the Symbian devices. As a software engineer, he knew how difficult it was to modernize outdated software code. Now Stephen was seeing just how deeply we were mired in development debt.

As software code ages, more elements in it need to be rewritten. This is called "development debt." The longer you wait to modernize the code, the more the debt grows and the more difficult it may become to make even simple changes. That's because you have to pay "interest" on the debt in the form of the additional work-arounds every time new features need to be added. Consequently, each time you make changes in the original platform, the size of the problem balloons. As the magnitude of the task increases, the time it will take to accomplish it also increases with a multiplier. If you miss the opportunity to overhaul the code for a few years, you're saddled with the software version of an underwater mortgage.

The problem is that doing a complete rewrite for a large piece of software often takes a couple of years, sometimes even more. When your customers are fleeing to other platforms and your business status is plummeting, you may feel you don't even have a year.

Also, where will you find the resources to do the rewrite? If you move your best people to the job, who will service your ailing current platform during the rewrite?

It's a gut-wrenching position to be in.

My own experience with development debt at F-Secure had caused me to conclude that there's only one solution: As soon as you realize you have fallen into this hole, create a separate team to start a complete rewrite of the source code or do the rewrite in stages. Assign separate resources for reducing the debt; otherwise it will never get done. Do this even if it means recruiting a new team or making a bigger investment than anticipated. The sooner you start, the sooner it's ready.

The next generation of Symbian—Symbian^3—made a valiant attempt to climb out of the black hole of development debt. It wasn't a complete rewrite, but large parts of the code base had been rewritten so that it was a real step in the right direction. This was the version that the company needed in 2008, which was scheduled for a 2009 release, and which we were finally preparing to bring to market in September 2010, nearly a year late.

Nokia's market share had slipped further in the first half of 2010. But in terms of smartphone sales to end users by operating system, the Symbian platform was far and away still the clear leader, with 41 percent market share (down from 51 percent in 2009).[5] Even though Android zoomed upward from 1.8 percent in 2009 to 17.2 percent of global sales, vaulting into third place behind RIM at 18 percent, it still commanded less than half of Symbian's market share.[6] The iPhone OS, meanwhile, had remained steady at 14 percent market share in terms of shipped devices.[7]

Hopes were riding on Nokia's N8, the first smartphone running on the Symbian^3 OS, and it looked as though they might just be answered. The N8 launch was delayed—again—but shipments of the sleek burnished aluminum slab were expected to start within the third quarter and preorders were reassuring. Operator commitments were bigger than ever before for a Nokia high-end device, and 90 percent of our survey respondents scored it higher than the latest iPhone. The initial reviews from testers were promising: "This is a good-looking phone with plenty of potential," the CNET reviewer wrote. "It needs a smooth, easy user interface to polish it off."[8]

That's exactly what we hoped the Symbian^3 would provide.

You Go, MeeGo

Meanwhile, MeeGo was waiting in the wings. Just a little more work, we had been told, and this new, unencumbered operating system would be ready to step onto center stage.

MeeGo solutions had been very much the focus of the business plan for the second half of 2010 and the first half of 2011 that had been outlined back at the July 2010 board meeting. At that meeting, Marko Ahtisaari, Nokia's head of product design, gave a presentation of Nokia's design philosophy centered on MeeGo devices. There were three in the pipeline, we were told. First up was Dali, with a sliding QWERTY keyboard, supposed to launch in 2011. (The original Dali launch was scheduled for summer 2010, but the device was felt to be noncompetitive and the launch was canceled.) Dali was to be followed by Lankku (the code name for what would become the N9), which would showcase a new "swipe" touch interface that enabled users to swipe their thumbs across the screen to call up their apps.

Marko's presentations were mesmerizing. He liked to paint enticing vistas for the listener, conjuring beautiful images by extolling "the craft in this design" and rhapsodizing that it was "precision-machined from a single piece of polycarbonate." He had a habit of caressing a new device as he described its attributes. People joked that his demonstrations bordered on erotic.

Designwise, these devices couldn't be beat. But for an engineer like me, the presentation was less strong on concrete actions. I asked Marko about the readiness of the MeeGo software and the likelihood of meeting our shipment deadlines. "I cannot comment. It's not my area of responsibility," he replied.

I pointed out that as he was working so closely with both the user interface and the hardware, he must have an opinion. "It would be valuable for the board to hear," I urged. Marko said he did not have access to the necessary data.

If Marko could not answer, perhaps Anssi Vanjoki would. As head of the Solutions group, which created the road maps for MeeGo devices, he could not say this was not *his* responsibility. So I asked Anssi. His brief answer contained absolutely no useful information at all.

I looked at Jorma, expecting him to direct Anssi to respond properly to the question. Nokia's future depended on us getting MeeGo to the market and winning with it. Jorma moved on to the next question from someone else.

I never learned what Marko or Anssi knew or suspected at that time.

Now here we were two months later with still no clarity. Would the new CEO be able to get an answer?

Bleeding Nokia Blue

Thanks to the enthusiastic feedback to his first-day e-mail, as well as having conducted town halls and small group meetings with thousands of employees, Stephen was well aware of the contradictions in Nokia's culture.

Plenty of employees were passionate about the company, insisting, "I bleed Nokia blue." There was certainly no lack of innovative thinking going on. On his visit to our facility in Salo, Stephen was given a phone and directed to toss it in a tank of water. The engineer dialed its number, and despite the device being submerged, the familiar ringtone burbled out. A nanoscale coating made the electronic parts water-resistant.[9] This was exactly the kind of knock-your-socks-off technology to be expected from the company that had invented the app store, built some of the first touch devices, and wowed the world with cameras in mobile phones. We still had what it took to make magic.

But many employees were frustrated and wanted Stephen to know, "Nokia is a company with talent and real capabilities. It is just not using [them]."[10] The e-mail Stephen found most telling: "At Nokia, everybody and nobody is accountable for nothing."[11] It encapsulated perfectly the challenges undermining our efforts to move forward as one coherent team.

Stephen was receiving similar conflicting messages from his meetings with operators around the world. They wanted Nokia to succeed, but at the same time, they were disappointed in our portfolio and exasperated by our inability to keep our commitments. And our execution was dismal: 38 percent of 44 recent product launches were more than four weeks late. The worst of it was that the most critical launches were the most late.

Many operators had also grown frustrated with Nokia's high-handed approach to supplying devices to the operators. During the good years before 2009, Nokia dictated the number of phones each operator was allowed to sell. Popular demand for Nokia devices was so intense that the word was that Nokia didn't have salespeople—it had supply allocation people. That approach breeds resentment, and when Nokia's position weakened, it came back to haunt us.

There was also a solid core of people who believed that Nokia should resist changes proposed by an outsider. At our first one-on-one meeting, Stephen told me about a run-in he'd had concerning his desire to rename the Group Executive Board. According to the feedback he'd received, the GEB, which comprised the top management team, had become a symbol within Nokia of leaders who sequestered themselves in an ivory tower, refused all connection with the real world, and made decisions that made no sense to the rank-and-file folks who had to implement them.

Since the term "GEB" had become fraught with negative connotations, Stephen wanted to change the name, but, he told me regretfully, that was impossible. "Why not?" I asked him. "You can change it, and you should." He had been told, he said, that our bylaws mandated that the top management team of Nokia *had* to be called the Group Executive Board.

I told him that was foolish. "Double-check," I urged him. "I am sure that our bylaws do not constrain what English term we use for the management team." And, of course, they didn't.

(Stephen was very careful not to reveal who had misled him, but a few years later he told me that it had been Jorma.)

The GEB was soon renamed the Nokia Leadership Team, or NLT.

Symbols and Signals

In the wake of the GEB episode, I told Stephen a story I had heard about a new leader in an organization that had become mired in doing everything by the book. This organization actually *had* a book that documented all the rules that everybody had to follow. All employees hated the book from the bottom of their hearts.

As the story went, the new CEO wanted to send a strong signal that things were about to change. He arranged for a video crew to film him as he tossed a copy of the rule book in an empty oil barrel in the company's parking lot and set it on fire. That symbolic act spoke louder than a thousand words.

Symbols are powerful. Any leader, especially one from the outside, who has to manage change should pay a lot of attention to symbols, and as well should be careful about what to change, how to change it, what message that change sends, and how to communicate it.

Much of the resistance to change that Stephen encountered came from the top of the company. Sometimes leaders who have created certain tools, processes, or behaviors are averse to having a newcomer change them. They take the proposal to change as indirect criticism and react defensively. This reaction may be even stronger if the company has actually been successful based on the old behavior.

Many times I have been told by experts that something I was considering was completely impossible. I pretty soon learned to push back. I'd say, "Even if it seems impossible, think of ways in which this could be done," or "Hey, I'm asking *how* to do this, not whether we can't do this." And I soon discovered that the same people who told me that something was impossible would come back to me with a gleeful grin to say that they had found a way to do it after all. This has happened over and over again.

A Breath of Fresh Air

The board meeting held on November 23 and 24, 2010, was a remarkable break with convention. It began with Jorma's usual analysis of macroeconomic trends. But then we launched into a strategy update.

We were now starting the meeting with the most important questions and dedicating a significant time to them. I felt this was a breath of fresh air.

The other welcome change was that almost all of the executive team members (i.e., the Nokia Leadership Team members) were invited to at least part of the meeting.

I thought I detected some tension between the chairman and the CEO. I later learned that the relationship was not evolving in a positive direction. Jorma had, for instance, forbidden Stephen to talk with the board members without the chairman present, and Stephen felt that was not a sustainable way for him to act. They also had a disagreement on Stephen bringing NLT members to board meetings. Stephen later told me that Jorma strongly disliked NLT members joining board meetings unless they were the presenters.

No wonder the new CEO seemed a bit on edge.

Our flagship N8 phone had—finally—launched. Sales were promising, but the reviews pinpointed a frustratingly persistent conundrum: The exquisitely designed hardware couldn't mask an exasperating user experience. "A slick case and great camera help to make this the best Nokia touchscreen phone ever, but it's just not fun to use," said the CNET reviewer, adding, "We blame Symbian for the N8's problems. This is the first phone with the latest version of the operating system, Symbian3, and, although there are improvements, it's just not good enough."[12]

Creating a Third Ecosystem?

It was against that backdrop that Stephen introduced the findings from Project Sea Eagle and McKinsey.

Three years after the iPhone burst on the scene, the mobile phone market continued to show healthy growth with a strong shift toward smartphones. But while Nokia was still overall the biggest player in the industry that it helped create, the high-end market was now dominated by Apple, the mid-range section was under attack by myriad Android vendors, and the low-end segment was under pressure from devices built on cheap MediaTek chipsets and, increasingly, on the Android platform. The number of Symbian phones worldwide was 50 percent higher than their Android counterparts, despite Android's explosive growth. But Android had conquered the North American market, and it was easy to extrapolate that it was only a matter of time before Android overtook Symbian to become the most used platform in the world.

There were no safe or secure markets remaining that Nokia could depend on.

The app usage statistics showed why. Two ecosystem giants were pulling away from the pack: Apple and Android. App developers showed very strong interest in Apple, which boasted over 300,000 apps. Even with just over half that number, Android had clearly reached critical mass with developers.[13] Meanwhile, Symbian notched barely 28,000 apps and Microsoft's Windows Phone just 2,000. MeeGo had practically no third-party apps.

Apps weren't just a measure of popularity; they translated into revenue. iPhone users spent a lot more money than users of any other platforms. For an app developer, the iPhone was the platform of choice because people opened their wallets more readily.

For Nokia, the big question was this: If Apple and Android already had momentum in building their ecosystems, could Nokia form a viable third ecosystem? Nokia's Ovi app store had an advantage in terms of reach—it sold paid apps in 190 countries, whereas Apple was in 90 countries and Android in 32. It offered operator billing in 90 of those countries—users without credit cards could charge their app purchases to their account and the cost would show up on their bill—something neither Apple nor Android had.

But Symbian was no longer competitive. MeeGo was in its infancy. Given the advantage that Apple and Android had, could Nokia catch up?

Even assuming that Nokia could build a competitive ecosystem, there was an unrelated portfolio challenge. The dynamics of the market shift made it clear that Symbian would continue to lose competitiveness. No longer able to command high prices, Symbian devices would relentlessly slide to lower and lower price points. But when you aim to compete at the low end, you design the device to fit that market segment and use as few resources as possible—a slow processor, not much memory, and therefore a lightweight operating system. Unfortunately, Symbian just wasn't designed for the low end.

Symbian was stuck in a no-win conundrum: It was no longer competitive in the market it had been designed for and could not be competitive in the market it was being forced into.

MeeGo was meant to replace Symbian in the middle market. But with Symbian sliding ever downward, a gap would emerge in the middle. As Symbian progressively slumped, the gap would inexorably grow.

Nokia did not have a competitive mid-range operating system to fill the gap.

There were three alternatives. We could bring MeeGo down to fill the gap, but that wasn't reasonable since all the development efforts were focused on making MeeGo competitive at the high end. We could try to stretch Symbian upward and stop its decline, but that wasn't likely to work out either. Or we could buy or develop another OS to fill the gap. But we were already developing the Meltemi OS to compete against Android at the rock-bottom $50–$150 range, and the last thing we needed was a *fourth* smartphone OS.

Somehow Symbian *had* to hang on in the medium market—not an easy task with so much competition and a product in shaky health—until MeeGo swooped in and saved the day.

A Second Opinion

At the December 2010 board meeting, it was clear that the N8, rather than reviving Symbian, at best provided only a slight improvement on usability. Our Symbian-based device families were becoming tarnished as a brand, in comparison with Samsung's glowing Galaxy, for instance.

The first MeeGo-powered smartphone—the N9—was scheduled for release in June 2011. That was admittedly late to the party, but Android had shown it could succeed emphatically as a "fast follower." With Nokia still a global heavyweight with sales in 160 countries,[14] our hope was that MeeGo would enable us to come out swinging and, over time, rebuild a strong market position.

MeeGo's vital importance made the McKinsey findings about its viability even more consequential.

They were as blunt as a fist in the gut. The products planned for the MeeGo portfolio, including the N9, already lagged behind Android competitors in the target price points in terms of both features and performance. These gaps would not only dissuade potential buyers but would also deter developers and other players from creating the apps and games that would draw consumers to the platform.

The MeeGo portfolio itself was paltry compared with Android offerings. MeeGo was aimed at the high end of the market. Meanwhile, the McKinsey findings noted that more than 80 different Android models were expected to hit the market below the MeeGo price points.

Furthermore, there was no strong differentiator between the "non-Android Android" (i.e., MeeGo) and the real Android. Or rather, the only differentiator was that it was a Nokia. But that was perhaps no longer compelling enough. And with Android now hitting the 200,000 apps mark,[15] the window of opportunity for MeeGo to create a viable alternative ecosystem was closing rapidly.

Stephen needed to be absolutely certain about MeeGo's health before proposing any decisions. In addition to doing his own deep dive to verify McKinsey's conclusions, he wanted a second opinion from a Nokia leader in the know.

One natural candidate was Kai Öistamö. It was obvious that Kai was technically capable. Now in charge of strategy after the previous spring's reorganization, Kai had coordinated Project Sea Eagle and sat in on every meeting. Through the course of those meetings, Stephen could see Kai's genuine pain and remorse about the Symbian downfall, as well as his desire to fix the mistakes of the past. He decided to trust Kai.

Stephen and Kai agreed that each would independently do his own deep dive into the MeeGo R&D organization. They would talk to coders, testers, and managers; inspect the bug reports; and make their own calculations on development velocity. They reserved a month to form an opinion and agreed not to compare notes during that time.

Curled Up in a Fetal Ball

On January 4, 2011, perhaps two weeks into the month-long assessment period, Kai called Stephen and announced that he was ready to express an opinion. Stephen replied that he, too, had made up his mind. "Come to my office," he invited Kai. "You'll find me under my desk curled up in a fetal ball."

The situation was even worse than McKinsey had warned.

The MeeGo team had somehow neglected to set aside resources to work on the next generation of MeeGo devices after the N9. At its current rate, Nokia could introduce only three MeeGo-based devices before 2014, far too slow to keep Nokia in the game. Three models over three years was a good strategy for Apple when it disrupted the market with touch. For Nokia trying to catch up, it was no strategy at all.

With just one MeeGo device per year, the volumes would not be enough. Without the volumes, the developer ecosystem would not believe in the platform sufficiently to start creating apps. Without the developers' support, MeeGo could not succeed.

It was like the Symbian compilation fiasco all over again—only worse. "MeeGo had been the collective hope of the company," Kai recalled, "and we'd come to the conclusion that the emperor had no clothes."[16]

There are two sides to any failure: making mistakes, which always happens, and, because of cultural flaws, not identifying the mistakes early enough to act decisively. Developing MeeGo was exactly the right thing to do, but when problems arose, as they always do, the news didn't get passed to the top. The issues ballooned until they were too big to ignore—and by then, were too big to solve easily.

Thanks to the earlier discussions about MeeGo's challenges, the board knew that all was not rosy. But no one had suspected that things were as bad as they were when Stephen dropped the bomb: MeeGo was a bust. The portfolio road map was a shambles. And with Meego being DOA, it would not cover the ground lost by Symbian.

The air went out of the boardroom. Without Symbian or MeeGo, Nokia didn't have anything to carry the company forward. I was so stunned by the news that I could hardly think straight. Looking around at the others, I could see they felt the same way.

How had these elementary mistakes been made? Why were they hidden for so long? MeeGo had been discussed for several years already with the board. We had been shown prototype devices for quite some time. We had all held them in our hands. They were *real*. It was hard to believe that now MeeGo suddenly had no value. We felt betrayed, but we didn't know whom to blame.

In just a few weeks, Stephen was due to speak at our Investor Day, an annual event in London where Nokia's top managers provided an update of the company's strategy, operations, and financial targets. In the past, Investor Day was the podium from which Nokia announced grandiose plans to an adoring audience.[17] Now industry analysts and major investors from around the world were eagerly waiting to hear Stephen's strategy to save Nokia.

At that moment, nobody in the boardroom had any idea what that would be.

7

TOUGH CHOICES

JANUARY 2011– FEBRUARY 2011

. . . .

The Windows Phone was a gamble, with a huge upside
but a fairly high probability for complete disaster.
Android's upside wasn't as high, but there was
significantly less likelihood of total failure.

. . . .

THERE'S ALWAYS AN option. It just may not be the option you prefer.

Back in October 2010, when Stephen Elop brought in a McKinsey partner to work on Project Sea Eagle, the consultant's primary brief was to render an objective assessment of Nokia's strengths and weaknesses based on its product portfolio, current plans, and organizational capabilities. But even as Stephen asked for an evaluation of Nokia's future based on the Symbian, MeeGo, and Meltemi operating systems, Stephen also asked him to look into other, non-Nokia operating systems.

This other line of investigation was called Plan B.

Knowledge of Plan B was strictly limited to a very small circle among the senior management. Plan B was a secret because giving up on Nokia's own platforms would be tantamount to a total defeat—an admission of having failed to stay competitive even while having by far the largest market share and R&D budget in the industry.

There was no question of settling for small plans. Nokia needed a strategy that would provide the most reasonable likelihood of Nokia retaining its identity as the industry giant.

There were only two alternatives: Android and the Windows Phone.

Why Android?

The Android ecosystem was zooming ahead with unprecedented momentum. Google reliably pumped out fully functional OS upgrades every six months (compared with Nokia's historical 12- to 18-month development cycles—plus delays), and each new version spawned myriad apps and services. There were already more than 25,000 developers churning out more than 200,000 apps—in some cases, attacking such traditional Nokia strongholds as maps and free turn-by-turn navigation.

Low- and mid-priced Android models were swarming our huge installed base. (In India alone, our market share slid more than 15 points to below 60 percent.) More than 80 different Android models in these price points were expected to appear on the shelves over the next 18 to 24 months. In contrast, Nokia had little in its bag.

Furthermore, the board was told that key operators, equipment manufacturers, and other technology companies that had earlier endorsed MeeGo had since shifted their stand. In meetings with our management, they said that it was important for Nokia to remain in the market but they were not certain whether they could support MeeGo without proof that it could truly be competitive. Technology companies like LinkedIn, Facebook. and Twitter, whose apps we needed to build our ecosystem, were not excited about having yet another operating system to support. Assuming that they would probably have to support Microsoft's Windows Phone in some way, their thinking went, "Okay, Android and iPhone are a given. But if we have to work with more minor operating systems like MeeGo and Windows Phone, let's choose one rather than both."

Meetings with other handset manufacturers were similarly lukewarm. Among the big manufacturers, only Samsung backed MeeGo.

Because Samsung was the king of Android, though, MeeGo was just an option; at the first sign of trouble, they could abandon MeeGo in an internet minute. (By the way, Samsung was doing exactly what I proposed Nokia should have done in my memo in late 2009. Samsung was hedging their Android bet and putting some pressure on Google to be on their best behavior.) MeeGo needed more support to break through, but the excitement just wasn't there.

Since we couldn't beat them, why not join them?

Android had definite advantages as an alternative future for Nokia. Partnering with Google would open up an avenue to the entire Android ecosystem: not just for phones but also for tablets and other emerging devices that were standardizing on the Android platform. It would free up technical talent and management bandwidth to help focus more on feature and product integration differentiation, rather than get further bogged down in building our own OS. We might even be able to leverage our expertise to influence the Android road map and differentiate ourselves from other manufacturers. It wasn't an unreasonable position.

Last but definitely not least, working hand-in-hand with Google might open a new revenue stream. If we did something to significantly boost Google's ad revenues, maybe we could get a cut. That would help Nokia create some financial headroom, an immensely reassuring proposition.

Why Not Android?

Google didn't see things our way.

At the January 2011 board meeting during which the MeeGo portfolio disaster was revealed, Stephen reminded us that Nokia had been in touch with Google several times during the previous months. Google's response was that they felt their current momentum and growing market share pretty much guaranteed that Android would take over as the biggest platform. Their message was clear: They didn't need Nokia because they had already won.

The vision of the future if we joined the Android ecosystem was grim from Nokia's vantage point. Instead of being the king, we would become just another vassal. And not only would we be one among many, but we would be the least experienced player on the platform. Samsung, the largest manufacturer of Android phones,[1] had been working on the Android platform for two years; we wouldn't be able to launch an Android device until late 2011 or early 2012, giving Samsung even more of a lead. And we'd be way behind Samsung in terms of volume.

We were especially keen on getting involved in the separate low-end version of Android that Google was working on. We tried to negotiate an exclusive head start on the project. But Google was not interested in giving us any preferred treatment.

It did not stop there. Since Google already had GoogleMaps, we'd have to sell Navteq. We expected Facebook and other major players to be future customers for Navteq, so the idea of having to sell such a valuable asset was not attractive.

We both knew that time was on Google's side. The longer the discussions took, the bigger Google would grow—and the weaker we would become. They didn't offer any concessions, and we didn't have any leverage.

MeeGo had hit the wall. Symbian, of course, was a total disaster. And now the Android option was starting to look like a no-go.

The Other Option

That left Microsoft and their Windows Phone.

Like Google, Microsoft didn't make devices themselves; they needed a hardware manufacturer to showcase their operating system. However, Microsoft's attitude was literally the flip side of Google's. Google's free Android platform had a plethora of manufacturers creating devices on it. Microsoft's Windows Phone was not free, and it was still trying to create a foothold in the market. Where Google signaled, "We don't need you," Microsoft had proactively proposed a relationship with us and throughout the winter spent significant time brainstorming how we could be persuaded to choose them. Where one party was withdrawn and reluctant, the other was excited and energetic about the possibility of partnering with us. Under the circumstances, Microsoft just felt like they'd be much more fun to work with.

Emotions aside, there were plenty of solid arguments in Microsoft's favor.

With the Windows Phone, Nokia would be unique and would have the pole position from the get-go. Nokia would be the biggest player and would be supported in a way that no other vendor in the Windows system would be. We would have unique access to and influence on the Windows operating system, with requirements defined by *us*. We would receive a significant marketing subsidy to the tune of $1 billion a year for four years. Of course, we'd be paying a license fee, which would eventually nullify the marketing subsidy, but since we were starting from zero volume, our initial licensing costs would be low.

Microsoft lacked some of the components we had—like our mapping and locations database—and we would be guaranteed the ability to differentiate in certain key areas, such as imaging, where we had lots of unique capabilities and intellectual property. We could build features and functionality that no one else had into the devices, and Microsoft would make certain features in the Windows Phone only available to Nokia for a certain time period. On Android, any unique ideas Nokia had would be supported equally by the OS for all vendors at the same time.

Together, Nokia and Microsoft could establish a viable third ecosystem with a real possibility to achieve a 30 percent market share. After all, Android had rocketed from nothing to its present position in just two years. Why couldn't a new system do the same?

Most conclusively, our internal calculations showed that gross margins for the Windows Phone would be higher than for Android. The large number of Android players could flood the market with lower-priced devices. With the higher-end Windows Phone, we would encounter less competition and have more pricing power.

In short, it would truly be an interdependent relationship. We wouldn't be begging, and Microsoft wouldn't be holding an ax above our head. If things went badly, Google wouldn't bend over backward to support us. Microsoft would.

At least, that is what we thought.

Moving Ahead with Microsoft

A leadership team meeting was held on January 22, less than a week before the decisive board meeting, to discuss and decide on the question of Android versus the Windows Phone. (Plan B was still a secret, but as the difficulties with MeeGo and Symbian became clear during the fall, it moved from being a backup plan to front and center.) Stephen was there, of course, along with Kai Öistamö, the head of strategy; Timo Ihamuotila, our CFO; the other NLT members; and the McKinsey consultant.

With one exception, they all voted for Microsoft. As I understand it, they genuinely believed that the Windows Phone was a better choice. Were they influenced by the sense that Stephen was leaning toward the Windows Phone? It's impossible to know.

The one person who disagreed was the McKinsey consultant. His argument went: "The difference between the two alternatives is that the Windows Phone gives us a black-and-white option. It has to succeed perfectly for Nokia to win; the alternative is the end of Nokia's story. With the Windows Phone scenario, Nokia would be the biggest vendor. For the ecosystem to succeed, it would have to achieve certain volumes. If it achieved those volumes, Nokia would automatically account for the majority of the market. But if that critical mass isn't achieved, then the Windows Phone will fail and Nokia will fail. There's no middle ground. With Android, there is middle ground."

The consultant felt that the Windows Phone option was a huge gamble, with a huge upside but a significantly higher than zero probability for complete disaster. With Android, the upside wasn't as high but there was much less likelihood of total failure.

The following Wednesday and Thursday, we held the board meeting. The first day, we focused on the Project Sea Eagle findings and the dire MeeGo news. The second day, we addressed our options going forward.

We were under the gun to make a decision. Nokia Investor Day, our annual get-together with our key shareholders and analysts, was just two weeks away, and the MeeGo story we had counted on to pump up investors had deflated like a punctured balloon.

The Windows Phone option sounded good. After all, in addition to the logical arguments from comparing what Google and Microsoft were willing to do with us, the Microsoft option was being recommended by a new CEO who came from the software industry and was thought to better understand the new world we were in. He had devoted all his time for several months to analyzing the situation, meeting with operators, technology partners, and our employees. And he was supported by every single Nokia management team member. They all said that the analysis was correct and that the Windows Phone was the better choice.

The McKinsey consultant was at the board meeting, but he didn't raise any red flags. He, too, wanted to support Stephen in front of the board. Also, the report that McKinsey created could easily be read in such a way that it actually supported the Windows Phone. The argument raised at the NLT meeting was not clearly presented.

The only other options were a combination of trying to push MeeGo, trying to fix Symbian, working on Meltemi, and/or doing exploratory work on Android—a real hodgepodge, which would spread our already thinning resources and further fragment them.

Microsoft looked like the only viable way forward.

Emotionally, we couldn't help rooting for Stephen. Just a few months into his term, here he was confronted by a crisis threatening the future of Nokia. We all wanted Stephen to be successful. We all wanted him to be right.

One of the key unresolved topics was getting Microsoft to commit to the low end of the market. Despite being a global business that made a lot of money overseas, Microsoft was predominantly an American company with an American management team. From Microsoft's point of view, there was just one important product-market fit, and that was for a device that the Microsoft people wanted to use themselves: a high-to-medium-category smartphone that had an English-language user interface and was equipped with the apps popular in the United States.

Due to Apple having swallowed the high end, Nokia's current strength was in the medium-to-low-end phones. We had millions and millions of customers on the streets of India, Pakistan, China, Brazil, Indonesia, Nigeria, Egypt, Russia, and many other developing countries. Many of these markets have local application vendors and lots of local requirements, the least of which is language. The initial version of the Windows Phone supported only eight languages—a ridiculously low number. But the management team was so determined to push ahead that these shortcomings didn't really register at the time.

Microsoft's Seattle-based engineering team assured us that they could deliver what we needed. We only realized afterward that they had no appreciation for the complexity of what we were asking.

Microsoft oversold, but we didn't do our homework on their international capabilities or even current features supporting the global market. Above everything else, we didn't dig deeply enough into the potential downsides.

In the January 26 board meeting, we de facto chose the Microsoft option. Very little effort, if any, was spent on developing the Android option after that. An ad hoc committee was established to support the final negotiations with Microsoft, which would still take weeks. Since the committee was established only after the choice had been made, it never explored any alternatives to the Windows Phone.

There was no time to waste. Fourth-quarter earnings were due to be reported the next day. The top 200 Nokia leaders would gather in London on February 9 in advance of Nokia Investor Day on February 11.

On the evening of February 10, the board held a conference call. It was too late to question whether we should do this or not. Stephen went over the plan in a very convincing way. He was analytical and open and answered every question. The team made notes of all the questions he couldn't properly answer, and they delivered more data without any delay on all those questions. It felt like a high-quality process under a very tight timetable.

The process wasn't perfect, but the facts led us to believe that the Windows Phone was the best choice.

Nokia could be blamed for shooting for the stars rather than settling for something smaller and safer. But as it fought to regain its past glory, it couldn't be blamed for lack of ambition. By this time, though, there was no room for mistakes.

. . . .

Always Look on the Dark Side

Logically, the argument to partner with Microsoft was very strong. Where the logic went wrong was that our analysis of the downside was not good enough. We simply hadn't had enough practice as a board doing this kind of thing; during my four years on the board, we had cumulatively not spent as much time on all technology topics as we did on this one. And we only spent perhaps two days total on this. Taking into account the complexity of the topic, that was not much. Technology was thought of as something that was too operational for the board and should be handled purely by management.

The other characteristic of our board work in those days was not to be critical, not to discuss negatives, and not to express doubts. I had received very direct one-on-one feedback a few times from our chairman for being too critical. I am sure my board colleagues had, too.

It's always more attractive to focus on how do we win, rather than trying to understand how we could lose. We spent 98 percent of the time thinking about how to make this a success. Very little time was spent on thinking through alternative scenarios: "What if this *doesn't* work? What would we do then? What might make this *not* work?"

If we had asked ourselves to think through a downside scenario, where we might have to resort to terminating the partnership, we would have had a better appreciation of the risk we were taking. If we had compared the Windows Phone downside scenario with an

Android downside scenario, we would have better understood the difference between the two alternatives.

When you need to make a decision that will decide the company's fate, consider appointing one or two team members to act as a red team. Their job is to focus on the downside, point out the risks, and keep everyone grounded. In our case, everybody belonged to the blue team.

As it was, the ad hoc committee identified 25 high-level risks on its risk map, of which the two biggest were that the ecosystem buildup would be unsuccessful and that the Windows Phone wouldn't be competitive. These were right on the money. But we didn't spend any time examining them. Nokia's mitigation plan for these scenarios was pretty much "We will work extra hard."

All of the above might not have changed the outcome. We might have still chosen the Windows Phone for the higher upside it offered. There was a lot of pressure to aim for a status that was comparable to what we had gotten used to.

Scenario-based thinking (which I'll describe in more detail in Chapter 11) would have helped the board and management explore the situation in more detail. A scenario-based approach forces one to be more methodical about alternatives. It imposes a discipline that compels the team to look at less-attractive options.

But in 2011, neither the board nor the leadership team had enough practice in this discipline. And because we weren't used to it, we didn't realize what we were missing.

• •

8

JUMPING OFF
A BURNING PLATFORM

FEBRUARY 2011–DECEMBER 2011

. . . .

Nokia had always been able to come up with a miracle
when the chips were down. The possibility of making
a miracle again was not completely unrealistic.

. . . .

ON FEBRUARY 8, 2011, Stephen sent out a companywide e-mail, the repercussions of which would rock our world.

Stephen wrote:

There is a pertinent story about a man who was working on an oil platform in the North Sea. He woke up one night from a loud explosion, which suddenly set his entire oil platform on fire. In mere moments, he was surrounded by flames. Through the smoke and heat, he barely made his way out of the chaos to the platform's edge. When he looked down over the edge, all he could see were the dark, cold, foreboding Atlantic waters.

As the fire approached him, the man had mere seconds to react. He could stand on the platform, and inevitably be consumed by the burning flames. Or, he could plunge 30 meters into the freezing waters. The man was standing upon a "burning platform," and he needed to make a choice.

He decided to jump.

Over the past few months, I've heard from our shareholders, operators, developers, suppliers and from you. Today, I'm going to share what I've learned and what I have come to believe.

I have learned that we are standing on a burning platform. And, we have more than one explosion—we have multiple points of scorching heat that are fueling a blazing fire around us.

Stephen summarized how Apple and Android had redefined the smartphone, incinerating Nokia's market share in both the high end and the low end. At the same time, he wrote, Nokia made one wrong decision after another:

The first iPhone shipped in 2007, and we still don't have a product that is close to their experience. Android came on the scene just over 2 years ago, and this week they took our leadership position in smartphone volumes. Unbelievable.

MeeGo's promise was thwarted by bad execution. Symbian had not been competitive for years. Meanwhile, the Chinese OEMs (original equipment manufacturers) were cranking out devices, as one Nokia employee said, "in the time that it takes us to polish a PowerPoint presentation." Stephen warned:

If we continue like before, we will get further and further behind, while our competitors advance further and further ahead. And the truly perplexing aspect is that we're not even fighting with the right weapons.

Stephen explained that the battle of devices had now become a war of ecosystems:

Our competitors aren't taking our market share with devices; they are taking our market share with an entire ecosystem. We're going to have to decide how we either build, catalyze or join an ecosystem.

Nokia's culture was partially to blame:

We poured gasoline on our own burning platform. We have lacked accountability and leadership to align and direct the company through these disruptive times. We haven't been delivering innovation fast enough. We're not collaborating internally. Nokia, our platform is burning.

Stephen concluded by alerting everyone to the announcement of a new strategy on February 11. He acknowledged that it would take a huge effort to transform the company. But, he wrote, we had no choice:

The burning platform, upon which the man found himself, caused the man to shift his behavior, and take a bold and brave step into an uncertain future. We have a great opportunity to do the same.

Stephen[1]

Board members were not on employee e-mail lists, so I heard about the memo from a colleague who sent me a link to an online news piece that included a copy of the e-mail.

I felt the memo was very strong and used some unorthodox language compared with the committee-approved, professionally polished messages I had gotten used to in Nokia. But while I was surprised, I understood the logic.

We had been doing things the wrong way for such a long time that our culture had become as unworkable as corrupt computer code. Stephen knew that in order to change a culture, you need to shock people into paying attention and make them understand the problem. He must have felt that the cultural problem was so pervasive and pernicious that he needed to make a strong symbolic gesture to galvanize change.

The need for the memo arose from the gap that had grown between the management team and the rest of the company over the months of analysis and research into Nokia's issues with Symbian and MeeGo. The management team had been on a journey toward the realization that Nokia had built its house on sand and the tide was rising. The rest of the company was still officially living in dreamland.

A webcasted all-hands meeting was arranged at Nokia House. Stephen introduced the challenging situation we were in and the burning platform story. The feedback from employees was hugely positive: "Finally, someone is telling us the truth" was a typical response. Not everyone had tuned in to the webcast, however, and the Nokia Leadership Team felt that it was crucial to bring everyone along on the journey. So the webcast was transcribed, edited, and checked over by the chief legal officer, and Jorma was briefed on the message. Then it was sent out to all employees, again to overwhelmingly positive feedback. (Many Nokia employees knew about Symbian's issues. They knew about MeeGo's challenges. Any presentations from the leadership that claimed things were good just reduced the credibility of the speaker. This is why Stephen's memo received such a good response from the staff. They already knew.)

It took about a week for the e-mail to leak—and then it went viral. But while Stephen received a range of approving responses—from the man who actually jumped from the platform (the story is based on a real-life incident) to Sir Martin Sorrell, then the head of WPP and one of the titans of marketing, who called it "some of the best corporate communications ever"[2]—the feedback was not all good. Although the media's reaction was balanced, characterizing the memo as "astonishingly candid,"[3] "brutally honest,"[4] and "one of the most combustible and gripping documents ever to emerge from a major corporation,"[5] some analysts and especially a multitude of bloggers took the opportunity to blame the memo for Symbian's rapid demise.

It is clear that Symbian did not die because of Stephen's memo, but no one will ever know how much the process was accelerated by the widespread negative publicity Symbian received because of the memo going viral.

Overcommunicate—But Be Careful What You Say

With hindsight, the mistake Stephen and the communications team made was disregarding the possibility that the memo would become a global phenomenon.

Was it right to hold the all-hands meeting and webcast? Absolutely yes. Bringing employees along on the journey was a must.

One of the toughest parts of leadership is that the leader is accountable for what happens, not just what was known when a decision was made and how good the intentions were. The main reason to criticize Stephen's memo at all is because of the outcome. It is much more difficult to criticize somebody for not predicting that.

Usually it's good to overcommunicate. It wouldn't have hurt to send the e-mail in advance to the board members and the full leadership team. There's no penalty in that. The penalty may be in *not* doing it.

One problem was that the board, with the exception of Jorma, did not know about the all-hands meeting or the great feedback from the employees. For some reason, Stephen did not explain the background, nor did Jorma. For the board, the memo seemed like a much bigger and different type of a mistake than it actually was as we only learned about the memo once it had already gone viral.

Surprising people with something major communicates mistrust. They're bound to ask: "Why didn't you show it to me before? Why did I have to see it at the same time as everyone else?" Stephen could have sent it to us as an FYI. Surprising your board like this gives people an unnecessary opportunity to disavow themselves not just from the message but also from the action it proposed.

When you're at the beginning of a major transformation, trust is your main currency. If you devalue it, you cannot hope to persuade people to wholeheartedly invest in your vision for radical change.

The board did not lose trust in Stephen. I believe we all felt that everyone is allowed a mistake. But the negative publicity created by the memo further fractured Stephen's relationship with Jorma, who was extra-sensitive to any public criticism.

During one board meeting that spring, I returned to the board-room after lunch. Stephen came in and sat down opposite me. He was visibly upset, with tears in his eyes.

"What's happening?" I asked.

He shook his head and said, "It's nothing."

He looked so shaken that I couldn't let it go. At the next break, I pulled him aside and said, "You look like you got a bad shock. What's going on?"

He took a deep breath. "Jorma attacked me about talking with board members."

Stephen had called each of the board members in advance of the meeting to brief them about the Microsoft relationship, so that they would be better informed. (I think that's a good practice. If something big is happening, I have long had the practice of either asking our CEO to call every board member before the meeting or doing it myself. People have a chance to formulate their questions and gain a more robust understanding of the topic. It makes for a more effective meeting.) Now Stephen said that Jorma had completely lost his temper. Stephen was used to the f-bombs and aggressive interplay at Microsoft, where CEO Steve Ballmer was known to fling office furniture around, but, he said, "I've never been in this kind of situation before."

Whatever trust existed between the CEO and the chairman was eroding fast.

A Three-Horse Race

On Friday, February 11, on the London stage at Nokia Investor Day, Stephen publicly announced the plan for Nokia's new future. "Nokia and Microsoft will combine our strengths to deliver an ecosystem with unrivaled global reach and scale," he said. "It's now a three-horse race."[6]

Stephen was joined on stage by Steve Ballmer, the bald and bombastic CEO of Microsoft. "This partnership with Nokia will dramatically accelerate the development of a vibrant strong Windows Phone ecosystem," Ballmer said. "This partnership is good for Microsoft and it's good for Nokia."[7]

The two clasped hands warmly and presented a picture of equal partners. Stephen had warned Ballmer that his trademark enthusiasm might erode the image of an equal partnership, but although Ballmer tried, he just couldn't restrain himself. He strode from one side of the stage to the other, his voice getting louder and even cracking a little in his excitement. Some viewers felt the event became a bit too much of a Microsoft announcement rather than a joint event. Speculation immediately started simmering: Could Stephen stand up to his former boss, or would Ballmer dominate his former lieutenant?

Among many of the Nokia faithful, the news of the Windows Phone partnership was like the announcement of a funeral. Symbian, which once commanded over 70 percent of the smartphone market and was still the number one smartphone platform in the world, was now officially on a deathwatch.[8] Stephen promised that MeeGo would continue as an "open-source mobile operating system project" and a MeeGo-related product would ship later that year, but it was clear that MeeGo was being sidelined. Almost immediately, Stephen was accused of being a Trojan horse, a Machiavellian plant who betrayed Finland's flagship company to an upstart from Seattle.[9]

Even though shares of Nokia slumped 12 percent on the news,[10] there were plenty of independent observers who approved. "There are no heroics in being the 20th Android phone at Best Buy," said one consultant. "Going ahead with Windows Phone 7 could actually serve as a differentiator for Nokia in the marketplace."[11]

Google had a different opinion. Sniffing at Project Sea Eagle, which advocated the switch from Symbian to the Windows Phone, Google senior vice president Vic Gundotra tweeted, "Two turkeys do not make an eagle."[12]

In Case We Need a Miracle

Against this background, negotiations with Microsoft continued at breakneck speed. (We wouldn't have a final contract until April.) The board's ad hoc committee monitored the contract negotiation process in a number of conference calls during the spring. But now that we had announced the deal, we *had* to accomplish it. If things broke apart during that period, Nokia didn't have anything to fall back on.

We eventually agreed on a 10-year deal. A "rip cord" was added to the contract, which allowed Nokia to terminate the contract after 3 and 5 years.

While we agreed that the Windows Phone would be our "main smartphone platform," we weren't bound to total exclusivity; in principle, we just agreed not to use Google's Android. And just because Symbian and MeeGo were off the table didn't mean that we didn't have other cards to play.

One project was the Meltemi operating system. This "mini-MeeGo" was a Linux-based addition above the low-end S40 operating system. We envisioned Meltemi becoming the platform that would bring the "internet for the next billion" smartphone users.

Project Serenity was the third pillar in our strategy, after the Windows Phone and the "internet for the next billion." The idea was to disrupt ourselves—and, in the process, Apple and Android.

Our labs around the world were already working on an emerging technology: HTML5. HTML is the descriptive language in which web pages are coded. HTML5 was a new standard that expanded HTML to enable developers to create applications that would run in browsers. Instead of having to customize an app for each operating system, developers could write an app once, and it would work on Android and iOS and Symbian and Windows Phone and every single device with a compatible browser. The team believed there was a chance that we would have a new device platform that would build on the promise of HTML5 in less than three years. These devices would basically be cloud phones, with all data and much of the functional logic in the cloud. All devices used by a single user would also share the same state. Whatever you did in one device would immediately be visible in all your other devices. This was an intriguing concept.

Over its 100 years of history, Nokia had always been able to come up with a miracle when the chips were down. The possibility of making a miracle again was not completely unrealistic.

Bridging the Gaps

The Microsoft deal closed on April 21. Within a month, changes began—and they were harsh. Nokia announced a round of layoffs, slashing 7,000 jobs, or 12 percent of our workforce.[13] Because Symbian would be terminated, the cuts targeted people who worked in smartphones—including about 1,400 employees[14] and some 2,500 subcontractors in Finland alone.

In towns like Salo, 60 miles west of Nokia headquarters, Nokia was the largest employer.[15] Working for Nokia in these communities was more than a paycheck. Our R&D facility in Salo was where engineers had shown Stephen the water-resistant smartphone. That's the sort of thing you could boast about to your friends and family. Now that would be gone—as would the corporate taxes that helped fund local social services.[16]

We knew these cuts would bite deep.

There are plenty of ways to handle huge layoffs that cause long-lasting harm to both the affected employees and the company. The "Bridge" program offered an alternative scenario.

Bridge was a comprehensive approach to helping employees find new employment opportunities and to continuing to support local economies where Nokia had been a major employer. The program was based on four principles:

- We would accept our responsibility, rather than blame others or the market.
- We would actively lead the program, rather than expecting the government or local community to step in.
- We would involve all relevant parties as full partners.
- We would communicate openly.

Bridge offered five paths, or bridges, to a new life. Employees could opt to transition: to train for a new job at Nokia, to go back to university or another educational institution, or to journey to "your own destination"—something dramatically different, like starting a nonprofit organization. Or they could choose the innovation lane by starting their own business. Or they could find a job in a different company. Nokia contributed training, career counseling, equipment, and considerable financial support: €300 million for the innovation bridge and €800 million for the rest of the program.

The Bridge program resulted in 60 percent of employees knowing their next step on the day they left the company. It also helped former employees start more than 1,000 new companies, supporting jobs in communities where Nokia was a major employer.[17] Some 18 months after Bridge was launched, a Finnish university surveyed the people who had been laid off: 85 percent said they felt the way in which they had been treated in the downsizing had been good or very good.

A Sad Spring

Bridge was a positive response to a sad situation. Throughout the spring, there were other reminders of our precarious circumstances.

We continued to be dogged by quality issues. The N8, our Symbian flagship phone, was a dud. Back in January, it had a return rate of 35.8 percent. In February, the return rate was 24.6 percent—one out of every four devices was being brought back to the shops. An acceptable return rate for low-end devices used to be less than 2 percent; for a high-end smartphone, it was between 5 percent and 10 percent. That's bearable; we gave the user a new device, and typically it worked and the user was happy. Anything above 10 percent is painful; it's a huge cost to us, and after a couple of faulty replacements, customers won't buy your products ever again.

Most of the returns were due to problems with Symbian^3. We were looking forward to shipping an updated version of Symbian^3 in March, but it was the same old story: delayed due to quality faults.

Our market capitalization was down 40 percent from the previous year. Apple's was up 40 percent in the same time frame. We didn't appreciate the symmetry.

The number of Android devices had leapfrogged Symbian phones in just two years, a remarkably short period of time. Bounding along at the front of the pack was HTC, a Taiwanese newcomer whose HTC

Dream, sold as T-Mobile's G1, had been the first Android phone on the market at the end of 2008. I couldn't help thinking that if Nokia had started an Android program a year earlier, it probably would have buoyed up our share price. Instead, in April, HTC surpassed Nokia's market capitalization, $34 billion versus $33 billion.[18]

Things weren't going well with NSN either. Back in November 2010, the board approved Project Nemo, a decision to sell 30 percent of NSN. Three private equity firms showed interest, and by the annual meeting in May, the due diligence had been completed and preliminary bids received. One of the private equity firms didn't have adequate funding, so we didn't know if we could take them seriously. Some of the terms in the others' proposals weren't acceptable.

Meanwhile, NSN was a money-losing sinkhole that now threatened to drag down all of Nokia.

Making the Marriage Work

Work had already begun on the Lumia 800, the Windows Phone model we hoped would start to win us back, if not yet market share, at least mindshare. The launch was scheduled for November, gut-wrenchingly soon. Our R&D teams had dived in back in February, even before the definitive agreement was signed, but the timetable was extremely challenging. There was so much to do and learn.

The Nokia and Microsoft teams worked well together. The Microsoft team quickly learned to respect Nokia's ability to do hardware, and the Nokia team quickly learned to respect Microsoft's ability to do software. This mutual esteem helped protect against infighting when negative surprises arose.

And they inevitably did.

The Nokia team soon discovered that Microsoft didn't have much experience in designing products for global markets. They didn't appreciate the complexity involved in supporting a myriad of languages and local applications.

The biggest surprise shouldn't have been a surprise. That was how strongly the chipset manufacturers bowed down to Android's dominance. By 2011, Android had muscled its way into becoming the top global smartphone platform.[19] Consequently, the chipset vendors put Android at the top of their priority list. The Windows Phone, being the younger cousin with the merest sliver of the market, was much further down the list.

Over the next years, this created an irresistible headwind for the Windows Phone, preventing the Windows Phone from claiming that it had the fastest chips and best performance. In a face-off, the Windows Phone was able to run faster than Android on the same hardware due to its lighter operating system, but the high-end Android devices always had dibs on better hardware. Our strategy of stealing a march on Android by launching Windows Phones on a different schedule quickly fizzled because we couldn't get the fastest chipsets first.

After a frantic eight-month sprint to the finish line, the first two Lumia phones hit store shelves in November. The €420 ($588) Lumia 800 and the slightly less expensive Lumia 710 were aimed squarely at the mid-market that was the Android sweet spot.[20] Showing off the Lumia 800's minimalist design and vivid colors, Stephen Elop proclaimed, "It's a new dawn for Nokia."[21]

But despite solidly positive reviews—"Today was about proving that Nokia can deliver," commented an influential industry analyst at the Lumia debut at Nokia World. "Today they showed they can"[22]—profitability plunged. Five years earlier, Nokia had been minting money, with an operating profit just shy of €8 billion.[23] By the end of 2011, the company reported an operating loss of €1.07 billion.[24]

Nokia, once the undisputed king of mobile, had been dethroned.

Change at the Top

Those weren't the only changes.

Earlier that year, Jorma had announced that he would step down as chairman at the Annual General Meeting in May 2012. In November, vice-chairman Marjorie Scardino invited me to her office in London to discuss the possibility of my taking his place.

I don't remember a lot about the discussion, but one thing stuck out. For some reason, I said that I hadn't yet encountered anything that I couldn't do. My unwitting boast so tickled Marjorie that she burst out laughing.

Finns typically don't brag—it is considered crass—so I sheepishly explained what I had meant. Like any programmer, I learned to believe that one can solve even the most difficult problem by breaking it down into manageable components and solving those one by one. With perseverance, one can overcome challenges.

As an entrepreneur, I have made all the mistakes in the book, but none of them prevented me from creating in F-Secure a company that I continue to be proud of. Inadvertent hubris aside, I told Marjorie that I sincerely believed that I had not yet encountered a challenge that I could not cope with.

Despite that answer—or, maybe, because of it—Marjorie recommended me for the chairmanship. In mid-December, she told me that if I were willing, the board would propose me as the next chairman.

I wasn't altogether surprised. Individual board members had raised the issue periodically. Nokia is a Finnish company. For the first time ever, it had a non-Finnish CEO, so the board felt we should have a Finnish chairman. There were only three Finns on the board, two of whom—Jouko Karvinen and Kari Stadigh—were sitting CEOs, so they really couldn't take on the role. That left me as the only option.

But when Marjorie originally asked me to come talk to her in London, I wasn't altogether sure whether I should take the position.

Just about every year I had considered leaving the board; I don't really know why I didn't. I suppose I stayed partially for the right reasons, partially for selfish reasons. Despite my frustration and disillusion, I had enjoyed the prestige of being on the board of a company everyone recognized. And I had to admit that the idea of becoming chairman of a global brand-name company was attractive. I wasn't very proud of these selfish thoughts, but they did have an emotional impact.

But I also hated the idea of giving up, of abandoning the company when it was in trouble. It's not how people should act. Then, too, Nokia had given me so much in my career as an entrepreneur that I was starting to bleed the Nokia blue as well. And like many entrepreneurs who don't know where our limits are, I never doubted that I would do okay, even if there was no rational reason to support that.

The same logic applied to being willing to take on the chairmanship: If I declined, how could I ask someone else to do it? Nokia epitomized everything that was great about Finland. I couldn't abandon it just because it was no longer at the peak of success.

At the heart of how all Finns see themselves is the concept of *sisu*, the uniquely Finnish quality that combines endurance, resilience, tenacity, determination, and perseverance. *Sisu* is about facing obstacles head-on, about not giving up. It's about finishing what you start and not quitting just because things are tough.

I really didn't have a choice about accepting the chairmanship. For both good and bad reasons, I had to say yes.

· ·

Why Nokia's Board Didn't Do Better

Why didn't Nokia's board of directors do more to stop the implosion?

That's a valid question. It speaks directly to the reality of being a board member versus what many people think a board member does.

To begin with, board members—both individually and as a team—have direct authority on very few topics and no formal authority on a multitude of topics. But even when the decision is not formally a board decision, the board has a lot of influence, if it chooses to use it. Why many boards either don't or can't is usually because they simply do not know enough to be able to have an opinion. They have limited access to limited information. People may think that board members are deeply involved with the company, even if not physically present every day. That's often far from the truth.

You come together at predestined dates for relatively brief periods of time. The agenda is created by someone whom you trust to know what's going on. And for each of those little pockets of time, yet another person—a management team member who has been delegated to discuss that issue—presents the information.

The management's approach veers between two extremes. At one end of the spectrum, the management team members use the board as a brain trust: They invite board members to engage deeply and share their expertise and experience.

At the other end, the members of the management team just want to escape unscathed: to give basic information but avoid unpleasant topics. Sometimes they mislead the board, or in the rare worst case, they blatantly lie.

As a single board member, you have very little influence on this. You may actually learn so little that you might not know at all what's really going on in the company. During my first few years on the Nokia board, we were inundated with data—the pre-read material usually measured hundreds of pages—but we lacked insight into what was happening and why. Data does not replace understanding.

That's often the case when the company has been doing well for a long time. The board falls into the mindset that, because things have been going so well, it's clear that the members of the management team are doing a good job, so let's not disturb or distract them; let's not destroy value by interfering. It's not that the board members are trying to shirk their duty; they naturally believe that the success will continue if they continue doing what they've done before. They also get used to taking it easy, and changing the status quo always requires force.

It's the chairman's responsibility to shatter that complacency. If the chairman is not awake, or even worse, is deliberately trying to avoid tough topics, it's really difficult for an individual board member to find out early enough if something is going truly wrong.

And because the chairman serves as the conduit between the management team and the board, if there's not a strong and open relationship between the chairman and the CEO, information won't flow through to the board.

I know other Nokia board members would have liked to ask tough questions. They were good people with plenty of business experience. During 2008 and 2009, Nokia's still recent overwhelming success swept aside doubts and created its own momentum to continue doing things the same way. It takes an enormous force to change the trajectory of a heavy object that is already hurtling in a certain direction. With a sharp-tongued and thin-skinned chairman at the helm, intent on maintaining iron authority, raising questions can be close to mutiny.

For a new, relatively inexperienced board member with little access to information, with someone else deciding how much time in meetings is spent on which subjects and when not much time is allocated to these meetings in the first place, it's going to take a while to understand what the situation really is. I offer this not as an excuse but as a challenge: How do we change that?

It was one of the challenges I began to address as soon as I became chairman.

· ·

PART TWO

TRANSFORMING
TO WIN AGAIN

9

TAKING CHARGE IN A CRISIS

JANUARY 2012–APRIL 2012

. . . .

The concepts of entrepreneurial leadership are necessary
for any person and any organization to adapt successfully
to today's complex and dynamic world.

. . . .

TWO YEARS EARLIER, toward the end of 2009, Nokia's leadership commissioned McKinsey consultants to assess and provide ideas to improve the organizational efficiency of the company. McKinsey's Organizational Health Index (OHI) is a methodology used by McKinsey on thousands of companies to evaluate the drivers of—and detriments to—creating a high-performing culture. OHI enables comparisons between the companies and can help a company understand its organizational health relative to that of others. Obviously, no company wants to be ranked in the bottom 50th percentile.

Nokia ranked down in the bottom *25th percentile.*

McKinsey's ability to compare a large number of companies meant the ranking was relatively objective. This was bad news for Nokia, as according to McKinsey historical data, there was a higher than 50 percent probability for companies ranked at Nokia's level to cease business operations within two years. (The report was not shared with the regular board members. I only learned about it in 2017.)

When I was asked to become chairman in December 2011, it had been two years to the month since the OHI report put Nokia on death-watch. According to the data, our time was up.

Nails in the Coffin

As McKinsey had predicted, we were sliding over the brink and hang-ing on by our fingernails. The year 2011 did not end well, and 2012 started even worse. Having set the 2012 financial targets just a few months earlier, at the end of January Nokia already had to reduce the first-quarter revenue forecast by €1 billion. For the full year, the fore-cast was sliced by over €3 billion. The full company's operating profit target was halved from €2 billion to €1 billion; for Devices & Services, the former money mill, operating profit was lowered from €640 mil-lion to *zero*.

There was no reason to believe the decline would stop.

Symbian was imploding before our eyes. Even if we had managed to turn out the perfect version of the Symbian OS for devices, it might not have helped. Users, app developers, resellers, operators—everyone was beginning to believe that Symbian was toxic.

China was hammering nails in the coffin lid. Our growth in China had been based on the GSM/WCDMA platform for cellular networks. But as China shifted to TD-SCDMA standards (these are all different radio standards, which require modifications to mobile phones), what had been a uniform GSM market in 2009 had become a market in which two-thirds of the networks were *non*-GSM. The market we could sell into (management having decided not to invest in TD-SCDMA in order to keep costs down and profits up) shrank from 98 percent to 55 percent—and in that remaining portion, we faced very tough competition.

All the Chinese mobile phone operators suddenly changed their criteria defining how they would subsidize products along the range of price points. They basically said, "We will subsidize a product at Price A that fulfills these stipulations: this much memory, this type of pro-cessor, and a display of the following specifications." Similar criteria were issued for other price points. In our industry, operator subsidies have a significant impact on sales. All the Chinese manufacturers were able to manage their portfolios so that they had products that fit the new criteria and could benefit from operator subsidies. Unfortunately, the criteria were defined in such a way that excluded Nokia, so we were not subsidized in what had been one of our major markets.

The collapse of Symbian sales intensified negative momentum. When sales cratered, everything needed to be downsized to fit that lower sales volume. Some future models had to be killed because the planned portfolio was too big and costly; canceled products resulted in overcapacity in R&D, which led to further layoffs; fewer products to sell automatically meant sales went down even further. We were in a vicious, vicious cycle.

In addition to gutting our profitability, Symbian's disintegration was wrecking our cash flow with a vengeance. In our model, we were paid by our distribution channel before we paid our component suppliers. In an up cycle, cash flows in like a flood tide. It's like being automatically loaned a lot of money by the suppliers. But when sales start declining, the financial tide turns. The loan becomes due. Money is no longer coming in from the distribution channel, but you still have to pay suppliers and cover your other bills. Thanks to Symbian's free fall, we were now facing strongly negative cash flows.

NSN was also draining cash. Nokia and Siemens, the two partners in the joint venture, had each put in a final €500 million. With that €1 billion and up to €1.5 billion from a revolving credit facility, the plan to restructure was a go. It's not always understood that it's hugely expensive to restructure. It is quite common for companies doing poorly not to have sufficient funds to restructure. Taking care of the employees who will be laid off and other actions is a double whammy to cash flow. "Workforce balancing"—the euphemism for layoffs—would be announced on January 27, setting off yet another negative news cycle around Nokia.

A few rays of light managed to sneak through the roiling clouds.

Nokia was doing well in the low end. We had shipped the 1,500,000,000th S40 device in December—that's quite a number!—

bringing in over €1 billion in profit in 2011. Maintaining that cash machine through a successful implementation of the Meltemi operating system was more important than ever.

And while the Lumia ramp-up remained slow and was dogged with significant quality issues, there was a lot of positive buzz around the Lumia 900. At the Consumer Electronics Show in early January 2012, it was dubbed "Best phone of CES."[1] AT&T would start promoting and shipping the Lumia 900 in March or April. One reviewer gushed, "It looks like a fantastic Windows Phone with outstanding hardware, design, and software. . . . This is definitely the Windows Phone to beat."[2] Expectations were high all around: from operators, industry analysts, the press, us, and, not least of all, Microsoft.

There was one other item of special significance to me on the board agenda. The invitation to the AGM was approved and issued. It included the name of the proposed next chairman. This was the first time people outside of the board knew of my planned future role.

But what kind of company would I be chairing? Things were going downhill so rapidly. I did not truly understand what our alternatives were—I just did not have enough data. Would I become chairman of a company with a future, or would I oversee Nokia's dismantlement?

Making Lists

As one of the youngest members of the board of directors, with little hands-on experience of running mega-sized companies and one who had been more critical than most about the way Nokia had been run, I was not an obvious choice for the chairmanship, especially as the current chairman did not support my election. (Even though Jorma never said anything to me about the topic, I sensed that he was not happy about the idea of me succeeding him. What I did not know at the time was that he actively campaigned against me. I am mentioning this here only because it influenced the dynamics in the board during the tough months ahead and made it more challenging for me to successfully start in the role.) Therefore, I wanted to be extra thoughtful about how I approached it.

As I started thinking, "How do I prepare?" I identified some things I could do to get a handle on the situation and ready myself for my new role.

I have long had a habit of keeping lists on various topics, ranging from thoughts about leadership, to potential problems and specific concerns I have identified, to particular interests. (I use Microsoft OneNote for these lists. That way I can access them from any device I have.) The items on the lists come from everywhere: from my own real-life experiences, from challenges I know I will have to face, from something someone else has lived through and talked or written about. Something rings a bell, and I think, "Hey, that's something I appreciate. Write it down."

One of my favorite lists is about leadership.

Professor James G. March from Stanford University maintains that people always have a target profile in their minds for any important activity that they engage in, and he believes that they subconsciously aspire to behave according to that profile. I believe it is much more efficient to deliberate on what the profile should contain than to allow that profile to build randomly based on one's experiences. I have been working for almost 20 years to collect leadership behaviors that I believe in and that I try to realize in the way I interact with people.

When I knew I would become the chairman, I once again looked over my notes about the kind of a leader I wanted to be. I thought about what that meant in terms of leading the board and working with the management team of a company in crisis. That helped me take some good steps in the early weeks and months of 2012.

The Courage to Break with Convention

One of the most important lessons from my lists was that whenever you start something important, your first move should be: Stop! Take a mental step back and distill the essence of the issue. Remember the traffic safety lesson you were taught as a child: Stop, look, and listen. Think of this as the leadership version. And the more serious the leadership challenge, the more necessary this lesson.

I know this sounds counterintuitive. In a crisis, it's natural to feel an urgent need to identify the core problem and come up with a solution. The more critical the situation, the greater the desire to act immediately. So as the storms around Nokia intensified, I deliberately forced myself to step back and engage in deep reflection.

This is not just about stopping to listen to people and looking around to examine the situation before taking action. What I am talking about is a rung higher on the abstraction ladder. Think: What should the dynamics and behaviors from yourself and others be like so that you can, together, comprehensively understand the situation and come up with the right actions? What kind of a working environment would enable you to find the best way forward no matter what you end up facing? What might hold you back? How can you address those issues?

My biggest concern was, of course, that I would fail and speed Nokia's collapse in some way. This was a real possibility, at least if I believed the current chairman. I couldn't erase four years of, "Risto, you come from a small software company. You don't understand how a global company the size of Nokia works." And, maybe he had a point. Regardless, if some of the other board members shared Jorma's opinion, it might be really difficult to be an effective leader of the board.

And if I failed to show the board that I could do a good job from the start, that would quickly erode the credibility and confidence necessary to do the job well. That, in turn, would affect the management and senior leadership. If the management knows that the chairman doesn't truly enjoy the support of the board members, it's difficult for the chairman to deal with the CEO and the management team as well.

Your authority is directly related to your actions. Without the right actions, you do not have real authority regardless of your position. On the other hand, a chairman needs to beware of behaving in a way that would reduce the CEO's ability to be effective. As a leader, you need to know what the boundaries are and where, so you can avoid breaching them. That's something I'd have to keep in mind as chairman.

The common denominator of my mental explorations was the *qualities* involved in trying to fix Nokia's myriad problems, not the actual *work* of fixing them.

To start with, I asked myself, "What am *I* accountable for? What is *my* ultimate duty? What are the limits of my responsibility? If my job is to lead the board, how can I do that in a way that will result in what we need?"

My first realization was that running the board based on traditional best practices would not cut it. I did not want the company to fail after I had done everything by the book. I realized that it was my duty to throw the "rule book for boards" in the trash and do whatever it would take to make Nokia successful again—within my personal values, Nokia's values, and laws and regulations, of course.

I reminded myself of one of my core beliefs: Don't let your role define you. Or in this case, don't allow yourself to be limited by conventional definitions of your role.

Everything flowed from the answers to those initial questions: my role, the role of the board, the relationship between the board and the management team, the way we should all conduct ourselves to accomplish our best work.

Without the courage to break with convention, we might no longer exist as an independent company.

Getting Acquainted with Management

Back in December, I had told Marjorie that I would like to get to know the members of the leadership team so that I could begin to learn enough of the details of the business to be useful. Her sole concern was that I might step on the CEO's toes. Now that I was officially chairman-in-waiting, I could freely engage with CEO Stephen Elop and start talking directly to the management team, something that hadn't been possible earlier.

I remember the wariness in Stephen's behavior when we first sat down to talk. I tried to impress on him that I truly understood that in order for the company to be successful, he needed to be successful and that it was my job to do what I could to make that happen. I invited him to talk with the CEO of F-Secure, the company I had founded and led for 18 years before moving on to become its chairman. (Transitioning from long-term CEO to chairman is one of the most demanding role changes.) I explained to him how the more I knew about what was going on at Nokia, the better I would be able to help him. If I proposed good ideas, he could adopt them as his own; if the ideas were bad, he could just ignore them.

I made it clear that because the company was in such dire straits, I wouldn't just watch from afar. But I promised that I would always be completely transparent. If I talked with one of his team members, I would try to always send him at least a short note summarizing the conversation. In turn, he promised to encourage his leadership team to talk freely with me.

Stephen may have been worried that I would intrude on his turf, but by the time I actually became chairman, we felt quite relaxed with each other—enough that I would regularly invite Stephen to join me in a kettlebell workout and he would just as regularly find an excuse not to.

I also interviewed all the board members about what they thought were the most important issues and what aspects of the board's role they would like to change. I got great ideas from both the old and the new board members.

We had brought in two new board members at the Annual General Meeting the previous May: Kari Stadigh is the CEO of Sampo, a Finnish financial superpower that owns the largest insurance company and 20 percent of the largest bank in the Nordic countries; and Jouko Karvinen was the CEO of Stora Enso, a global Finnish-Swedish forest industry giant whose origins date to before Columbus discovered the New World. Both are strong characters and seasoned business leaders. Kari had been elected one of *Harvard Business Review*'s 100 best-performing CEOs in the world in 2014. We were golfing buddies from back when I still had time to play golf. He is always good company and has a quirky sense of humor, but best of all, he has very strong opinions—especially about the importance of always working on behalf of the shareholders—and is never afraid to share them.

Jouko liked to put on a humble facade, but like Kari, he had strong opinions and didn't try to hide them. Jouko was the epitome of a grumpy old man—lovable and obstinate. I respected both of them tremendously. I was very happy when they joined the board because I knew they would not kowtow to anyone. They were good role models for the kind of a board I wanted to build. (Jouko stepped down from the board in 2016 after providing an invaluable contribution to Nokia's transformation. Kari is still a board member in 2018.)

With Stephen's support, I arranged meetings with management team members during the spring. I learned something from every conversation. As an example, one of the conversations was with Juha Putkiranta, Nokia's master of manufacturing, logistics, and supply chain management. Juha explained to me that Lumia 900 had 800 separate components—twice as many as a Symbian smartphone and a painful indication of how difficult it was to create devices on the new platform. The testing efforts for Lumia were 10 times what was involved for Symbian. Were these indicative of a bigger trend? Had we gotten ourselves into an even worse mess than with Symbian, one I would be held accountable for if it failed?

In each of these conversations, I asked, "What should I change? And how could I change it?" After each conversation, I made notes and added them to my lists.

It's perhaps unusual for a new chairman to get involved with so many leaders, but this is what any sensible person should do, especially in a company in crisis. Not knowing something is a poor excuse for failure, if by working a little bit harder and smarter, you could have gained the required information.

A Drumbeat of Despair

It's fair to say that I didn't realize how bad things were when I agreed to become the next chairman of Nokia. As the early months of 2012 unspooled, and I had more access to data and people, I began to understand just how precarious Nokia's situation really was.

Symbian continued to disintegrate; at the March board meeting, we began to discuss plans to end its life. Samsung was smelling blood and pouring money into programs targeting Nokia in every market with the goal of a final take-down. Samsung officially unseated us as the world's top handset maker at the end of April.[3]

Despite positive feedback from the public and press, the hard facts about Lumia sales were depressing. Our blind shopper tests showed why: In a typical interaction, the sales clerk would ask an interested customer, "Do you want the iPhone or an Android?" Lumia wasn't even mentioned.

Worse, now there was bad news about Meltemi.

It was originally assumed that Meltemi, the OS for low-end smartphones—a sort of MeeGo-minus—would be a straightforward project integrating MeeGo components for a simplified OS. Instead, it turned out that the MeeGo components were too "fat," i.e., designed for a system with more memory and processing power, to fit into the slimmed-down Meltemi criteria. We'd been assured in previous updates that Meltemi development was on track. Now we were told that the program would be delayed by five months.

History was repeating itself in the most depressing way. Just like the Symbian and MeeGo calamities, there was no single reason for the delay. It was the familiar frustrating refrain: a program spread among different development sites with different cultures, a lack of communication among the sites, a reluctance to raise red flags, and a program leader who purely relied on reports from his lieutenants rather than also talking directly to the developers.

Nokia's worsening financial situation raised the question of whether we could afford a five-month delay—and then, perhaps, *another* delay— or whether we should just cut our losses and kill the Meltemi program. Meltemi was a key pillar in our mobile phone strategy. Would killing it eviscerate the one business in which Nokia was still making money?

Warning Bells

On April 11, Nokia announced that it expected financial results to miss prior forecasts:[4] first-quarter Devices & Services revenues would be about €4.2 billion, a 40 percent year-on-year fall.[5] Our operating profits from D&S were down by approximately €800 million.

Nokia's market cap had shrunk to around €10 billion. Apple's had grown to almost $600 billion.[6] Nokia and Apple had been roughly even in 2008. Now Apple's market cap was 60 times as large as Nokia's.

A public company typically issues a profit warning when there is reason to believe that the actual results will deviate in a material way from the original guidance. Guidance can be given on almost anything: revenues, cash flow, the launch of a new product, or earnings.

Sometimes profit warnings are positive, but more often they're negative. The implications of a negative profit warning are bad on two levels: The bad news is obvious, but a profit warning also indicates that the company's management was caught by surprise. It opens up questions about whether the company's forecasting processes are good enough, or if something dramatic happened that made this a surprise, will it continue? Will this be a single event or a long-term trend? How will it affect employees', customers', suppliers', and investors' opinion of the management of the company?

Nokia's April 11 announcement that it expected bigger operating losses in its devices business and that the losses would continue for the first six months of the year caused its stock to plummet 16 percent, closing at $4.24—a 14-year low.[7] And it accelerated a cascade of bad news. Our credit rating was slashed to "junk" status,[8] analysts downgraded the stock,[9] and share prices slid even further—this time below $4.[10]

The first rumors that Nokia might go bankrupt had appeared in January. Sparked by the demise of Kodak, another 100-plus-year-old company, a columnist for Gigacom asked, "Is Nokia the next Kodak? I hope not—for I like those guys—but Nokia is a likely candidate."[11] Now a new wave of negative stories surged in the media. "Nokia has a new problem—it might go bankrupt," announced star analyst Henry Blodget on April 19.[12]

The April profit warning was the second in less than a year—the previous one had been issued in May 2011[13]—and it would not be the last. A third warning would be issued in June. That came out to one in each of the first two quarters of 2012, along with the announcement that Nokia would cut a further 10,000 jobs.[14]

The June warning drove shares down to $2.35 on the New York Stock Exchange,[15] the lowest point since 1996. Our market value was now 92 percent lower than where it stood when Apple released the iPhone.[16]

In addition, Nokia's bad news hit all the companies that were suppliers and subcontractors to Nokia. Their share prices sank too, as investors unloaded shares all along the value chain.

Nokia had once been able to boost a sagging market or calm volatility with our announcements. Those days were over.

Entrepreneurial Leadership: The Way Forward

Looking back, this period was the darkest six months in my entire time with Nokia. The company's leadership was being attacked by the press and investors; employees were demoralized and afraid of continued instability, potential reorganizations, and tight cost cutting. Finland's flagship company—a source of national pride—was in danger of disappearing, and nothing the management did seemed to help.

It was a tough moment to become chairman. I was fully aware that if the worst happened, it would be my face and my name that would be forever linked to the event. That would have painful consequences not just for me but for my family as well.

How did I keep going? By drawing on my philosophy of entrepreneurial leadership.

My ideas about what I call "entrepreneurial leadership" were forged and honed during my 18 years at F-Secure. But you don't have to create a company to adopt an entrepreneurial mindset. While some of the concepts of entrepreneurial leadership are, I think, fundamental to a leader, they're also completely applicable to anyone in any role, from a receptionist to the CEO and everyone in between. I believe those qualities are necessary for any person and any organization to adapt successfully to today's complex and dynamic world.

You should cultivate those qualities whether you're in charge of a company of many or a company of one.

There are 10 components in the way I think of entrepreneurial leadership:

1. Hold Yourself Accountable

First and foremost, you need to care—and care deeply—about everything that happens: the business, your colleagues, the customers, the products. And you need to show at every turn that you have a sense of ownership.

What do I mean by ownership? One question I often ask audiences is, "How many of you have ever rented a car?" Almost everyone raises a hand. Then I ask, "Who here has ever washed a rental car?" Most people don't, because they don't have a sense of ownership for that car. If you feel your workplace is the equivalent of a rental car—that it's just something to get you from one place to another in your life—then you don't feel any ownership. You won't go the extra mile or care about what the company does. But when you feel ownership and you see something that doesn't work, you feel accountable, regardless of your role. You'll wash the dirty car.

You can think of work as a job, a career, or a calling. If you work in order to earn money to be able to do what is really meaningful for you, you drive a rental car. If you are motivated by progressing in your career, you have a deeper connection with what you do. If work feels like a calling, you don't have to struggle to find motivation. You care deeply. I believe that we all are entitled to seek out and find our calling.

Here's a small but illustrative example of something that happened at Nokia. A computer screen was installed next to the main elevator bank at Nokia HQ with a running display of weather forecasts, market news, Nokia values, and infomercials—the usual things. About a week after it was put up, I noticed it was displaying an error message. The next day, it hadn't been fixed. The third day, it still hadn't been fixed.

When people see the same error message every day, it tells them that something is broken in our world and that it's fine with us to let it remain that way. I flashed back to the Symbian build-time fiasco. Would people again feel that other unacceptable things could become acceptable?

I felt a real pressure on myself to make sure the error got fixed. In the afternoon of that third day, I sent a message to the people in the IT department asking, "When are you going to take care of this?" They, of course, answered, "Today." (Typically, when the chairman calls about a computer problem, they say they will fix it immediately.) But the question was, why didn't they fix it earlier or at least shut the display off? Why did they allow it to flash the same error message for 72 hours straight?

While the display was not even close to the seriousness of the Symbian build-time example, it was a good opportunity for me to show that I cared about the company.

It is important to think of the various broken things around us as symbols of caring, symbols of pride in what we do—and, if we allow them to remain broken, as symbols of lack of pride and not caring. When you have an entrepreneurial mindset, *everything* is your responsibility. You truly care, and your actions communicate that loud and clear.

2. Face Facts

When you feel accountable, you can never escape from facts. Everyone else can hide from the facts, but you know that if you try to avoid them, they will be back to haunt you. Because even if the problem stems from someone else's department, you feel accountable for what you did not do when you identified the problem, or what you did do to allow the circumstances for the issue to exist.

Facts are always a welcome opportunity, *never* a negative. That's why one of my favorite sayings is, "No news is bad news. Bad news is good news. And good news is no news." Embracing bad news is the only way to make sure people will tell you and the rest of your team what's really happening. Never grow angry at facts or, especially, at the people who bring them. The worse the news is that people bring, the more grateful you should appear. This way you encourage them to share the bad news early in the future as well.

When you can help people to fix the reason for bad tidings, you provide the motivation for them to continue to bring you bad news.

3. Be Persistent

You don't have to like the facts. But especially when you don't like them, you need to face them immediately to find a solution. An entrepreneur never has the luxury of giving up.

There's *always* a solution. I have gone through so many crises over the years that I know in my heart of hearts that if I just keep putting one foot ahead of the other, I will get through. If a challenge is insurmountable, we will figure out a way to go around it. If a particular battle is impossible to win, we will fight a different battle. Once you absolutely know that you will come out on the other side in the end, you can keep pushing through all the hard stuff. Others will see that in you, and they will gain faith as well.

4. Manage Risks

An entrepreneur takes risks. Nothing significant can be achieved without exploring new territory.

Taking risks doesn't mean diving in blindfolded any more than managing risks doesn't mean avoiding taking chances. Risk management does not mean minimizing risks; it means choosing which risks to take, with open eyes and in a deliberate, analytical fashion. The list of things you do is important, but the list of things you decide *not* to do is sometimes even more important.

5. Be a Learning Addict

Every challenge, every problem, every piece of bad news is an opportunity to learn and improve. Cultivate your learning addiction and try to infect others with it. To stop learning is to stop living.

Beware of losing your drive to learn as you are promoted to more senior roles or become accustomed to having things explained to you. There are always topics of such importance to your company that you need to personally "go back to school" to study. (I describe one such topic in the Conclusion.) Don't ever feel that you can delegate learning to others!

6. *Maintain an Unwavering Focus*

If you really think about it, not all that many things are truly important. One way or another, *everything* comes down to your products and
your customers.

When you understand what your focus should be, then you should
review everything you do through that lens. It's easy to be distracted.
There are small fires everywhere, and if you only focus on putting those
fires out, you'll spend your time fixing small problems and never get the
big things done. Ask yourself, "How does the amount of time I spend
on these activities actually contribute to what is truly important?"

You might think that my concern about the broken display screen
at the Nokia House elevator bank was a case of being distracted by a
small problem. But to my mind, the broken display sent the wrong
message to our people, which would, in turn, affect our culture and
therefore our customers and our solutions. When seen through that
lens, a seemingly small thing was, in fact, a big deal.

7. *Look to the Horizon*

Always look to the horizon, even when putting out the fires at your
feet. That's really difficult, especially for a leader. But if all your colleagues say they need your help to figure out today's problems, you'll
be mired in minute details. Your duty is to raise your head and look
to the horizon. Because if you don't do that, no one else will! When
you are focused on strategy, competition, future core technologies, and
your customers' future needs, you have your eyes on the horizon. In a
healthy organization, the top management spends a large portion of its
time worrying about the more distant future.

8. *Build a Team of People You Like and Respect*

An entrepreneur knows that she or he will win or lose because of the
team. But even more important, people are the only source of real happiness, whether they're within your family or your workplace. If you
don't surround yourself with people you genuinely like and respect,
then you won't be as happy as you deserve to be.

Happy people also do better work for a longer time, and loyalty breeds loyalty. My problem with certain well-known entrepreneurial companies is that I don't believe that success is worth leading people through fear. I do believe that for the vast majority of companies, the way to be successful is to build a team of people who truly enjoy what they do.

9. Ask Why

This is a very simple thing that people often forget. We tend to ask "What?" way too often, especially compared with how often we ask "Why?"

For example, in strategy work, when a team presents its strategy, the typical questions are "what" questions: "What are your primary objectives?" "What is your action plan?" But the question that really forces people to think is, "*Why* do you think this is a good strategy?"

That is really difficult to answer unless you have defined some criteria for a good strategy beforehand. If you know that at the end of the strategy process you will have to explain *why* the outcome is a good strategy, you will run the process differently and think about what defines a good strategy at the very beginning.

10. Never Stop Dreaming

As Robert Kennedy (basing his statement on a quotation by George Bernard Shaw) famously said, "Some men see things as they are, and ask *why*. I dream of things that never were, and ask why not." That encapsulates the entrepreneurial mindset. When you dream about things that never were and ask, "Why not?" and then set about creating what never was, that's being an entrepreneur. You're building something new. And in doing so, you can change the world.

The Power of Paranoid Optimism

The core of entrepreneurial leadership requires behaving as a paranoid optimist. Paranoid optimism sounds like a contradiction in terms, but it's not. It's really two sides of the same coin.

Being a paranoid optimist means that underneath all the fear and confusion that are swirling around you, you can be optimistic because you are convinced you will find a solution to the problems confronting you. At the same time, though, you're paranoid about what might go wrong. So you prepare for problems because there *must* be problems, even when people say there aren't. When you find them and examine them, you understand how to avoid or minimize them. Even if you're not able to preempt them, as an optimist you're damn sure you can deal with them.

Being a paranoid optimist is a good way to navigate through hard times. You combine vigilance and a healthy dose of realistic fear with a positive, forward-looking outlook.

In practice, paranoid optimism calls upon leaders to explore a full spectrum of scenarios: the best case, the worst case, and the options in between. By imagining the unthinkable, you won't be surprised and can generate strategies that will help you avoid it. As a result, you can radiate an unwavering certainty of eventual victory because you have already imagined the worst that could happen and have constructed a response.

Practicing paranoid optimism sharpens your foresight, expands your options, and strengthens your ability to lead in a fast-changing world. It helps you respond to crises and cope with change.

Infecting your organization with paranoid optimism will create a high-performance and strategically thinking organization that will not be taken by surprise.

In 2012, I was both scared and optimistic. But I trusted in the components of entrepreneurial leadership. They were the compass that had guided me through countless challenges over the course of my career. They gave me the confidence that I could help guide Nokia through the chaos confronting us and enable the company not just to survive but to succeed again.

Little did I know that things would get a lot worse before they got better.

10

THE GOLDEN RULES

MAY 2012–JUNE 2012

. . . .

The eight rules laid out a framework for how we would
operate and the principles we would apply as we tried
to control the chaos confronting us.

. . . .

THERE'S AN OLD saying that a leader without followers is just a guy taking a walk. Transforming an organization's culture requires commitment from the top. But you need to convince people to change their habits and follow you.

All the Nokia board members wanted to do a good job. I never saw any maliciousness or laziness. The problem, as I saw it, was that the board had not been enabled to work effectively.

From my conversations, I sensed a hangover from all those years when the Nokia board had been told that things were under control, only to discover that was obviously not true. Those were years of never getting to the heart of the problems and always being forced to take the management's recovery plan at face value. These experiences had left people feeling fragile and unsure both of themselves and of the board as a team. We all felt, rightly so, that we had not done a good job.

Our confidence about being able to do better was low. As we had failed collectively, there were also understandable questions on board members' minds regarding their own role in the future. And while they didn't *not* trust the new chairman to lead, the jury was definitely out. The board members needed to be convinced and reassured that we could prevail.

Many companies fail to have a fundamental discussion about the role of the board. Boards often believe their primary duty is to appoint and evaluate the CEO. That's not wrong—it's very important—but it falls far short of the full potential of their contribution.

As I see it, a board should do whatever is necessary to ensure the company's success. It's that simple. That includes hiring and firing the CEO but so much more, depending on the issues the company is facing.

Nokia was teetering on the edge of a precipice. Everyone—including the board—would need to work together to pull us to safety.

As I looked over my notes from my conversations with board members and senior management, and as I studied my lists of leadership lessons, I thought it would be helpful to try to distill the essence of the behaviors that I would like to see in the board. I probably wrote 10 different drafts of what became the Golden Rules. I proposed the rules to the board in my very first board meeting as chairman when we convened immediately after the Annual General Meeting on May 3, 2012.

The AGM Gauntlet

Nokia AGMs were always big shows. They were held at the Messukeskus Helsinki, Finland's largest convention center. The usual audience size was around 1,500 attendees. At my first AGM four years earlier, the attendees had been a relatively happy bunch. This year, some 3,000 people had registered, and they were out for blood.

I couldn't blame them. Our operating loss was over €2 billion during the first half of 2012. Our mobile phone revenues were almost in free fall. We had laid off thousands of workers, and more layoffs were planned for the coming months. Our share price was barely €3, down from about €28 just four short years earlier. Our credit rating had recently been downgraded to junk status. Rumors were flying about when—not if—Nokia would declare bankruptcy. (We were not really short on cash; we were short on credibility.)

If I were in the audience, I would be demanding answers, too. From now on, I would be responsible for providing them.

Actually, for this meeting, I was still pretty much in the audience; I would become chairman only after the AGM. Jorma gave his last speech to the AGM as chairman, and Stephen gave an update on Nokia business during 2011 and answered a ton of questions from the shareholders.

In addition to Jorma Ollila, two long-time members—Bengt Holmström and Per Karlsson—were stepping down. They were replaced by Betsey Nelson, Bruce Brown, and Marten Mickos. Betsey, Bruce, and Marten were the first members I recruited to the Nokia board. They all coupled a technology background with strong business experience: Betsey was a long-term CFO in Silicon Valley software companies, an experienced audit committee chairman, and an active investor in start-ups; Bruce was the chief technology officer of P&G and had been on its leadership team for many years; and Marten had been a CEO at numerous tech start-ups, MySQL perhaps the best known of them.

I felt confident they would be strong contributors as we began Nokia's transformation. They all proved themselves able to maintain a highly professional and completely unselfish attitude under the most difficult circumstances. Betsey and Bruce later became chairmen of our Audit and Personnel Committees, respectively. (HP acquired Marten's company in 2014, and he joined HP's management team. As Nokia and HP play in the same markets, Marten had to step down from our board.)

A Model for Board Behavior

On the evening of the AGM, at the first meeting of a newly appointed chairman and the board of directors of a company in the midst of an all-out conflagration, you would expect the agenda to focus on what the board can do to help the company put out the fires.

We didn't.

The only real item on our agenda was how the board should conduct itself: how we would want to behave.

This idea grew out of my conviction that the smartest thing to do when confronted with a crisis is to step back and take a deep breath before considering all the options. A board—or any team facing a crisis—naturally wants to jump directly to fix-it mode: What's the core problem, what's the solution, what's the plan, and when do we start?

But people will have different opinions. And because of the urgency of the situation, there will be raised voices and bruised egos and hurt feelings that can resonate for a long time.

So my message to the board was this: We're in this together, and we will work together to make Nokia successful again. Let's start by talking about the principles of how we make decisions. Let's consider the values we share. Then we'll be free to address the practical problems we face.

For example, we might agree, "We will conduct our business in a way that respects our people." When you start talking about layoffs, there's a huge range of approaches and an equally large range of associated costs. But if you have decided that you want to show respect to your people in all events, then doing layoffs in the cheapest possible way isn't just a non-option—you don't even consider it. If you limit your options according to an agreed-upon set of beliefs, they will naturally guide you toward a certain way of doing things and, as a bonus, will reduce conflict among the board members as well.

These types of discussions are often dismissed—if they're even thought about—as not being pragmatic or addressing the urgency of the situation. But they will pay off for years and years in a board that is more effective, one that does a better job advising the management team, and one that is more pleasant to work with.

The Golden Rules

The guidelines we came up with crystallized into the "Golden Rules." The eight rules laid out a framework for how we would operate and the principles we would apply as we tried to control the chaos confronting us. The rules were a little different in 2012, but the core philosophy has remained untouched. The latest version of them is:

1. **Always assume the best of intentions from the actions of others. Operate openly, honestly, and directly, and expect others to do the same.**

    Give everyone the benefit of the doubt. When someone says something you don't want to hear, it's natural to want to lash out. But rather than warping into DefCon 1, stop and remind yourself, "I'm committed to assuming the best of intentions from that guy." Ask a clarifying question. If you can follow that rule, it will change how you and others behave.

    Of course, this is easy to agree to but more difficult to actively live. But agreeing to this rule provides the leader with the opportunity *after* a verbal annihilation to take the criticizer aside and have a constructive discussion: "Let's talk about what happened in the meeting. Did you really assume the best of intentions from that person?"

2. **Our philosophy is data-driven and based on analysis. We always aim to analytically map out the alternative future scenarios for the company and strive to understand the triggers and levers related to those scenarios. This sometimes leads us to invest more time in our board work than some other boards do, but we believe this effort pays off in the long term.**

    The "data-driven" element may sound obvious, but it obliges you to find out how things really are. It forces you to ask questions, and not to shy away from, ignore, or soften something you don't want to hear. It returns to my saying, "No news is bad news. Bad news is good news. And good news is no news."

    This rule gives me, as chairman, the right and responsibility to require the team to do the necessary analysis. The focus on analysis is also an agreement to put in the extra hours when necessary.

    This rule was especially important for the Nokia board, as it required us to change our behavior from the habits we had gotten used to. To be successful, this also required the management to change how it worked with the board.

3. **Be well educated in the company's business and deeply engaged in the discussions with the management. Expect the management to support you in learning more and to be open, straightforward, and engaged in its dealings with the board.**

   Learning about the company's business is important on so many levels, not the least of which is something boards often don't get involved in: the management of the company. I'm not talking about second-guessing the CEO or executive team or trying to do their jobs. I'm talking about becoming familiar with the issues and the people handling them, so that the board can serve as a brain trust, ready and able to support the management by strategically sharing the benefits of its collective experience.

   Culturally, this was a huge change in the relationship between the Nokia board and the management team. Now, instead of the board being safely above the fray while the management team is fighting in the trenches, we all stand side by side. When something fails, we're both accountable and we will bear the consequences together. And instead of pointing fingers, we'll move on and try something else.

4. **Be prepared to debate, but do it in an informed, unemotional, respectful way. Affirmatively support the decisions, even if you did not win the debate.**

   We can disagree about the business and business issues. We *need* to disagree. The last thing I wanted was board members who wouldn't air their concerns in a meeting and then later confess, "I was worried that might happen, but I didn't want to say anything."

5. **Firmly and respectfully challenge the management while keeping in mind that the board is successful only when the management is successful.**

   We want to assist top management to come up with the best possible strategies, but we can't help them by just agreeing with them. We need to challenge their plans and thought processes. But we have to do it in such a way that the members of the leadership team know in both their head and their gut that we're trying to maximize their success. The firm is successful only if the management team is successful. Absolute challenge and absolute support.

6. **We seek to constantly improve in everything we do. All board members are expected to contribute to the improvement of our work, tools, and processes as well as the way we work as a team.**

   The Japanese concept of "kaizen," or continuous improvement, is usually applied to manufacturing. But there's no reason that it can't also apply to the work of the board. Therefore, all board members are expected to contribute to strengthening our work, as well as how we function as a team. To ensure that happens, periodically ask everybody how we can improve. I often ask every board member at the end of the meeting to give their thoughts on what we could have done better in that particular meeting.

7. **We encourage the management and board members to engage with each other outside the board meetings as well.**

   Under the previous regime, the CEO was unofficially forbidden to meet with the board members outside of board meetings. Board members meeting with the CEO's direct reports was even rarer. But in order to delve more deeply into the challenges confronting the company, it makes sense to talk outside of the formal forum.

   We deliberately created a rule saying that it's fine for board members to have those conversations—with one major caveat: It's very important that the management team members understand that they should regard the board members as highly paid consultants whose opinions and ideas they are free to use *if* they so decide. However, it's *their* call. An individual board member doesn't represent the voice of the board, and there's no pressure to agree. And on the flip side, board members are obliged to share their observations with the rest of the board and the CEO by writing a memo soon after their meeting to enable everyone to learn.

   All meetings are also shared with the CEO and chairman in advance. We coordinate and ensure that we are close to the optimum in the number of meetings and who meets with whom.

8. **Our board is light on formality and heavy on substance.**

Any meeting where we don't laugh out loud is a miserable failure! This helps you balance between optimism and paranoia. Otherwise, you fall into the trap of just being paranoid. I always aim to get the board to laugh out loud during the first 10 minutes of a meeting. That gets things moving in the right spirit. The darker the tidings, the more important it is to find a reason to laugh as well.

And by the way, suits and ties are not mandatory at board meetings.

These are healthy things to talk about in any company, but especially a company in crisis that's facing the need for radical change. Ironically, Nokia's chairman-centric history worked to my benefit. My suggested rules weren't challenged. Over time, people realized that those changes paid off, and they began to implement them on their own initiative.

The rules also provided a backstop against backsliding. On a board of directors, everyone is a high-profile person, and many have a big ego. How do you rein in these alpha personalities? When somebody deviated from our agreed-upon behavior, it was very easy for me to have a chat offline. "I understand that the pressure is high. I understand there's a lot of emotion at stake," I might say. "But you do realize how (the person receiving the broadside) felt and what that does to our board dynamics that we have agreed to nurture." I was not criticizing that person; I was just referring to what he had already committed to. Because there was a solid foundation of mutual respect, all the board members eventually changed their behavior. At least, a little.

The rules aren't etched in stone. They're a living, organic framework that's flexible enough to adapt to different situations and be customized for the particular demand of the moment. (In 2012, for example, there were only six rules.) Every year before the Annual General Meeting, I review the rules, ask for ideas from my colleagues (that definition includes the CEO and the board secretary), and try to think if we can or should change the rules to better reflect the challenges we're facing right now, the mistakes we made over the past year, and the misunderstandings that occurred.

The rules serve as a checklist in times of roiling disruption as well as ordinary ups and downs. They guided us through the tough days we faced in 2012 and continue to guide us today.

The Journey to Transparency

By approving the Golden Rules, the board endorsed a certain way of working and gave me the freedom to begin our transformation. It was a relief to put the cat on the table, as the Finnish saying goes—although our problems were so much bigger than cats that we joked about "putting the moose on the table." No one could doubt we were in crisis. No one could argue that we needed to change our ways: to create an atmosphere of transparency and trust.

From the outset, when planning the 2012 board calendar, I deliberately added 30 percent more time to be dedicated to board meetings. I pulled the number out of thin air, but that didn't matter. I knew that we were in trouble and that the more time we spent together, the better we would understand and trust each other.

The best way to run any team and get the team's support is to give all the members a chance to state their opinion. In the old board, dissenting opinions were often ignored or squelched. That's something I insisted on changing immediately. At the first meeting, for a particular topic of importance, I went around the table asking everyone to state his or her opinion. It was not voluntary: Everyone *had* to speak up. As a result, our sense of teamwork and trust started to improve.

We also needed to persuade the management team to trust the board. During the months before my confirmation as chairman, Stephen Elop gave me a lot of access to his top team. Our joint message was: "If you want us to respect you, you'll level with us. If you tell us, 'I have a big challenge and I don't know how to tackle it,' or 'I have three plans but I'm not sure which is best,' we will respect you far more than if you don't ask for our advice. If you come in with only one solution and try to sell that to us, you may get our support but not our respect."

Forging an Agenda for Success

I also knew we would have to change the content of the board meetings. We needed to forge an agenda that would put us back on the path to success.

To that end, Stephen and I worked to reduce time spent on topics of secondary importance: corporate governance, share price, compliance, media coverage, and social responsibility. These are meaningful topics but not as important when the ship is sinking. Instead, we focused on fundamentals: our technology, our products, our people, our customers, and our competition, as well as our competitiveness now and in the future. These are the right things to talk about in any company but especially a company in distress.

We tried to teach the management to explain to the board what defines our success in the market. This was not just about stating, "This is *what* we need to do now." It was understanding *why*: Why do we think this technology or this feature will be important? Why will these actions make us good in these things? Why do we assume we're on the right path? Why is this approach the best way to track our progress?

For each of these topics, the goal was always to find alternative paths forward. If you have only one path forward, you become a passenger. If you have several alternatives, you can make choices. You are in control.

A member of the management team crystallized the difference between the old board and the new board. The old approach was "Don't you dare bring bad news to us without a solution"; the new one was "Bad news is good news. We will help you find a solution."

That's the factual side of enacting change. We also took our first steps on the cultural journey to transparency.

A bit later, the board started having breakfast with rising stars of the company. Before every board meeting, we scheduled a one-hour breakfast meeting with four high-potential managers. They each were given 15 minutes to talk about themselves and the top issues they were facing. Our question was always the same: "What would need to change for you to be more successful in your job?" We are basically trying to get them to complain, so the board could understand what should be improved in the way the company operated.

Strategic Symbols

Other changes were symbolic, but their message was no less strong.

Nokia tradition was that individual board members always had a personal chauffeur to drive them in an Audi 8 or Mercedes S-class luxury sedan to board-related events. But after the 2012 AGM, they all rode to dinner in a mini-bus—and I rode with them. It was a small thing, but it demonstrated a different approach to creating a board culture. The old way focused on appearance and protocol; our way emphasized building a team and getting results.

The next morning—my first as chairman—I started moving the furniture. Most people at Nokia headquarters, including the CEO, sat in an open office setting. The previous chairman, however, had his own office. It was nicknamed "the blue room" because of the color of the glass facing the rest of the office space. People referred to time spent there as "a blue moment."

I asked for the walls to be moved and the space changed into an open office. I had a table installed like everyone else. In that open environment, I started meeting with people, asking questions, listening, and learning.

During the months preceding my chairmanship, I learned that the previous chairman, following a Nokia tradition of having his official portrait painted of himself before leaving office, ran a global search for a talented portrait artist. He picked an American painter and had him move to Finland for several months and finish two portraits, one for the company and one for his home. The idea of spending a significant amount of money on an individual portrait during a time of crisis did not feel right. I informed the staff that from now on a photograph of a departing CEO or chairman would be sufficient.

These and many other small actions combined to send a strong emotional signal of a cultural shift gaining speed.

Then, on June 18, 2012, Microsoft knocked us flat.

. . . .

Turnarounds Start with Trust

During those early days, there were a lot of things I instinctively did right without fully understanding why I did them. Only later did I realize that the core goal of every interaction was to build trust.

Laying down a foundation of trust is absolutely paramount. In times of trouble and complex circumstances, trust both greases the gears and is the glue that holds everything together.

Instilling trust started the moment I welcomed everyone to our first board meeting. It may not have been explicitly stated on the agenda, but implicitly it was my first order of business. Each board member had to be able to trust all the other board members. The board as a group had to trust the chairman. The CEO and the management team must be able to trust the board. Trust must flow out to our employees, suppliers, partners, and investors.

Trust is built on two pillars: transparency and equality. Transparency encompasses sharing data, developing the discipline of analysis, encouraging board members to talk with the CEO and management team, and sharing the content of those discussions. Equality means a lot of different things ranging from giving everybody an equal opportunity to be heard to nurturing a team spirit by riding in the same bus.

In the spirit of both openness and equality, we started to evaluate the board members much the same way management is evaluated in a 360 degree–like process.

I launched an annual anonymous numeric evaluation process. All board members receive a personal grade for their contribution during the past year and a grade for their expected ability to contribute in the future. The board members' contributions are also evaluated by the management team members with whom the board had meaningful engagement. Suddenly, the board members were no longer untouchable. The fact that management could safely give feedback on the board's behavior in general, as well as on the individual board members' behavior, gave the board the right to contribute more actively to secure a future for the company. Trust is often about balance. Or in this case, checks and balances.

Trust must constantly be reinforced. It cannot be taken for granted. That reinforcement can only be done by unfailingly setting an example: by encouraging people to seek out and share bad news, by not punishing them when they do, by constantly rewarding accountability, and by recruiting people who already think accordingly.

I also made changes that required trust. One was starting a regular evaluation of the CEO where I interview the CEO's direct reports one-by-one. (I do this in all companies where I am chairman.) Naturally, I discuss my observations with the board. The board should have a strong understanding of the type of CEO they have and what his or her strong and weak areas are.

I hold these interviews at least annually, and for new CEOs more often. We go through five areas: how the CEO develops the culture in the company; how she leads the management team; how the relationship between the individual being interviewed and the CEO is evolving; how the board could better support the management team; and, last but not least, what future plans does the individual have and is there an interest to, one day, perhaps serve as the CEO of the company.

I ask a lot of pragmatic questions about how the management team meeting agendas are created, how the CEO deals with conflicts, how easy she is to get in touch with, how she supports personal development, etc. In the course of these discussions, I get to know the CEO in a different way, but also learn to understand the team dynamics better. Once the interviews are completed, I think deeply on what I learned and how I could best help the CEO. I then go through all my findings and thoughts with the CEO in a spirit of brutal honesty, while maintaining anonymity for the management team members.

I remember that neither Stephen nor Rajeev were exactly happy with the process when I first discussed it with them. Over time, though, it became part of our standard routine, I believe, and helped both CEOs to manage the company better.

As trust filters across an organization, you will see clearer communication and greater transparency, all of which will lead to a greater range of ideas and suggestions from your employees and colleagues. These are the innovative ideas and suggestions that are necessary to jump-start a company's turnaround.

· ·

11

PLAN B . . . AND PLAN C
AND PLAN D

JUNE 2012–DECEMBER 2012

. . . .

Scenario mapping enables you to minimize the likelihood
that you might overlook something important
and maximize the likelihood that you are prepared
for whatever scenario eventually occurs.

. . . .

NO ONE SAW it coming.

On June 18, 2012, Microsoft announced it was launching the Surface tablet. This was more than a stunning surprise. It was a shot across the bows of all Microsoft's hardware partners.

Throughout the nearly 40 years of its existence, Microsoft had been a software company. Its empire was built on DOS and Windows, sold through PC vendors. Microsoft had dipped a toe into hardware through mice, keyboards, and the Xbox, but most people thought of Microsoft as a software company and assumed that it would stay a software company forever.

The previous September, Microsoft CEO Steve Ballmer had hinted in his annual letter to shareholders that Microsoft would increasingly view itself as a devices and services company.[1] That letter introduced the unwelcome possibility that the company, whose partnership we had just bet our future on, might become a competitor. When Nokia signed an exclusive relationship with Microsoft to manufacture Windows-based smartphones, our agreement didn't restrict Microsoft from producing its own devices for the simple reason that no one imagined that was even a theoretical alternative.

Then in June, Microsoft introduced the Surface tablet. It was a huge shock to the PC manufacturers and OEMs (original equipment manufacturers), which paid immense royalties to Microsoft to include its software in their devices and whose alliance had been the backbone of the personal computer industry for decades. Michael Dell called me to share his feelings both at what Microsoft had done and at how it had done it. HP's head of PC business was similarly stunned that Microsoft had not trusted its closest partners enough to give them a heads-up earlier. The fact that Microsoft had kept Surface a closely guarded secret, only telling some of its closest OEMs less than two weeks before going public, was felt as a hostile act throughout the industry.

The news sent tremors throughout Nokia, too. If Microsoft started making tablets, why wouldn't it start making smartphones? And if it started making its own smartphones, what would happen to us?

Thinking in Alternatives

The Microsoft shock galvanized our determination to map out alternative scenarios.

Most people and all management teams are at least remotely familiar with the concept of scenario mapping, or scenario planning. It has its roots in military intelligence where people were able to safely learn from mistakes by playing simulated war games. Some companies, like Royal Dutch Shell, create very long-term scenarios spanning tens of years as they try to predict and prepare for the future.

I like to use the same concept also at a micro level. For almost any challenging situation, we can name a few different paths the future might take based on what individuals or companies decide or how large numbers of people vote with their feet or their wallets. By naming those possible paths, thinking about them one at a time, deciding whether they are positive or negative for us, and defining specific actions that we can take both right now and later to influence that future, we are more likely to be successful.

Thinking as a paranoid optimist almost forces you to do scenario planning. You can't stop your imagination from coming up with different scenarios of successes and failures—or ways to influence the outcomes.

Scenario planning is a method of bringing discipline into thinking about the future and a tool for dividing big problems into manageable pieces, enabling you to deal with each piece separately. The strength of the exercise depends on the breadth and depth of your perspective: listing all the relevant alternatives, then diving deeply into the key details of each possibility.

Sometimes the complexity of all the possibilities is so vast that it can be difficult to obtain a cohesive picture. Your mind jumps from one scenario to another, from one sub-branch to another. A good way to attain both the necessary depth and a holistic overview is to think of the scenarios as a tree. The present time is the lowest part of the trunk. From there, you delineate the future alternatives that grow from the trunk. If the branches are complex, you can assign separate teams of people to expand each branch. Then you pull everyone together and go through the findings.

The scenario tree is a living, growing organism. Each time you discuss your findings, you'll find new sub-branches that need to be explored. New possibilities are constantly revealed, both positive and negative.

And that's the point. Scenario mapping is not just about identifying existing options but about constantly imagining and manufacturing alternatives, then identifying the actions associated with each option. In other words, this is not just about listing realistic scenarios and coming up with related action plans. You can also come up with actions that will make an unrealistic positive scenario feasible. Feel free to envision the best possible scenario from your own point of view and add that as a branch in the tree.

The actions are aimed at increasing the likelihood of a positive outcome and decreasing the probability of a negative one. Ultimately, this way of thinking brings a systematic process to your work.

Scenario mapping is a healthy discipline for a board or management team to engage in. It forces you to dive much deeper into what is happening to your company and the industry and to go through the same learning process. It enables you to minimize the likelihood that you might overlook something important and maximize the likelihood that you are prepared for whatever scenario eventually occurs. Even considering scenarios that will never happen teaches you about industry dynamics and sharpens your thinking.

A Driver or a Passenger?

Scenario mapping epitomized the kind of data-driven, analytical approach that we agreed to in the Golden Rules. Inculcating it in our behavior was a gradual process that coalesced over the course of 2012.

The board, of course, was in favor of it. Up until now, we had suffered from feeling out of control and lacking visibility to key data. If you can describe the company's future in a discrete number of scenarios, then everyone can see the big picture. And seeing the big picture means being able to make choices. Making choices gives everyone a sense of being in control.

The management team carried the heavy burden of doing all the homework. It was easy—and fun—for the board, together with management, to come up with a long list of questions and possibilities, ask the management to do the analysis and make recommendations, and then review the results and come up with new scenarios. Not surprisingly, there was some pushback at times from the management team about the extra work piled on top of an already large workload. But we all agreed that it was very, very important for us to think ahead and not be caught by surprise.

We were all really tired of being surprised. We had been surprised by Apple, by Android, by Symbian, by Meltemi, by MeeGo, by Microsoft—by so many things. We were just fed up with that.

Scenario mapping offered the promise of avoiding unpleasant surprises. We could get to that place by asking the management team to bring alternative scenarios to the board. We emphasized that fully baked plans without alternatives were no longer acceptable; instead, we explained, we would rather have a selection of alternative half-baked plans. Then, management and the board could engage in a robust discussion about which direction to take. This enabled the board to share the journey with the management team and help the management identify the risks and rewards of various scenarios at an early stage.

You can think back to almost any of the major challenges that Nokia had faced during the last few years and conclude that paranoid optimism might have helped us identify what could go wrong: Symbian overall, Symbian Foundation, MeeGo, touch, Android, China . . . the list of surprises is long. Imagine how differently things might have turned out had we engaged in scenario planning for these issues early on.

It's natural to want to spend more time examining the likely scenarios, but what makes this exercise robust is dedicating a decent amount of time to exploring *unlikely* scenarios. It takes mental discipline to list lots of scenarios without prejudging their plausibility too much. It takes even more discipline not to short-shrift the improbable ones, yet a deliberately non-critical approach is key to opening the mind to possibilities. Consequently, during the time reserved for thinking about Option B, you're not allowed to think about Option A, even if you think Option B is a waste of time. Under this agreement, when it's time to explore a winning scenario, even if that scenario requires a miracle, people will turn their brains to figuring out how to make it happen.

Mapping scenarios is all about opening the mind to possibilities. You realize that there really *are* alternatives.

I can't emphasize how important that is. If you don't have alternatives, you're not making decisions—they're being made for you. Conversely, the more alternatives you can create, the more you realize that your fate is in your hands. Whether you're in the midst of a crisis or you're dealing with day-to-day decisions, scenario mapping is the difference between being the driver or being a passenger.

Getting into the habit of creating alternative scenarios has multiple benefits: It reduces anxiety, because crafting an action plan is not as scary as an amorphous or unarticulated threat. Having a plan gives you control. And finally, it makes you very quick to react to whatever happens as, even in the worst case, you have a plan ready for a scenario that at least resembles what has actually occurred.

I thought about nominating a "designated Cassandra." Cassandra was a Trojan princess who was cursed to speak true prophecies that no one believed (such as the fall of Troy). In a business setting, the designated Cassandra has everyone's permission to imagine really bad scenarios. It's useful, but I didn't feel it was necessary. No one needed a "get out of jail free" card: We had achieved enough trust that *everyone* felt comfortable bringing up negative scenarios.

That was good, because there were plenty of them.

Remembering the Corporate Orphan

Over the years, so many issues central to our competitiveness had been only lightly addressed in board meetings. Our meetings now focused on strategic issues. We quickly realized that two topics in particular demanded concentrated interest. We set up two special committees on the board to explore them; by splitting forces, we were able to do twice the work. The Industry Dynamics Committee focused on our central business of smartphones and mobile phones; its title was a euphemism for "What the heck is Microsoft going to do and how do we respond?" The other committee examined our sideline investment in Nokia Siemens Networks (NSN).

Under the previous Nokia board, NSN had been treated as the forgotten stepchild, or as one of the board members called it, a "corporate orphan." It rarely made it onto the board agenda; when it did, it was so far down the list that it was barely talked about. In September 2011, at the same time we put in €500 million, we recruited Jesper Ovesen, a hardcore restructuring expert, to serve as executive chairman and help CEO Rajeev Suri get the company back in shape. Then Nokia's problems eclipsed what was happening at NSN.

NSN was not part of Nokia. It was an independent company owned 50-50 between Siemens and Nokia with Nokia having a golden share, i.e., holding one share more than Siemens. NSN had its own board, brand, culture, and destiny. When I joined the Nokia board, NSN had the same number of employees as our handset business and one-third of its revenues. As Nokia's handset business tanked, however, NSN's proportion of the combined revenues grew. None of us really understood NSN's business, and that just wasn't right. We had a responsibility to be good caretakers of the asset.

One red flag waving from NSN was the possibility of a breach of debt covenants. NSN had issued bonds whose covenants were close to being triggered; the last thing we wanted was for the covenants to be breached during NSN's restructuring. However, our own situation made it difficult to consider bailing NSN out if a breach became imminent.

As we dug deeper into NSN's issues, we began to realize, too, that the joint venture with Siemens was in jeopardy as its first phase approached completion. In order to do the best possible job in the forthcoming negotiations, we needed to approach NSN with more understanding and thoughtfulness. That meant getting to know the members of the NSN management team and having them get to know our board. Among other things, we wanted them to be loyal to us and not any more loyal to Siemens than absolutely necessary.

Microsoft's Double Whammy

In early July 2012, the price of Nokia's American depositary shares slipped below $2,[2] bottoming out at $1.69 in anticipation of our second-quarter earnings report.[3] The company's market capitalization was roughly €5 billion, and the company had net cash of about €3.5 billion; the actual value of the business was only €1.5 billion, almost nothing for a company of our size and our brand. Our IP licensing business alone was easily more valuable than the whole company.

After our results announcement, both Stephen Elop and I bought shares to communicate our faith. Many people feared Nokia would eventually go bankrupt. It wasn't an impossible scenario, so even at that valuation, buying was a risky investment.

After a few weeks, the share price slowly rebounded, bolstered by some positive news. We were on track to report better-than-expected results for the third quarter.

Perhaps the most amazing positive development was that we had improved tremendously in the McKinsey Organizational Health Index. Due to Stephen's relentless efforts to bring the company's issues to light and deal with them, we had turned the corner and started a steady upward climb in the rankings. We were nowhere near where we wanted but at least we had pulled into the better half of companies. What was amazing were the circumstances under which this was achieved. In the middle of constant layoffs, negative press, and worsening results, our employees were rapidly regaining their spirits. This is one of the most under-appreciated achievements of Nokia's entire history.

Our high hopes for Lumia, though, had slammed into a wall—a wall unintentionally built by Microsoft.

Toward the end of spring, Microsoft announced that upgrading to Windows Phone 8 would cause a binary break with Windows Phone 7.5. Basically, that meant that all apps would have to be rebuilt for the new OS version. It also meant that none of the new apps built for the latest and greatest devices would work on the older devices. The early Lumia devices ran on Windows Phone 7.5. They had been out not even a year, and now they were obsolete.

At the same time, Microsoft announced a delay with the release of Windows Phone 8.[4]

We knew the break was coming at some point, but Microsoft announced it without consulting us. If Microsoft had alerted us, we would have said, "You are telling today's customers to invest in a platform for which *nobody* will be creating applications anymore. Anyone who wants a Windows device will wait until Windows Phone 8 is available. But you also announced that Windows Phone 8 would not be available for some time. You are forcing people to choose another platform for the time being." That platform, of course, was Android or iPhone.

Business is often all about momentum. It's much easier to maintain momentum than to get it going in the first place. News like this was a millstone around our neck, killing the momentum that we had been slowly building.

Alternative Smartphone Scenarios

With Microsoft's news about the Surface and the binary break weighing heavily on our minds, for our board meeting in mid-September, I asked Stephen and the management team to come up with alternative scenarios that would enable Nokia to survive in the mobile phone business, especially in smartphones, no matter what happened. They presented four options:

Scenario #1: Renegotiate the Microsoft Partnership

We were in a fixed relationship for 10 years, but our agreement included a "rip cord" allowing Nokia to terminate the contract after three or five years if sales volumes were below certain jointly agreed-upon levels.

The rip cord could, at the earliest, be pulled in November 2014, assuming volumes did not start accelerating rapidly. Microsoft could already see the likelihood that the targets might not be met and that Nokia could decide to pull the rip cord.

If we did decide to pull the rip cord, we would need to prepare for that alternative well in advance so that we would already be executing our new plan at full speed by the separation. The worst thing for Microsoft would be if we started a secret Android program. They would be moving full steam ahead with us until the date when we could pull the rip cord, when they'd get a call from us saying, "Sorry, guys. We're terminating." Then after a mandatory contractual three-month delay, we'd launch a full range of Android devices. They'd be caught by surprise, and the Windows Phone would be toast.

Microsoft could imagine that scenario as easily as we could. What could *they* do? They would have to renegotiate with us much earlier, to see if we would agree to remove the rip cord. To make that scenario appealing, they would have to make concessions.

We knew that they knew that we knew this. We had some leverage, so we could approach them and ask to renegotiate. Knowing that our goal was to save the relationship with Microsoft, our next step was to create a strategy for renegotiating.

Scenario #2: Disrupt the Whole Market with Project Serenity

Serenity was our code name for a new cloud device platform based on HTML5, an open web platform that enabled developers to create applications used by all browsers across all operating systems. Back in 2011, we had estimated that we could develop this platform in less than three years.

Renegotiating with Microsoft and launching Serenity were not mutually exclusive. Only Google's Android was mentioned in our agreement with Microsoft. So we could move ahead with Serenity, renegotiate with Microsoft, or do both.

Scenario #3: Explore Other Non-Android Options

Despite its dominance, Android wasn't the only player. A number of other platforms had potential and had attracted big bets from large companies. Firefox OS, for example, was strongly supported by Telefonica, Sprint, and Deutsche Telecom, before it turned out to be a dud. Facebook was considering introducing its own devices; we were exploring a partnership using a Meltemi-like platform that would help Facebook attract more users in developing countries where lower-priced products were key.

All three options—the Windows Phone, Serenity, and a Facebook phone—could happen at the same time, but that would fragment our focus and our resources.

Scenario #4: Android

There were actually two sub-scenarios involving Android.

Option 4A was what we called the "organic Android plan": We could build an Android-based device family ourselves. However, this would be very difficult under the terms of our contract with Microsoft.

If November 2014 was the earliest date we could pull the rip cord, we would need to have a range of devices ready for an early 2015 launch. But building a device on a new platform would take at least 9 to 12 months, so we'd need to start no later than the end of 2013. We were now approaching the end of 2012.

The first generation of devices is like your beta version. It's when you make mistakes and learn from them. The first generation of Lumia phones was not the greatest, but we had since ironed out the wrinkles and the Lumia 920 was supposed to be pressed to perfection. Even if we assumed our Android devices would be perfect, the best-case scenario wouldn't have us turning a profit until 2016 at the earliest. The worst-case scenario would be very bad indeed.

Furthermore, it would be almost impossible to keep such a program a secret. Between us and the ODMs (original design manufacturers), hundreds of people would be working on the Android devices. The news would inevitably leak. We could just imagine the headlines: "Nokia Has Lost Faith in Windows Phone." We had *not* lost faith. Yet.

Option 4B was the "nonorganic Android": We could buy an organization that had already shipped a number of Android devices and had everything it needed to create them. These players included Huawei, Motorola, HTC, and, perhaps, Xiaomi; we had already had "getting-acquainted" discussions. Of course, such an acquisition might also mean loss of control. Our cash was low, and our shares did not have much value. We could not acquire anything meaningful without losing our independence.

We decided to start acting on all five options, not doing anything that would be impossible to reverse but quietly moving ahead laying plans, gathering intelligence, and weighing options.

This is the beauty and curse of scenario-based planning. You can start traveling down all the identified paths, accumulating understanding and laying plans, so that when the time comes to act, everybody is already on board, there is no hesitation, and everyone knows what to do. That's the beautiful part. The curse is that you end up doing the same work several times as you are preparing for many different futures. Finding the balance between taking on an onerous workload and being prepared for any future scenario is a difficult skill. There is no tried-and-true playbook; you just have to feel your way forward, trusting that you are doing the right thing.

These first six months of the new board worked wonders. By engaging in scenario thinking, the impenetrable fog that had been the future was replaced with an imaginary landscape mapped with a number of clear paths. For the first time since I had joined the Nokia board, I felt I knew what our issues were, what we were doing about them, and what alternative futures lay ahead.

It was not that we had fewer problems—we might even have realized we actually had more—but we had visibility, could choose our focus, and felt we had more control of what lay ahead.

Spotlight on Lumia

As the 2012 holiday season approached, all eyes were on the Lumia 920, our flagship smartphone. Everything we knew was packed into the 920. If it sold well, our marriage with Microsoft might be saved. If not, we would have to admit defeat. This was, for many of us, the final test of the viability of the Windows Phone franchise. The 920 launched in November to rave reviews in both the United States and the United Kingdom, two important signaling markets. "It's Nokia's greatest Windows Phone yet," declared the Engadget reviewer.[5] The headline in the U.K.'s *Independent* proclaimed, "It's Big, It's Beautiful and Probably the Most Advanced Smartphone on the Market."[6] The *New York Times* aptly summarized, "Excellence has been attained. Now it's up to market forces."[7]

Those market forces looked good. Sales were seriously constrained by supply, because of chipset availability, which was not good, but it was a great feeling that customers were so eager to buy the Lumia 920 that we couldn't satisfy the demand.

Surfing the Lumia wave, Devices & Services posted better-than-expected financial results. Combined with good performance by NSN and the sale of Nokia House headquarters (which we promptly leased back) bolstering our cash reserves by €170 million, in early January 2013, Nokia did what had seemed unthinkable the previous spring: We announced a *positive* profit warning for the fourth quarter. Instead of reporting a loss as large as 10 percent, as analysts expected, we predicted that we would break even or even turn a profit.[8]

Our share price immediately surged nearly 19 percent in the United States.[9] A number of analysts rated our stock as a buy. GigaOm told readers, "You'd better sit down for this: Nokia is actually doing reasonably well."[10] "The Lumia smartphones are night-and-day different from Nokia's old Symbian handsets," said an influential International Data Corporation analyst. "I think what we are starting to see now is what will be a steady turnaround in Nokia's fortunes."[11]

Inside the company, there was a sense that Stephen Elop's plan was finally kicking in. The latest Nokia employee survey gave us a score of 65 percent for people engagement, 71 percent for leadership, and 71 percent for visible cultural change—healthy on the average, a tremendous improvement over the previous two years, and amazing progress for a company fighting for its survival. As Stephen wrote in his CEO letter at the end of December 2012, "All told, I feel a sense of measured optimism as we close 2012 and prepare for what's next."

My optimistic half did, too. But its paranoid twin was not ready to yield, either.

. . . .

Baking in Scenario Thinking

It is not enough for leaders to learn to think in alternatives. You need to bake this into your culture. That's simple to say but much harder to learn to do consistently. Here's how I start the ball rolling:

Every time someone presents a plan, it is a great opportunity to ask, "What are the alternatives?" If the response is, "I am sorry, this seemed such an obvious way forward that I didn't think of alternatives," you can strengthen alternative thinking as part of the culture by spending a little time together to come up with some different scenarios. Even if the person didn't have a selection of alternatives *this* time, I'm sure he or she will the *next* time. And *that person* will ask for alternatives the next time one of his or her team members presents a plan.

What starts as a leadership approach becomes an inseparable part of your culture and strategic thinking. If I ever heard somebody answer a question about our culture by saying, "Well, we always think in terms of alternatives," I would probably swoon with happiness.

. . . .

12

CAN THIS MARRIAGE BE SAVED?

JANUARY 2013–APRIL 2013

. . . .

You can win or lose a lot depending on how you play the game.

. . . .

"CAN WE TALK?" That's what Microsoft CEO Steve Ballmer asked when he called me late in the evening on January 30, 2013. Our conversation lasted barely five minutes: Could we meet in person at the upcoming Mobile World Congress in Barcelona at the end of February to discuss the future of our partnership?

I wasn't surprised to hear from him. I knew to expect this call.

Stephen Elop often talked to his former boss about the Windows Phone partnership. This was very helpful for Nokia, because the two connected easily. Toward the end of 2012, Stephen had started hearing hints that Microsoft wasn't happy with the way things were going. We were not exactly happy either. There had been rumors that Microsoft was interested in putting their own brand on smartphones.

As we understood that Microsoft's plans might have weighty consequences for Nokia, we raised the bar a little bit for Steve Ballmer. Stephen notified him that any discussions beyond our current partnership should happen with me.

Steve's request to meet sent a signal that the situation was getting serious.

We had decided that should there be negotiations regarding structural arrangements, I would take on the role of lead negotiator and all critical communications to Microsoft should go through me only. Usually, CEOs negotiate with CEOs. But at Microsoft, Stephen Elop had reported to Steve Ballmer. We didn't want the perception that Steve might be able to influence Stephen. We were both concerned and convinced that he would try. I was an unknown quantity to Steve, and that might work to our advantage.

Trying to Preserve Our Partnership

It wasn't clear where our partnership was heading. The Windows Phone was definitely not a success, but it was still too early to call it a failure. The partnership had been in practice for two years, but we were barely a year into shipping products—a fairly short time period in which to establish ourselves—so ups and downs were to be expected.

So far, for every "down" there had always been a strong reason to believe in a soon-to-be-realized "up"; for every disappointment, there was an explanation that encouraged us to maintain our energy. The first Nokia Windows Phones were created in a hurry by an ODM (original design manufacturer), so they weren't really Nokia devices with Nokia-specific differentiators. The Lumia models in the second batch were more Nokia, but were still running a very young operating system missing a lot of critical features. The Lumia 920, our third-generation flagship device, was a great device with the best OS that Microsoft could make and lots of unique Nokia differentiators, but sales were initially hampered by supply constraints.

Opening a third ecosystem was proving more difficult than we had expected. Android and Apple had started spinning their virtuous circle so much earlier that it felt almost impossible to match their velocity, let alone catch up with them. Their head start boosted them far ahead on the growth curve, with volume shares of 75 percent and 15 percent, respectively, compared with the Windows Phone OS at just 2 percent.[1]

We kept trying to jump-start our own virtuous circle. Our devices were good; the user experience was good; the feedback from industry experts was good. The meetings with telecom operators were overwhelmingly positive. We were excited about the features we planned to pack into the next generation of Windows Phones.

But we just couldn't seem to break through with consumers. Our weekly activation numbers were climbing steadily from a flat 200,000 per week all across the summer months to 300,000 during October and November and peaked at 550,000 immediately after Christmas. That was respectable growth, but Android saw over 300,000 activations *per day* already back in 2011. After Christmas, Lumia activations declined to roughly 300,000 per week. Android activations were over a million. Every day.[2]

The first quarter of 2013 was expected to be below plan as well, as our Lumia 920 supply constraints continued to haunt us.

Mapping Scenarios for Our Survival

In his treatise *The Art of War*, the ancient Chinese military strategist Sun Tzu counseled that the best way to win a war is to win it before it starts. In advance of my meeting with Steve Ballmer, the Nokia team and our bankers had a number of discussions to explore alternative scenarios and plan how we should play the meeting.

Our initial approach analyzed our options from Microsoft's perspective. Our thinking developed over time as events unfolded and as we shifted our perspective to our point of view. However, the basic framework remained as follows:

Plan A: Microsoft acquires Nokia.

- A1: We end up making a deal. The various different deal perimeters are the following:
  - A1a: Microsoft acquires all of Nokia.
  - A1b: Microsoft acquires all of our handset business plus our HERE mapping and navigation-related services (formerly known as Navteq).
  - A1c: Microsoft acquires all of our handset business without HERE.
  - A1d: Microsoft acquires only our smart devices business.

- A2: We fail to make a deal.
  - A2a: We manage to agree to a new contract that releases us from the exclusive Windows Phone partnership. We embrace Android in addition to the Windows Phone OS.
  - A2b: We continue in the exclusive relationship but get Microsoft to make a bigger financial investment in marketing. We get Microsoft to support only Nokia instead of trying to create competition between different Windows Phone licensees.
  - A2c: We continue with the current contract.

If Plan A moved ahead, we would need to decide whether we were willing to make a deal. At the same time, we would need to start negotiating to prevent Plan B and Plan C.

Plan B: Microsoft acquires some other handset company.
It was widely known that Steve Ballmer was a fan of HTC, the Taiwanese consumer electronics giant. Its devices were thinner than Lumia models and, at that time, thinness was a prime feature that the media focused on.

- B1: Microsoft acquires HTC.
  - B1a: We manage to agree on a new contract that releases us from the exclusivity. We embrace Android in addition to the Windows Phone OS. Microsoft provides us with reasonable compensation.
  - B1b: We sue Microsoft.
- B2: Microsoft acquires another handset company.
  - B2a: We manage to agree on a new contract that releases us from the exclusivity. We embrace Android in addition to the Windows Phone OS. Microsoft provides us with reasonable compensation.
  - B2b: We sue Microsoft.

Plan B would be the worst outcome. We would stay locked in our binding contract with Microsoft (because, stupidly, we did not think to specifically remove this option from Microsoft during the original contract negotiations). As a result, Microsoft would know all our plans and would work hard to build better devices in competition with us. Therefore, this option had to be prevented at almost any cost.

Plan C: Microsoft becomes a mobile manufacturer organically.
If that occurred:

- C1: Basically the same as B2a.
- C2: Precisely the same as B2b—we sue Microsoft.

Plan C was more unlikely. Even if Microsoft outsourced to the maximum, it would take a long time for them to ramp up to a global scale. Nevertheless, this would throw a huge wrench into our relationship.

For each scenario and sub-scenario, we could do the following:

- Launch an ongoing intelligence-gathering project around the scenario so that our information on the topic was as accurate as possible.
- Launch an ongoing program to come up with bigger and smaller actions we could take to influence the likelihood of the scenario. Implement those actions in a strategic way. For example, one action might be to reach out to HTC's CEO to open our own M&A discussions with the company and complicate things for Microsoft at the same time.
- Prepare for the possibility of having to sue Microsoft:
  - First, we would need to know how strong a case we might have. If it was very strong, that could provide leverage in negotiations and could be used if negotiations turned ugly. If it wasn't strong, it was still important to understand that.
  - Second, by being prepared, we could sue Microsoft soon after they announced plans to acquire HTC. We would not be completely caught with our pants down.
  - We also prepared skeleton press releases for the different scenarios. If nothing else, this is a good practice to clarify your

thinking and ensure everyone understands what the outcome would look like from the outside.

Playing the Game the Right Way

You can win or lose a lot depending on how you play the game. Of course, this was not a game—this was an extremely serious situation for Nokia. Any outcome would impact tens of thousands of people directly and millions or even billions of people indirectly. This was an engagement where both sides needed to have a lot of integrity in how they interacted. At the same time, though, you can interact in a skillful way or a non-skillful way, and there's a huge gap between the two.

We felt that, within certain constraints, time was on our side at that stage. We still believed that the latest generation of Lumia smartphones had a chance to change the game and that there was a possibility we could weather the storm with our own devices and our own business model. Our first priority was to avoid the scenario where Microsoft would buy HTC or another handset company. That would be a disaster for Nokia.

We really wanted to find a way to communicate to Microsoft the feeling that we were not ready to engage in a yes-no situation just yet, that we needed time to seriously consider their proposition. But we didn't want to be so negative that we would push them into the arms of another company. Our goal was: Open the door but don't allow them to come through.

One of the lessons for me, from the extensive deal making of 2013, 2014, and early 2015, was the realization of the power of the right words at critical junctions. This lesson was first drummed into me as we were discussing tactics for the forthcoming meeting with Ballmer in Barcelona. How could we play for time while preventing Microsoft from moving forward with alternatives hostile to our interests? What could I tell Ballmer to accomplish this?

We spent quite some time discussing this. Finally, Gary Weiss, one of the two senior bankers from JPMorgan Chase whom we were working with, suggested that we say something very simple: "You are much farther down this path than we are, and you have taken us by surprise. You need to give us the opportunity to think through what you are suggesting and what we should do. Secondly, as we are joined at the hip in a deep business partnership, we owe both ourselves and each other the opportunity to see if we can make this a real win-win partnership. So, what we would like to do is launch a management audit to analyze what in our current partnership is making it impossible for each party to achieve what they really want out of this."

Ballmer Gets Down to Business

In Barcelona, Steve Ballmer and I first discussed how each company was doing. We were like two fencers getting a feel for their opponent. I mentioned that I'd heard rumors that PC volumes were being hit hard by growing sales of iPads, tablets, and mobile phones, affecting Microsoft's core software business. Steve seemed uncomfortable.

I talked about the pain that Nokia had gone through in 2012 with our huge layoffs and the public speculations about bankruptcy. I emphasized the positive business developments in the third and fourth quarter. (We didn't know at the time that we had sailed into the eye of the storm and the worst was yet to come.) Basically, my message was, "Nokia is moving in the right direction. We just need more time."

Then Steve got down to business.

As a latecomer to the smartphone game, Steve estimated that Microsoft needed to sell 100 million devices just to break even. He couldn't justify spending that kind of marketing money, he informed me. "If I need to invest $20 to sell a Windows Phone in order to get $10 back in royalties, where's the sense in that?" Steve asked.

I could see why Steve was under pressure to either get Microsoft out of the mobile phone business or acquire a company to start making phones under the Microsoft brand. But I didn't want the discussion to go one step further down the M&A path, so I went into a rapid-fire brainstorming mode. I asked a lot of questions to understand how he thought about the handset business and Microsoft's objectives. I suggested different scenarios in which Microsoft would have a reason to spend much more in marketing and we could share the gross margins of those extra volumes. I proposed options that ranged from minor tweaks to different business combinations.

The media often describes Steve as "big, brash and bullish,"[3] "fiery," "impassioned," and "crude,"[4] and "flamboyant"[5]—pretty much the opposite of my personality. But we actually got along quite well. Our joint brainstorming established a foundation of trust and mutual respect.

However, I sensed that Steve had already decided to pursue a vertical business model of Microsoft producing their own devices one way or another. It wasn't clear exactly what he was proposing, but Microsoft's Plan A seemed to be, buy the smartphone division of Nokia. Plan B was to look elsewhere.

I asked Steve about his timeline. "If Nokia drags their feet," he told me, then he would need to move to Plan B. I made it very clear that if Microsoft went for HTC, we would be forced to consider legal actions. But I also reiterated that this was a scenario we would prefer to avoid.

I gave him the preplanned "You are much farther down this path . . ." pitch and suggested that we have a management audit to examine the existing relationship and try to form a plan in which the two companies could achieve their respective objectives within the current partnership.

Steve did not believe this would change anything and was adamant that we accomplish the audit in two to three weeks. He probably also understood that I was deliberately trying to delay the proceedings to buy us more time, so he put counterpressure on us.

I flew back to Helsinki feeling as though we were zooming at warp speed into a new reality. Could we maintain our partnership with Microsoft? If not, how could we ensure that Nokia remained their primary acquisition target, not HTC or another company? Would an acquisition be our salvation, or would it sink us?

Nokia was made up of three business divisions: Devices & Services, aka the handset business, which included both smartphones and mobile phones and supplied 90 percent of our revenue (if one excluded the consolidated revenues of the joint venture NSN); HERE, the location mapping service; and Nokia Technologies, our valuable portfolio of patents. But in terms of our revenues and in the eyes of the public, Nokia *was* handsets. If we *did* agree to the acquisition of all or part of the Devices & Services division, what would be left of Nokia?

The blunt answer was, not much. That might be the end of Nokia.

Playing for Time

Throughout the month of March, management teams from Nokia and Microsoft met a few times in Reykjavik, Iceland. Why Reykjavik? Because it's roughly midway between Seattle and Helsinki, and even more important, it's a fairly secure place to meet.

We were paranoid about leaks. Nokia's business was challenging enough; we did not need intense public speculation on our relationship with Microsoft. Despite a positive Q4, our overall mobile phone business was doing badly, and we continued to have serious issues in China.

We were also paranoid about the possibility of a deal between Microsoft and HTC. Microsoft indicated that they had given up on the in-house option: Organic development would take too long, given that Microsoft didn't have the competence or capabilities. That knocked out the original Plan C. (As if we didn't have enough letters in the alphabet, as we shifted the perspective of the scenarios to Nokia's point of view, we reused C and, for the rest of the process, Plan C referred to continuing our cooperation with Microsoft based on an amended partnership agreement.)

Plan A was some sort of a deal between Microsoft and Nokia. But we suspected Microsoft was prioritizing Plan B, which was a deal with HTC. (We later found out that Microsoft had gone far enough to send a team to Taipei to do some preliminary due diligence.)

We also met with HTC ourselves later on in the spring, trying to sniff out whether Microsoft's noises about HTC were just a negotiation tactic or whether they were a credible threat. While HTC was a licensee of Windows, they were predominantly an Android player and, as such, not a perfect partner for Microsoft. So while we were still in a tremendously precarious position, we felt we held some strong cards in this discussion.

The management audit process enabled us to buy several weeks and amass lots of data about Microsoft's objectives and thinking. On April 1, with the audit completed, Steve Ballmer and I had a conversation. I suggested that as Nokia and Microsoft had both entered our partnership with the serious intention of making it hugely successful, let's both make one final effort: Give us two more weeks, and we'd give our best proposal on the concessions we were willing to make to continue as partners. Steve reluctantly agreed.

During that period and throughout the process, our chief legal officers were in regular contact. (Louise Pentland was our CLO, a great colleague and one of the best lawyers I have ever worked with; her counterpart at Microsoft was Brad Smith, whom I also learned to respect.) This was a useful back channel to find out what each party wanted the other to learn, and it also served to build trust between both sides.

We presented our proposal for a new relationship with Microsoft on April 11, a Thursday. They listened very carefully, and we agreed that Steve Ballmer would call me the following Sunday to share their feedback. We fully expected Microsoft to reject our proposal, and that's just what happened. But we had bought a bit of extra time that we feverishly dedicated to preparing for the real negotiations.

Steve wanted to start M&A discussions immediately. We agreed to meet a week later in New York.

As part of the preparations, we had spared no effort to analyze how Microsoft might value us, both stand-alone and in comparison with HTC. Let's assume that Microsoft was serious about acquiring either us or HTC. If we could calculate what our market value would be in case Microsoft did the deal with HTC, we would know a floor value for Nokia. Any offer above this floor would theoretically be worth accepting, as, for our shareholders, it was better than forcing Microsoft to embrace the HTC option. If we said no and drove Microsoft to buy HTC, we would be worth less.

Our JP Morgan M&A team helped us with the analysis, and together we had ended up with a valuation of our Devices & Services business (post Microsoft doing a deal with HTC) of between a downside value of €1.6 billion and an optimistic upside value of €5.5 billion. Therefore, if Microsoft offered us more than €5.5 billion, we should accept. If they offered less than €1.6 billion, we should decline. If they offered something within the range, we would need to decide whether we believed in the optimistic case more than the downside case.

"We Seem to Be on Two Different Planets"

Between the core management teams for Nokia and Microsoft, lawyers representing each side, bankers from Goldman Sachs (for Microsoft) and JP Morgan (for us), and a phalanx of support personnel, there must have been close to 30 people crowding into the room for our first negotiation session, on April 22, 2013, in New York.

There's a certain process that the bankers and lawyers, especially, are familiar with. Since, for many, only one side can win, there's an adversarial undercurrent to the proceedings from the get-go. Then add all the big egos trying to intimidate the opposite party and posturing for their retinue. I was reminded of classical Chinese theater, where each actor played a set character and the audience knew what to expect from each role. Steve Ballmer, towering over the room, his bald head gleaming and his characteristic assertiveness barely leashed, was an easy contender for the biggest and baddest.

As Microsoft had approached us, etiquette stipulated that they speak first. I welcomed everyone to the meeting, Steve echoed my remarks, and I told him that the floor was his.

Steve launched into a short description of Microsoft's strategy in handsets, gesticulating broadly, his voice rising to just below a shout. I'd heard that this was how he expressed himself when he got excited, but this was the first time I experienced it live. (I had seen the video of him doing what became known as "the monkey dance,"[6] which was, of course, excitement on a completely different level.) He seemed a different man from the one I had met with in Barcelona.

Then Microsoft's banker from Goldman Sachs presented the proposal. The banker had his role down pat. He was a master of his trade, representing one of the most powerful banking firms in the world, a veteran of lots of landmark deals, used to overawing people as a matter of course.

The room was dead silent as he began to speak.

Microsoft was known for paying serious money for companies they wanted to buy. A few years earlier, they had offered close to $50 billion for Yahoo!, a more than 60 percent premium over an already overvalued stock price.[7] Our expectations were high. We believed we would get an offer of, at least, €8 billion.

Instead, the offer was in the range of €4.25 billion to €5.25 billion for our Devices & Services business plus HERE and a large patent license as well. This was well below our lowest expectations. Assuming that they valued HERE at over €2 billion and the patent license at over €1 billion, their valuation for all of Devices & Services was between €1 billion and €2 billion. This was close to our Plan B downside valuation of €1.6 billion.

We were all stunned. Hiding our surprise, we asked questions, because every engagement is an opportunity to gather more data. Then I suggested a breakout so we could discuss the proposal in a separate meeting room.

The usual dynamics of these deals are that an offer is made, you make a counteroffer, and after perhaps weeks of negotiations, the outcome is close to the midpoint unless that outcome is simply unacceptable to either party. It was obvious we couldn't agree to their offer. But we could not get to where we wanted by way of a counteroffer either: Their offer was so low that our counteroffer would have to be absurdly high for the midpoint to be where we wanted it. For instance, to get to €6 billion for D&S and an IP license, we would have to make a counteroffer of €12 billion to €13 billion. And such a high counteroffer would be read as completely unrealistic and set the wrong tone.

We felt that the only way forward was to clearly communicate to Microsoft that their offer was completely out of the question, but we had to do it without any grandstanding or antagonism.

I went out to find Steve Ballmer and pulled him aside. "Hey, Steve," I proposed, "we would like to discuss your offer but with only you and your leadership team members in the room. Let's have all the bankers, lawyers, and junior team members leave, and just have a small core team to talk through the situation."

At exactly that moment, Microsoft chief legal officer Brad Smith arrived from a meeting he had to attend in Washington, D.C. We gathered our chief legal officers, chief financial officers, Stephen Elop and his counterpart Terry Myerson, who ran the Windows Phone program, and Steve Ballmer and myself—eight people in the room.

As firmly and politely as I could, I said that their offer was a no-go. "We seem to be on two different planets in terms of valuation, and the distance is so vast that there is nothing to discuss," I explained. I sincerely thanked the Microsoft team for taking the effort to fly to New York and for having a good discussion, but said that we needed to figure out a new way to restart. I tried to say this in the nicest possible way, but the message was pretty tough.

Steve Ballmer took it relatively well. He stood up and thanked me for the feedback, then responded, "Since there's nothing to discuss, we might as well go home," adding somewhat ominously, "Be prepared for awkward moments in the weeks ahead." (I assumed he was referring to the HTC threat.) Brad Smith, who had sat down just five minutes earlier, tried to joke that this was the shortest M&A negotiation he had ever attended.

But as we filed out of the room, no one was laughing.

. . . .

"It's *Always* About the People"

People often say that business is business. But in my experience, business is never just business: It's *always* about the people.

The first meeting between the parties was a jungle of tangled personal dynamics: lots of people used to others being silent when they talked; lots of people with external pressure to perform.

If my meeting in Barcelona with Steve resembled two fencers crossing swords for the first time, the meeting in New York was like two armies confronting each other on the battlefield.

In hindsight, we should have invested in building personal contacts before that first meeting. I should have sought to have dinner with Steve the previous night. We should have made sure our bankers had a deep conversation with their counterparts. Maybe the CLOs and CFOs could have had their own dinner.

These situations are very delicate, as neither party wants to reveal its cards fully, but both parties need to be able to communicate certain expectations in order to avoid a disastrous surprise. M&A negotiations are often as much an art as science, and it is the people that make it an art.

This was our first major transaction process with this team. Over the next few years, we became much better at both the science and the art of deal making. I'll talk more about those lessons in the next chapters.

· ·

13

HITTING "RESTART"—AGAIN AND AGAIN

APRIL 2013–JUNE 2013

. . . .

We worked out a better way to negotiate: the 4 x 4 approach.

. . . .

I THINK EVERYONE was shocked by the impasse in our negotiations. We took the risk of refusing Microsoft's offer because it was so important to send a clear message to Microsoft that their approach was not the right way to think about this deal.

At the same time, it was important to emphasize that we intentionally tried to avoid becoming adversarial. Even if our negotiations failed, we would have to continue working together, at least for a time. Both parties knew we couldn't afford to burn bridges.

That was what the principals on both sides reiterated to their counterparts: "We're still partners. Let's be calm and rethink and reconnect. Let's not lose hope."

(Microsoft code-named the negotiations Project Gold Medal. It called itself Moses, after the great American hurdler Edwin Moses; Nokia was dubbed Nurmi, after Paavo Nurmi, the famous runner nicknamed "the Flying Finn." It was nice to know that Microsoft took a win-win approach, at least when it came to code names. On Nokia's side, the key players were Namu (the name of a famous whale), Minnow, and, for HTC, Halibut.)

On April 24, two days after the talks broke down, I spoke with Steve Ballmer. What happened in New York was my fault, your fault, and both of our teams' fault, I said. The management audit had focused on maintaining the current relationship. Consequently, the teams had not covered the topics necessary to understand each other from an M&A perspective. "There were lots of misunderstandings about what each party was seeking," I explained. "Let's go back a few steps and see if we can help each other to fill in the blanks."

He agreed, and we were back on track. But this time, we would do things differently.

Regulating the Bankers

We agreed that our bankers had allowed both parties to come unprepared. Bankers are incentivized to make a deal, regardless of which party it benefits, and they may sometimes steer a deal toward closure on terms that are biased. Microsoft's bankers had allowed Microsoft to make a proposal that was almost offensive to us. They should have understood that we were still hoping to be successful with the Windows Phone. Paradoxically, if, as their valuation suggested, they doubted the Windows Phone's viability, perhaps they should not have been interested in the deal in the first place.

In considering how to deal with our own bankers, we reminded ourselves of one of the rules of entrepreneurial leadership: Don't be defined by your role. And as a corollary: Don't let your bankers be constrained by *their* conventional role.

Consequently, we transformed our advisors into real partners. We did this by being completely transparent and including our two bankers and our external lead lawyer in all our deal-related strategy discussions. At the same time, due to certain signs that might indicate a biased analysis, I had a straightforward discussion with the global chairman of JP Morgan's TMT (Telecom, Media and Technology) area. I told her, "We can only continue to work with you if we are able to fully trust you." (M&A advisory work is like selling houses. The advisors make a lot of money when the house is sold. To an advisor, the selling price doesn't matter so much as long as there is a deal. To the house owner, on the other hand, the selling price matters a lot and it is often better to walk away from a bad deal and keep the house a bit longer.) Even a perception that JPM's analysis was influenced by their own earnings model would lead to negative consequences, I warned. I told the actual team the same thing.

I had nothing to complain about after that. JPM's Marcus Boser and Gary Weiss led a high-quality process, and never have we ended up being so satisfied with a deal team. We could not have hoped for a harder-working or more talented team.

The 4 x 4 Approach

Steve Ballmer and I agreed that the management teams should get together to clarify the earlier misunderstandings by exchanging more information on the business. We called this meeting an "information-sharing event."

Meanwhile, we worked out a better way to negotiate. I suggested to Ballmer that the first meeting failed partially because too many external team members were roiling the waters. We agreed to keep them out of the room from now on.

That's how we created the "4 x 4" approach: Steve Ballmer and I made up one pair, Stephen Elop and Terry Myerson made up another, and the two chief financial officers and two chief legal officers rounded out the quartet. We worked in pairs and had joint meetings together.

Each of the pairs had a good functional chemistry. Steve Ballmer and I, especially, hit it off very well. He was always very logical and extremely honest and demonstrated good integrity. I have a lot of respect for him. Although Steve is famous for screaming, he never raised his voice with me in any of our sessions. I was later told that the Microsoft team called this "the Risto effect."

Trust is best created in a smaller group with regular one-on-one sessions between the individuals. Because we knew we did not have all the expertise in the room, we kept the larger teams close but not in the inner circle.

Interestingly, we heard through Microsoft's bankers and team members that they did not want Steve Ballmer negotiating on his own. Although I never saw any indications of anything but completely logical thinking from Steve, he had a reputation of occasionally being a loose cannon. We understood that in some instances, the Microsoft team and board had no idea what Steve might spout off in a private discussion with me until he told them afterward, "Hey, I proposed this to Risto."

This was not something we did at Nokia.

The Nokia board discussed everything in advance. It was well versed in all the details and had debated all the alternatives a number of times. We knew—and agreed on—exactly what would be acceptable. I always had a clear, albeit sometimes broad, mandate to close a deal according to the terms that we had defined, with preset target outcomes and minimum limits.

It was, of course, natural for me to keep the board members up to date in almost real time, as they were *my* core team. However, I also felt it was necessary since Nokia's situation was becoming so precarious that any internal distrust or confusion might be fatal. I decided to err on the side of over-communication and too many meetings than allow the deal to fall through because of ruffled feathers or misunderstandings.

Of course, I never told Steve that I walked into every single meeting with the unquestioned authority to shake hands on a deal. Sometimes it's useful to be able to say, "Let me come back to you after I've discussed this with the board."

Time Runs Out

When we started our discussions with Microsoft in March 2013, we felt that time was on our side. The fourth quarter of 2012 had been strong, and we expected sales of the Lumia 920 Windows Phone to accelerate. The more we could slow down the negotiations, the higher Nokia's valuations would rise and the better deal we could make.

Spring snuffed out all our hopes.

The first-quarter results were horrible. We missed our Devices business top-line target by almost 20 percent and burned €18 for every

€100 of smartphone revenue. In mobile phones, we had targeted a volume share of 30 percent and missed that by a quarter. Our net sales were €500 million below plan, and we stood to lose €500 million in net cash.

Our Q2 results were expected to be at least as bad, with Devices & Services sales forecast to slump another €400 million.

But all that misery paled to insignificance as we continued to analyze the Lumia sales results. Demand for the Lumia 920 started to drop. Our earlier plan had been to reach a value market share of 2.8 percent in smartphones priced above $300. Our latest outlook had predicted reaching 2.2 percent. The reality was even worse: 1.3 percent.

It was time to face reality. We had bet the company on Lumia. We had failed.

We had set two triggers for automatic action should certain metrics be met. There was a trigger for additional cost cuts if the D&S division did much worse than planned. There was also a trigger for a complete strategy change if Lumia performed below all realistic expectations. (This is also an outcome of scenario planning. You can create plans in advance and define triggers for their execution within a certain scenario. This way you can act immediately when the trigger is pulled by events.)

The May financial forecast indicated that we would likely breach the Q2 trigger we had set to change our strategy. The trigger was an operating margin of –18 percent, and the forecast was –19 percent—a narrow miss, but a miss nevertheless. Hitting the trigger meant further layoffs, deeper cost cuts, and significant changes to our Windows Phone strategy, including even giving up on the Windows Phone altogether.

Time was no longer on our side. The question was, did Microsoft realize this? The more they could delay, the worse our situation and the more desperate we would get. Microsoft had all the device volume data and knew as well as we did what the Lumia 920 trajectory was. But did they realize what the data meant?

When we met with the Microsoft team in April, the lowest offer we felt we could theoretically accept was in the neighborhood of the higher end of the Plan B value analysis range of €1.6 billion to €5.5 billion. By May, our low-end valuation of €1.6 billion was looking grimly realistic. And if our situation continued to deteriorate, that worst-case valuation would actually look optimistic.

There was one glimmer of hope: If Microsoft wanted to acquire Nokia, it would be better to acquire a healthy company. After all, Microsoft wanted to build on Nokia's base, not destroy us. Microsoft, too, would suffer if they waited.

Increasingly, it looked as though it would be in both of our best interests to come to an agreement—and sooner rather than later.

A Triangulation of Value

On May 1, the management teams held the information-sharing meeting. One of Microsoft's main concerns was head count in Europe. In Microsoft's opinion, Nokia was less valuable *because* of our European employees. Finland, especially, with its labor unions and presumably expensive layoffs, was a bogeyman for Microsoft. We needed to educate the Microsoft team on the real costs of reducing head count in Europe. (This is a reminder to politicians as well as business leaders that perceptions and prejudices make a difference in foreign direct investments. Over the course of various deal negotiations, I have been surprised how often national or regional stereotypes were unchallenged by business leaders and decisions were made partially based on unverified assumptions.)

More importantly, a big sticking point was that we felt that their valuation calculations were off by a large margin. We took all the data points Microsoft had cited in the first meeting and came up with a method to calculate the value of Nokia from three different perspectives. We called this method "a triangulation of value."

The first scenario started with Microsoft's initial offer back in March: It was both a data point showing how much—or how little—Microsoft valued us and an insight into how they thought. We believed that there were mistakes in the calculations. Certain elements had been overlooked or not taken into consideration or simply missed. If all these incremental categories were added up, they would result in a much higher value for Nokia. We wanted to show Microsoft what valuation their own approach would lead to based on correct data. (Some of their assumptions regarding the future were also more positive than what we believed, and I must admit that we challenged some but not all of those.)

The second scenario looked at the costs if Microsoft didn't buy Nokia and acquired HTC instead. What would Microsoft get for the price? We compared Nokia's strengths with HTC's, checking off a long list of the areas in which Nokia was better. Our conclusion: Microsoft should be willing to pay several billion euros more for Nokia than they should be willing to pay for HTC, because we were that much of a better fit for what Microsoft wanted.

The third scenario looked at the intrinsic value of Nokia, i.e., what our shareholders saw. Basically, it was a discounted cash flow model of Nokia as a stand-alone business. This led to the highest valuations, as we had not yet had a chance to update our official long-range plan to reflect the unfolding failure of the high-end Windows Phones.

In a perfect world, the three different avenues would end up at the same price point. We saw them as three paths on a journey leading Microsoft to the right valuation of Nokia. The way it worked in practice was that as we presented each of these different points of view, the Microsoft team was forced to explain why they disagreed. With each explanation, we learned more about Microsoft's model of valuing Nokia. In this way, we were able to reverse-engineer the financial Excel model the company had built for Nokia.

On May 3, I had another call from Steve Ballmer. We discussed the situation and agreed that our differences were not insurmountable. We agreed to restart the process with a new round of face-to-face talks in London over the weekend of May 24 and 25.

The "Goddammit!" Meeting

Both of our small core teams showed up in London trailing lawyers, bankers, security, and support staff. But the staff stayed in their own meeting rooms while we started the day's first 4 x 4 meeting.

Steve had a habit of drafting Excel spreadsheets when he wanted to break down the details of a particular business. Trying to better understand the value opportunity in our mapping business, he started a spreadsheet for HERE. Seven people in the room sat and watched as he added formulas, totted up more calculations, and built more spreadsheets.

After what seemed like ages, we proposed that instead of watching Steve exercise his Excel muscles, we would try to do something useful and retired to our own break room. Steve estimated he'd be done in 30 minutes. He finally delivered Microsoft's latest version to our team two hours later.

It was a complicated proposal, and we needed time to go through it and debate our response. At some point, there was a knock on the door and Microsoft's banker popped his head in to ask how long we would take. With the memory of waiting two hours while the Microsoft people played with their spreadsheets, I curtly said, "As long as it takes." He shut the door and headed back to the Microsoft team to deliver the message.

Suddenly, we heard Steve yell, "Goddammit!" I thought, "Well, that's one less banker." We cautiously opened the connecting door and peeped out. Steve was flat on the floor with blood smeared on his face, cursing at the top of his lungs. It turned out he had tripped over a low glass coffee table and cut his head. Fortunately, his security detail had a first-aid kit and patched him up.

Despite the gash on his forehead, Steve insisted on continuing the negotiations. We all had a good laugh about his misstep, and the meeting became known as the "goddammit! meeting."

Still, we were not in a good mood as the day ended. We had spent a lot of time debating without making real progress. I invited Steve and his core team to join us for dinner, and a jovial gathering made a difference. It set the tone for a constructive atmosphere. After dinner, the Microsoft team returned to the meeting center for further work. The Nokia team stayed at the restaurant to discuss our plan for the next day.

After a full second day, we sensed that we were narrowing down our differences. As we closed the meeting, for the first time, both parties felt positive that we could actually achieve a deal.

On May 27, Steve called me with a revised offer, one a little higher than the first offer. From our point of view, though, the offer was, in a convoluted way, actually lower because it didn't take into account the additional valuation data that we had provided and that the Microsoft team had agreed with. Here's how it worked: Let's say their first number was $1,000. Our hard data showed undiscovered value worth $500, which they agreed with. As their new offer was $1,200, it meant that they had reduced their original offer to $700 and then added the mutually acknowledged $500 on top of that. We couldn't accept it.

However, Steve and I had a good discussion. And at the end of the call, he told me, "We're not there yet, but we know where we have to get to." That sounded encouraging.

On May 30, I agreed to talk with Steve at 1 a.m. Finnish time. The phone didn't ring until an hour later. Steve was in an ugly mood: He told me that he had just concluded an awful meeting with one of Microsoft's biggest partners. Given that, it may not have been the best moment to make a counterproposal that Microsoft could bridge the gap between the hypothetical $1,200 and $1,500. Perhaps because Steve was so upset, I had to repeat our counteroffer and the reasoning behind it three times.

Perhaps also because Steve was so upset, he became impatient. He stressed that because Microsoft's board meeting was scheduled for June 12 and 13, we had a deadline of June 11 to come up with an agreement or all bets were off.

Time was running out for a deal.

Time was also running out for Nokia. Our second-quarter forecast had sunk yet another €200 million, forcing us to drop our forecast for the first half of 2013 by €2.2 billion in the Devices & Services top line— a sickening 25 percent plunge. If our forecast was right, we'd blow right through the triggers activating further layoffs, cost cuts, and strategy changes.

Microsoft's response came a couple of days later. They didn't like our counteroffer. The essence of Ballmer's message was, "This isn't going to work. Let's stop wasting time."

For the second time, the deal was off.

All scenarios, even the worst ones, need to be considered. No news is too bad not to be discussed. The board had, of course, reviewed the worst outcomes as part of our scenario planning. Now, for the first time, our CFO Timo Ihamuotila, a colleague I valued very highly, and I privately raised the possibility that Nokia might not make it, not just as a theoretical scenario, but as a real fact.

Desperation Is the Mother of Invention

Over the next few days, we frantically tried to figure out how to get back on track. Stephen Elop came up with a winning suggestion: Instead of meeting halfway between the two headquarters, as had been our practice, let's sacrifice what was most precious to us: time.

"We'd like to meet once more, but you don't have to fly to London, New York, or Reykjavik," I told Steve Ballmer. "You don't have to travel anywhere. What's most important for us is to understand your point of view. We'll come to you next weekend, if you accept."

Steve did, even though it meant taking time away from his son's high school graduation party. And so the weekend of June 1, our team flew to Microsoft's offices in Redmond, Washington, to talk on their home turf.

The parking lot at Microsoft headquarters was deserted, with everyone out enjoying the bright early summer Saturday. Our steps echoed in the empty halls as we walked to a meeting room near Steve Ballmer's office. A pristine smartboard waited for us to cover it with scrawled graphs and charts.

We continued with our 4 x 4 approach but with a slightly different structure. First, all four pairs met together to identify the big issues. Then while each pair examined different issues through the lens of their expertise, Steve and I had a one-on-one discussion in his office. After Steve and I were done, we each pulled our teams together for a private huddle. Then the entire group reconvened to summarize what had been accomplished. We rotated through this process, chipping away at the remaining pain points, patiently, painstakingly, and in the spirit of partnership.

And in the end, Steve and I reached an agreement on the deal value. The result comprised Devices & Services in full, HERE, and the necessary patent license. The price was €6.25 billion and an earn-out over the next five years. Assuming Microsoft could achieve a reasonable market share, the earn-out would be worth €900 million.

We shook hands and went to tell our teams: We had a deal.

After general back-patting between the two teams, we flew back to Finland, tired but satisfied, although a bit shaky with the magnitude of what we had agreed to. Our deal still had to be approved by the Nokia and Microsoft boards. But the Nokia board had been informed every step of the way and had given me authorization before the meeting, so its approval was a formality. We were fine, I thought.

Except we weren't.

The Microsoft Surprise

On June 13, Steve Ballmer called me: The Microsoft board had rejected the deal.

I only learned the details years later. On the first day of Microsoft's two-day board meeting, Steve had presented the term sheet we negotiated and the board approved the deal. Steve's son was playing in a high school basketball game that evening, so Steve skipped the board dinner to watch the game, certain that everything was under control.

During the course of the dinner, the board had second thoughts. It seemed that while the board members knew of our discussions, they hadn't been apprised of the details and hadn't immersed themselves in the why, how much, and other aspects of the deal. The board felt that the price tag was too high, that the structure was unclear, and, especially galling, that they hadn't been kept in the loop. Led by Bill Gates, they revolted. Brad Smith, the chief legal officer, frantically alerted Steve in the middle of the basketball game: "Something is happening. You should come back here."

But it was too late.

It's very unusual for a CEO to shake hands on a deal and then get a red light from the board. Steve was so upset that on the second day of the board meeting, he did something unwise. Instead of working with Microsoft's board members to figure out their problem with the deal and come up with a solution they could accept, he issued an ultimatum. He told the board, "I'm going back to my office. You have until the end of the day to come up with a proposal to Nokia."

They did, but no one was happy with it.

Third Time Lucky?

When Steve called me, he was terribly apologetic. He had given his word and now he couldn't do what he had promised. He felt so bad that he offered to fly to Helsinki the next day to present an alternative offer in person. I asked, "What are you going to propose?" He wouldn't tell me, only saying that he needed to work on the details.

Stephen Elop was just sharing what he thought was good news about the Microsoft deal with the full management team when I called to inform him, "No, we don't have a deal." Stephen later told me the mood plunged from relief to outright despair. It hadn't been easy for the management team to concede to selling our crown jewels and to acknowledge that the company had sailed into such a bad situation under their watch. They had only just come to terms with that first obstacle on their emotional journey. Now they were hurled back to square one.

I reassured him that this was not the end of the story. "We will continue the negotiations, and we will do this deal," I said. "I don't know how, but we will do it."

When Steve Ballmer walked into the Nokia training center in the lush Finnish countryside on June 14, I was ready to do a little playacting. I overemphasized our board's outrage that we had shaken hands on a deal that then fell apart. Steve was contrite, apologizing over and over, and taking responsibility for not having kept the Microsoft board sufficiently in the loop throughout the spring.

We had spent five months building trust, not just between Steve and me but between all the pairs in the 4 x 4. We had endured an abnormally high number of breakdowns in the negotiations, but those were due to circumstances, not to distrust. That we had always recovered and restarted was entirely due to trust. When you construct the right kind of relationship, people want to do right by you, even in adversarial situations.

Clearly, Steve did not want to betray our trust. That's why he insisted to his board that he owed us *some* proposal. And that's why he flew to Helsinki, which is quite a flight from Seattle, on a day's notice to present it in person.

The proposal was very complicated. It boiled down to not an acquisition, but an equity investment in Nokia, involving lots of changes to the current partnership agreement. Unfortunately, it was not acceptable for Nokia at all. It would have eliminated all optionality for us and tied us irreversibly to the Windows Phones. By now, some of us no longer believed in the viability of the platform.

For the third time, the deal was off.

One bright spot was that Steve told us that the HTC plan was also off the table. At least, we didn't have to fear the worst. And the fact that he shared that news was yet more proof of our having been able to create a good relationship.

"We *Must* Move Forward"

It would have been easy to give into despair.

When Steve Ballmer told me that the Microsoft board had rejected his offer, I felt flooded by a maelstrom of emotions. Surprise, because it's so abnormal for a board to turn down a deal that the CEO has shaken hands on. Curiosity about what this would mean for Microsoft. And frustration at Steve for not having kept the board fully committed every step of the process.

But never for a minute, not even for a second, did I believe, "This is the end of it." It was more a question of, "We *must* move forward. How can we do it?"

Our team collectively pulled our socks up and dug in. One major sticking point was that Microsoft's board did not like the thousands of people working in HERE or the many thousands working in our manufacturing and logistics. They hated the operating expenses and were afraid that reducing head count would be a nightmare. We brainstormed how we could make changes to the deal structure that would take into account Microsoft's concerns.

One suggestion by Stephen Elop was to sell our smart devices business only, i.e., Windows Phones, and continue on our own with "non-smart" mobile phones. Nokia remained the world's second-largest handset maker, producing nearly 80 million devices every quarter.[1] The low-end mobile phones didn't produce the high profit margins that smart devices did, but they were doing well for us in India, China, and Africa—big markets all.

We examined different scenarios, but it was difficult to imagine how we could implement this strategy. We had one sales team, one distribution channel, and one supply chain. If we split our entire phone business in two, we'd be half an entity. Half a being wouldn't live very long.

Still, it was a start. On June 20, I called Steve Ballmer to propose that Stephen Elop discuss the smart devices option with Terry Myerson. Steve agreed.

There were problems. Nokia had licensed intellectual property rights from Qualcomm that couldn't exist in two places at once. If we were to sell the smart devices business to Microsoft and keep mobile phones, one of these two would be unlicensed, and it would be extremely expensive to acquire the license for it.

At the end of June, we agreed that the smart devices option wouldn't work.

The Lumia 1020 was due to launch in just a few weeks. Analysts and reviewers who got a sneak peek were stunned by a photo experience that was leaps and bounds beyond that offered by our competitors. "We're smitten," announced The Verge, describing the 41-megapixel camera as "awesome."[2] "Nokia's Lumia 1020 is the Windows Phone camera king we've been anxiously awaiting for two years," CNET wrote.[3]

But I no longer believed that the Lumia 1020 would kick off a Nokia comeback. It was so frustrating. We were producing great products, but they were just too late.

Still . . . we weren't dead yet. There *had* to be a way to salvage the situation and restart negotiations. Nothing less than the future of Nokia was at stake.

. . . .

Leveraging Emotions to Support Strategy Formulation

It's tempting to want to dismiss emotions and insist on making decisions on a purely rational basis. Tempting—but not realistic. We're not robots, and our reasoning is naturally affected by our emotions, especially when the stakes are so high.

Rather than seeking to weed out emotions from the strategizing process, we leveraged them to support strategy formulation. (This is described in detail in a research paper published in the *Academy of Management Annual Meeting*.[4]) For example, the shared guilt over past mistakes both helped the board and management team work more intentionally and motivated them to generate a wider variety of alternative scenarios.

Our practice of iterating, reiterating, and analyzing all the different scenarios brought the emotions to the surface early on. People can make really stupid decisions in the heat of the moment, and there were a lot of highs and lows as we went through the negotiations. We were, after all, discussing the fate not just of our company but of a Finnish national landmark. But as one of the board members later noted, "By allowing emotions to emerge during the process, we ensured that the decision would be made based on facts."[5]

Deliberately not suppressing negative emotions enables you to acknowledge the guilt and fear and move on. A board member noted, "When the worst possible outcome could be talked about, it actually removes the fear and then we can plan and prepare ourselves."[6] Instead of being paralyzed by paranoia, you can encourage the optimism, which will, in turn, facilitate positive actions.

. . . .

14

BOLD MOVES CAN BE YOUR BEST BET

APRIL 2013–JULY 2013

. . . .

Microsoft had hoards of offshore cash.
They needed to invest it somewhere. Why not with us?

. . . .

THE MICROSOFT NEGOTIATIONS were not the only thing on our plate. On April 1, 2013, Siemens publicly announced their intention to sell their share of NSN.[1] That spring, the 2007 joint venture agreement that had formed Nokia Siemens Networks was due to enter a new phase in which either party could force the other one to sell its share. Siemens had already quietly informed us that they would prefer to sell rather than remain a shareholder. However, by making a public statement, Siemens created pressure on themselves to follow through—and put Nokia in a tight spot.

After years as the ignored distant cousin, NSN had begun to metamorphose into perhaps not quite yet the heir apparent but certainly something that looked increasingly and intriguingly attractive.

It had been a long slog. When the telecommunications network businesses of Nokia and Siemens were combined, NSN struggled to gain traction, burdened by a poorly managed integration, shackled by high costs and head count in an industry dominated by Sweden's Ericsson, and threatened by cheaper equipment from China's Huawei

Technologies. Over six years, it had posted a cumulative reported operating loss in the billions. We had been ready to put it on the block, but the offers were so low that neither Siemens nor we were willing to sell. In September 2011, we had each injected €500 million in fresh capital as a last-gasp measure.

Since we were stuck with NSN, in late 2011, Nokia and Siemens authorized the management to launch a massive restructuring plan, slashing staff by almost 20 percent in an attempt to save €1 billion a year in expenses.[2] To demonstrate that every euro counted, the company stopped providing free coffee for employees; if you wanted a cup, you had to pay for it.

There are three steps to surviving a situation where a company fights for its financial life. First, cut costs enough not just to survive, but to be able to increase investments in key future solutions. That's what we did through laying off part of our workforce and divesting our not-profitable businesses. Second, continue to develop the core business for the long term, looking to improve growth and profitability. We picked the highest-gross-margin regions (Japan, South Korea, and the United States) and prioritized R&D and customer operations for those customers over lower-margin regions. Finally, invest in the future. In our case, that meant 5G and cloudification. This process began in late 2011 and was starting to show results in early 2013.

And, of course, always take care of your people! Especially during a crisis. Treat the people you are forced to lay off with respect, and give your remaining team members ample reasons to have faith in the integrity of what you are doing.

Looking for an Exit

Jesper Ovesen, the executive chairman, had been brought in to NSN in September 2011 to drive the restructuring. A Danish bulldozer, Jesper was a numbers guy through and through. If there was a way to save money to make the company healthy again, he wouldn't take no for an answer.

Rajeev Suri was the CEO. Born in India, Rajeev started working at Nokia Networks in 1995, then steadily moved up the ladder, eventually heading up the Asia-Pacific region and global services, first for Nokia Networks and then for NSN, before becoming CEO in 2009. Like Jesper, he has a great head for numbers, but he has a very different personality. Rajeev is always extremely polite and rather soft-spoken. But despite being somewhat introverted, Rajeev reaches out to people. As a salesperson, he was known for trying to keep his word to customers under all circumstances, and he gained a lot of trust from teleoperators because of that.

In the early fall of 2012, I set up a special committee of the board of directors in order to significantly increase the time allocated to understanding the network infrastructure business and get to know NSN's management team well. Within a couple of months, we had a good enough sense of what was happening at NSN that we could map a series of strategic scenarios. All involved getting rid of NSN one way or another. The idea at the time was to focus our energies on Nokia's handset business.

Plan A was a full or partial merger with Alcatel-Lucent (ALu) to leapfrog past Huawei into second place behind Ericsson. Merging NSN with ALu, which was a publicly listed company, would automatically make NSN a publicly listed company as well, after which we could sell our shares, dust off our hands, and be done with it. There were lots of reasons that this option made sense: Primarily, ALu complemented NSN's scale in mobile broadband with the scope to deliver end-to-end solutions. (In fact, these reasons convinced us to eventually buy Alcatel-Lucent ourselves, as I'll describe in Chapter 18.)

Plan B was the private equity solution. Our idea was to sell a majority stake to a private equity investor, continue NSN's transformation, and then make a series of acquisitions—most likely Alcatel-Lucent plus several other companies—in a process we called "a string of pearls." This was essentially a rehash of what we had failed to achieve earlier. But now that NSN was showing signs of life, perhaps this time the plan would work. We would remain a minority investor as this new company consolidated the industry, and in a smaller way, we'd reap the benefits of whatever happened.

Plan C was the Nordic solution. That idea was that we would gather a group of investors from the Nordic countries that we knew well and buy out Siemens's share of NSN. We would complete the transformation to a publicly listed company and list the entity on either the Helsinki or Stockholm stock exchange.

As time went on, we refined the scenario into a sequence involving two, possibly three, steps:

The first step involved buying out Siemens. Nokia didn't have the funds, so we would need to raise them through either a private equity investor or a Nordic consortium.

After having bought out Siemens, the second step could be a full or partial merger with Alcatel-Lucent, after which NSN would be a publicly listed entity under ALu's name and provide an exit strategy for Nokia to sell its shares.

Or we could just skip trying to find a financing partner to buy Siemens's share and start with the ALu merger.

Meanwhile, though, NSN came off life support and began to breathe on its own. The results of the restructuring were starting to become visible. And thanks to a growing demand for new mobile broadband infrastructure to support ever-growing and ever more bandwidth-hungry internet services, NSN inched back into the black.

By early 2013, NSN had improved so much that its business was propping up Nokia's slumping Devices & Services division. This was a result of two things: great work done by Rajeev Suri and his team under difficult circumstances and the 4G investment wave.

I had followed NSN's finances more closely than most of the board, first from the perspective of being the chairman of the audit committee and then, as Nokia's chairman, ensuring that we wouldn't breach NSN's debt covenants. But it was very difficult even for me not to question how sustainable its recovery actually was. We had been too badly burned by NSN for years. We had to ask ourselves, could NSN continue to gain strength, or was this just a momentary hiccup?

We did what was becoming our habit: Together with the management team, we relentlessly analyzed the data and explored different scenarios. We took a systematic approach, digging up new data points and peppering the NSN management team with questions and more questions. In the spirit of paranoid optimism, we were still preparing for negative scenarios, but the balance started to shift toward planning to fully exploit the positive opportunities we were starting to see.

Gradually, I and most of my colleagues—although not all—became convinced that NSN's positive momentum could last.

Changing Our Mind

Siemens made it clear that they weren't interested in hanging on to NSN.

In dealing with Siemens's desire to dump their holdings in NSN, we had four immediate options:

1. We could let Siemens buy out our 50 percent stake, knowing they would turn around and sell NSN as quickly as possible.
2. We could buy out Siemens's 50 percent stake, although our cash position was getting lower and it would not take much to push our already jittery investors into taking action against the board.
3. We could find someone else to buy Siemens's stake—most likely a private equity firm—and jointly own NSN together, basically swapping Siemens for another partner.
4. Or we and Siemens could distribute NSN's shares to the Siemens and Nokia shareholders, essentially throwing up our hands and throwing in the towel.

We were still thinking in terms of divesting NSN according to Plan A, B, or C when in one of our one-on-ones, Timo Ihamuotila, our CFO, came up with yet another angle: What if we bought back our share of NSN—and kept it?

NSN's improved cash position and strengthened profitability now made it an attractive addition to Nokia's business portfolio. Timo suggested that NSN had the potential to become the core of a new Nokia, if we divested the Devices & Services business or had to run it down. (The thought of building a new Nokia around NSN had occurred to me as well, but at that moment I didn't think it a very likely outcome.)

Siemens was set on getting out and had hired bankers to determine NSN's valuation. In response, we hired a consulting firm to help us analyze NSN's asset value and to get a second opinion. The consulting firm's finding was surprisingly simple: We had a great opportunity to buy NSN at a bargain-basement price. And owning the company completely would increase its value, because a joint venture is always more difficult to manage, and so its value is automatically discounted.

In June 2013, we devoted one board meeting entirely to the NSN issue. (That was in addition to discussing it in every one of the numerous meetings we held that crazy month.) We went over the scenarios, combing through every detail and piece of data. The rationale for an acquisition boiled down to two elements: It would create certain shareholder value because we would be buying under market price, and it offered option value through the opportunity for Nokia to build a new company around the infrastructure business.

Members of the management and board were split. Some were swayed by the transformative possibilities of the second element. Some just wanted to get a good business at a discount and flip it later at a profit. Despite the different—and occasionally conflicting—opinions among board members, we eventually reached consensus: We agreed unanimously that we should try to buy NSN ourselves if we could persuade Siemens to agree on a reasonable price, but we should deliberately leave the door open to sell it later if a good opportunity presented itself.

All of this was happening in parallel to our negotiations with Microsoft, which led to another big "if": Could we actually find a way to finance the deal without adding unnecessary risk for the whole company? While it was a great deal, we did not want to add more uncertainty by funding it from our dwindling net cash reserves. And because of the possible sale of our handset business to Microsoft, we no longer had the ability to tap the public markets until the sale was resolved.

Multiple Deals in the Air

Interestingly, another company was sniffing around. Alcatel-Lucent, the fourth-largest player in the wireless infrastructure market, approached *us* out of the blue. Just like us, ALu thought that combining with NSN or outright buying it would enable ALu to leapfrog Huawei and butt right up against industry leader Ericsson.[3]

It was enough to leave one breathless. In the course of one month, we had spent an enormous amount of time on the Microsoft and NSN deals, and now we had a third opportunity open up. In hindsight, it seems almost unimaginable that we eventually ended up successfully doing all three of those deals. If someone had suggested as much that June, I would have personally escorted that person to a padded room.

We managed to negotiate an equity value of €3.4 billion with Siemens. To buy the half of NSN we didn't already own, we would pay €1.2 billion in cash, fronted in bridge financing by JP Morgan with Siemens loaning us the last €500 million to pay the balance.[4] (Timo had called Siemens's CFO Joe Kaeser and told him that we would do the deal if Siemens would loan us €800 million. Joe Kaeser was not pleased with the proposal and hung up on him, but then called back 30 minutes later and promised €500 million.) But the bridge financing and the Siemens loan were short-term, expensive money.

From the stock market's point of view, it was a good move. Within days of announcing the deal on July 1, 2013, Nokia's share price shot up 10 percent.[5] For our part, we felt we had made out like bandits: The value of NSN in sell-side analysts' SOTP (sum of the parts) analysis varied between €4 billion and €10 billion. We believed NSN was worth at least €6 billion. Paying for an equity value of €3.4 billion felt like a good day's work done for our shareholders.

Going Where the Money Is

In early July, I called Steve Ballmer at Microsoft to update him about the NSN deal. Steve saw the NSN deal as positive, and when I told him about the expensive financing we had taken on to fund it, he was sympathetic.

That was reassuring because I was about to ask him for an enormous loan.

Our finance team under Timo Ihamuotila's leadership had brainstormed a number of ways to reduce the risk caused by our overburdened balance sheet. One of the alternatives that Timo brought to me was gloriously gutsy: Ask Microsoft to fund our NSN deal.

I couldn't help thinking of the story of the bank robber Willie Sutton who, when asked why he robbed banks, famously replied, "That's where the money is." Microsoft had hoards of offshore cash. They needed to invest it somewhere. Why not with us?

Despite the ground suddenly disappearing from under our feet two weeks earlier when Microsoft's board of directors rejected the agreement that Steve and I had shaken hands on, our determination and hard work to maintain open communications between both companies' principals paid off. After considering carving D&S in two (probably killing at least one of the halves in the process), we explored a less extreme option: restructuring the deal perimeter to propose something that Microsoft hadn't already turned down.

Our way forward consisted of one simple change: We removed Nokia's HERE mapping business from the equation. (This actually was Plan A1c in the scenario mapping described in Chapter 12.)

Getting rid of the mapping business made the deal seem different enough that the Microsoft board was willing to take another look. We didn't really want to sell the mapping business anyway, so this new approach was fine with us. (We were right about its intrinsic value. Eighteen months later, we sold HERE to a consortium of German automakers for €2.8 billion—a little over $3 billion.[6])

We were back in business with Microsoft, and there was a sense of real momentum. At the same time, we were also in the middle of working on buying Siemens's share of NSN.

That's when I made the completely unconventional proposition to Steve.

"You know, we have agreed to meet in New York in six days. Our team will be there, but there are certain things we need to discuss first," I said. Then I laid it out: "There are five things we really need to continue negotiating this deal. They are so important that it doesn't make sense for us to come to the negotiating table unless we can agree on all of them. I know that this is unorthodox, but don't get alarmed. These are all very rational and pragmatic asks."

Our business was going so badly that we had one foot in the grave and the other on a banana peel. Our latest Lumia smartphone, despite featuring wireless charging, a touchscreen so sensitive that you could swipe it while wearing gloves on your fingers, and the best camera on the market, just couldn't make headway against the iPhone and Samsung Galaxy armada.[7] Our combined Symbian and Windows Phone share of the global smartphone market had plummeted to barely 3 percent.[8] We were hemorrhaging cash.

We literally couldn't afford Microsoft to succumb to "negotiations fatigue." But I felt we had some leverage because I knew that Steve felt guilty that the Microsoft board had dumped the previous deal at the last minute. If I presented things the right way, I thought, I might possibly get Steve to agree to my requests. Furthermore, agreeing to the preconditions sent the message that both companies were serious, and it might prevent other eleventh-hour surprises.

The preconditions were:

- **The negotiation meeting structure.** We would retain the 4 x 4 model in which only four representatives from each side would meet for the negotiations.
- **Separation of HERE.** We would take HERE off the table. This was complicated but possible if we agreed to license the technology to Microsoft, something we and Microsoft were both willing to do.
- **Due diligence conditions and timing.** The due diligence would have to be completed in just two weeks. I pointed out that a longer due diligence period was unnecessary since Microsoft already knew us well and a shorter period would minimize potential leaks.

- **Financing.** Microsoft would loan us €2 billion unconditionally at market interest rates—I could hear Ballmer inhale sharply at that—to help us out of the financial hole we were in from the NSN purchase, and this financing would be available for us regardless of whether the Microsoft deal succeeded or not.

- **A "get out of jail free" card.** Microsoft would allow us to terminate the contract between our two companies and embrace Android. This would provide us with optionality if the negotiations ended without success.

The way I looked at the conditions, some were easy for Microsoft to accept and some were not easy at all. But Microsoft knew we were far beyond mere gamesmanship. Our request was rooted in common sense and an honest desire to come up with the best solution for both companies.

I "just" had to convince Steve Ballmer to agree.

It was a tribute to our hard work in building a foundation of trust that Steve heard me out, then said, "These aren't unreasonable from Nokia's point of view." He didn't say the preconditions were reasonable from Microsoft's point of view—actually, he was rather indicating the opposite—but the discussion ended on a semi-positive note.

I asked Louise Pentland, our CLO, to send a document outlining the preconditions to her Microsoft counterpart, Brad Smith. Brad promised to get back to us in 48 hours.

Selling the Crown Jewels

We had already scheduled a meeting with Microsoft for the weekend of July 20 in New York. There was a sense of "now or never" among the members of our negotiating team. The understanding was that if the Microsoft team didn't agree to the preconditions, we would stay home.

If we had to stay home, it would be a disaster for Nokia.

Our teams were speaking daily. It was clear that Microsoft was trying to find a way to do what we were asking, although they still hadn't definitively agreed to it before we left for New York. But we had made enough progress to gamble that the trip wouldn't be in vain.

Even after all these months of negotiating, selling our entire Devices & Services division still seemed unimaginable. Our handsets were not just our core business; they had put Nokia—and Finland—on the map. They were a source of pride that had shaped the identity of a generation of Finns.

Now we were, once more, trying to sell the crown jewels of our company and our country.

Throughout the discussions among our board members and the leadership team to get to this point, I had seen how painful this decision was. It was a massive blow to admit that continuing the handset business was no longer a real option. All of us felt guilty that this had happened on our watch. It was also immensely sad to witness the death of a beloved institution that everyone had believed was invincible.

What offered consolation was our strategizing process. We had gone through all the options with a fine-tooth comb. We had negotiated and discussed every aspect of the situation and tried to understand what was possible, what could be realistically expected, and what was unrealistic. We had fully investigated and exhausted every alternative.

I myself had initially questioned and, to be honest, feared the idea of divesting the entire phone business. But by the time we made the final decision, I had no doubts. My certainty was not based on being psyched about doing the deal; it was based on the fact that we spent so much time analyzing the other options that I *knew* it was the very best thing for our shareholders and our employees.

The Now-or-Never Meeting

We arrived in New York to a record-breaking heat wave with temperatures topping 100 degrees and smothering midsummer humidity.[9] The streets were deserted; anyone who couldn't escape the city was holed up next to an air conditioner.

Our four pairs gathered around the conference table in Microsoft's lawyers' office. I couldn't help flashing back to the disastrous "different planets" meeting that had taken place in this room just three months earlier.

The negotiation issues were almost black and white: Either we would do the deal at the highest possible value acceptable to Microsoft or the deal would fail if Microsoft was unwilling to pay more than our minimum requirement for the asset within the context of our alternatives.

Over the past few months, Lumia's failure to thrive, especially at the high end, had made it painfully clear to us that the worst-case stand-alone scenario was the most likely to occur. If we couldn't accomplish this deal, the Windows Phone would drag Nokia to the brink of the grave or straight into it.

Lumia had a clearly negative value for Nokia. Mobile phones, on the other hand, still had a positive value despite sales declining dramatically over the previous two years. From a purely financial point of view, we should have been willing to give away D&S to Microsoft without any compensation or even pay Microsoft a dowry to make them interested. This fact was the most closely guarded secret of the negotiations on our side.

Our plan was to start negotiations from €4.75 billion with an earn-out potentially worth €900 million over 5 years, assuming that sales targets were reached. The board discussed giving me the authorization to accept a price all the way down between €1 billion and €2 billion. I did not want that. It was better that I have a bottom limit to my authority in case we had to start negotiating at those low levels. Then I could have told Ballmer, "€3.6 billion in cash and the already-discussed earn-out on top is the lowest I can go."

If that wasn't low enough, our board was standing by and ready to authorize me to go lower.

Once again, we had agreed that Microsoft would speak first. And this time, to our relief, we were not just on the same planet, but in the same ballpark. Even better, Microsoft's offer was comfortably above the price our team had decided we could accept as a minimum. Their offer was actually higher than what we would have proposed as our opening bid had we spoken first—taking into account what we know now; i.e. the earn-out would have been practically worthless. If we got nothing more than Microsoft's first offer of the day, we would still have a great deal. It was a wonderful start to the meeting.

We kept our poker faces and followed the protocol that worked so well, alternating meetings with all four pairs in the room, then between the pairs—sometimes just Steve Ballmer and me, if the others had nothing to work on—then separate meetings of the two teams, then everyone reconvening to assess our progress. Inch by inch, we hammered out the details, adding a hundred million dollars here and a hundred million there to the price tag. Having learned our lesson back in June, both companies committed to have pre-approval from their boards of directors before agreeing to anything, and asked both boards to stand ready for an immediate board meeting, if necessary.

On Sunday, July 21, Steve and I shook hands on a deal for a second time. Nokia would sell all of its Devices & Services business and the required IP license to Microsoft for €5.44 billion ($7.17 billion) in cash. Compared to the €3.6 billion and an almost worthless earn-out, the outcome was very good. Compared to how low we were willing to go, the outcome was a dream come true. Compared to not getting a deal at all and being forced to continue running a business struggling to survive—well, it is difficult to even make that comparison.

The fact that we could no longer see ourselves succeeding with the Windows Phone did not mean that Microsoft couldn't do it. There is always an inherent friction in two companies working together, and bringing the whole operation under one roof can make a big difference. Even more importantly, Microsoft's deep pockets enabled them to invest in marketing in a way that was far beyond our capacity. Therefore, it was quite possible that both parties did a good deal. At least, that was my sincere hope.

There were a few more sticking points mostly related to the loan, but they were resolved by Wednesday evening. I finalized the high-level loan terms with Steve Ballmer over the phone on my way to the airport.

It was a bittersweet moment.

Comparing apples to apples, we came from the first bid of €4.75 billion (the average of the price range of €4.25–5.25 billion) to the final deal of €8.24 billion (including the final price we got from selling HERE 18 months later). That was a good outcome, especially considering how rapidly our internal estimate of the value of D&S (as part of Nokia) declined during the process. Had Microsoft realized how desperate our situation was, the outcome could have been truly ugly. We were lucky in so many ways.

At the same time, there was no denying that we were selling a piece of our—and Finland's—heart.

Yet I had no doubt that this was the only way to save Nokia as a global technology giant. Now we could regain control of our destiny. We had a future.

Just what that future might look like was something we'd have to work out.

. . . .

The Paranoid Optimist's Successful Negotiation Tactics

It's astonishing to consider that the Microsoft deal nearly dissolved three times—four, if you count the five preconditions for our final meeting, which were really hard for Microsoft to accept. The pattern we created—some of it by design, some of it by happenstance—not only helped pull us through to a happy ending with Microsoft but then successfully guided us through future negotiations, including our €15.6 ($17 billion) takeover of Alcatel-Lucent two years later.

M&A negotiations tend to be somewhat adversarial, like two teams facing off against each other. What I try to do in these situations is to view myself more like a referee than a player. If I play my role well, the teams on the field play the same game, they follow the same rules, and they play in such a way that the sport becomes enjoyable. After a well-conducted process, the teams would be happy to engage again. If I can facilitate that, I have been successful.

A higher objective is to guide the main principal from the other team to join me slightly outside the fray. If we both are thinking about the big picture, instead of focusing only on a single game, we are much more likely to achieve a win-win outcome.

The key success factors are:

- Maximize face time in the negotiations.
- Keep the negotiation teams small and the feel of the discussion intimate.
- Team up a negotiator who matches the counterpart. For example, our two CLOs and CFOs were natural pairs. I was the right counterpart to Steve Ballmer.
- Plan your negotiation tactics in advance. Prepare for all scenarios.
- Be systematic and clear in what you ask. Know your limits, know your deal breakers, and know when to give in.
- Keep your board with you every step of the way.
- Keep up momentum in the negotiations. Make sure that there is always a next step agreed to by both parties.
- Ask boldly for what you need. Explain clearly the why of it. Don't be afraid to push the envelope, but focus your energy on doing so in a way most likely to produce your desired outcome.
- Relationship building is an important part of negotiating. Trust keeps the lines of communication open, even when negotiations break down, and enables you to restart proceedings. Trust is the oil that makes everything run more smoothly.
- Obstacles are an opportunity to create trust.
- Leave your ego at the door.

The underlying lesson: Don't become a captive of the traditional ways of negotiating and doing deals. Instead, use your brains to do what makes sense according to the circumstances. Be bold and humble, eager and patient. Don't play a role but be yourself. Combine intuition with rigorous analysis and a hefty dose of caution. Be prepared for any alternative and you will never be surprised.

That's the paranoid optimist's approach to negotiation.

• •

15

DOING THE DEAL

JULY 2013–NOVEMBER 2013

. . . .

This transaction makes all the sense rationally,
but emotionally it gets complicated.

. . . .

THE CLOCK BEGAN ticking as soon as we signed the term sheet, loan agreements, and some other documents.

Steve Ballmer and I had shaken hands on the high-level terms of a deal, and our respective boards had given their blessing. But agreeing on a deal and making it happen in practice are two completely different things. Just because the most important terms had been laid out didn't mean that there weren't a multitude of potential complications that could still sink the entire proceedings.

A deal like this is defined by two significant events. There's the public announcement that we have signed a more or less irreversible purchase agreement. Then there's the closing event when the assets are actually transferred. Closing depends on satisfying whatever requirements were agreed to between the parties, receiving shareholder approvals, and fulfilling regulatory demands. Achieving these three elements can take months—sometimes even years—and the failure of any one of them could destroy the deal.

We agreed to target September 3, 2013, as the date for the announcement. One major reason for the rush was that the risk for leaks grows exponentially as more time and more people are dedicated to the due diligence process and completing the final contracts. For our part, the longer it took, the more opportunities there were for Microsoft to change their mind. Also, in thinking like a paranoid optimist, in the scenario where the deal would fail, any time delaying that realization was time taken away from working on other options.

The Countdown Begins

We had lots of things still to negotiate, many of them high-value items.

For instance, the price adjustment. This relates to the business results during the period when the old owner is still responsible for the business but cannot necessarily conduct things the way they normally would because they have to manage the business for the new owner, whose interests may be different. In our case, we had a nonperforming handset business that was bleeding money. If we ran it based on our selfish interests, we'd minimize the cash bleed, which meant squelching marketing efforts, pruning back R&D, and cutting costs in general. But that would leave Microsoft with a lame horse that had been starved in the bargain.

We needed to come up with a model where we would manage the business the way Microsoft wanted but without Nokia shareholders footing the bill. It was a very, very complicated dynamic.

In most price adjustments, if the business performs better than expected, the buyer usually pays more as the value of the business goes up. We reversed the convention and proposed that Microsoft would pay more if the handset business performed worse. That's counterintuitive, because typically the buyer wants to incentivize the business to do better. But our business held a significant risk of a very steep decline, and we wanted to manage our risks. So we told Microsoft that there was no way to predict our customers' response to the announcement of this deal, and it would be completely unfair to penalize us if our customers reacted negatively because of Microsoft. We didn't see why we should have to pay the delta if sales dropped, so we insisted that Microsoft should compensate *us* if sales missed the planned target and our cash flow was less than expected.

One very important consideration from our point of view was protecting our people. We had a duty and a responsibility to take care of them, even if they moved to another company. We insisted that Microsoft agree to honor Nokia's severance practices for 12 months after the closing and that *all* our people—from India to China to Finland to the United States—would be covered by Nokia practices after they moved to Microsoft if Microsoft had to restructure. (Microsoft did restructure; in fact, they laid off almost 50 percent of Nokia employees within months of the deal closing, so we were glad we had insisted on this.[1])

Due diligence was another issue. We worked hard to limit the due diligence process to make it as quick as possible and suppress potential leaks. We also refused to give any guarantees on our business performance. Basically, that reduced the possibility of Microsoft walking away from the deal after it was signed.

Then there were numerous systems and service agreements that had to be hashed out. For example, we did not have an issue turning over our ERP system to Microsoft. Microsoft simply needed it more, and we would not have a manufacturing business anymore. However, our internally built advanced cash management system (which we called the Payment Factory) was something Nokia needed and Microsoft wanted, and it could not be bought from the market. In the end, we agreed to run the Payment Factory as a service for Microsoft for a reasonable fee.

We also had a debate about the Nokia brand. Initially, Microsoft wanted to include the brand in the deal. Microsoft's thought was, "You guys won't have any phone business left, so why do you need the name?" We said that selling the name just wasn't possible. Nokia had to remain Nokia. Steve Ballmer sensed that this was a nonnegotiable, and didn't really push.

We knew from our previous experience with Siemens that beauty—or the devil—was in the details. We had to ensure there were no explosive conditions that might blow up in our face later.

The amount of work was just enormous—and all of this was happening in the middle of the summer, so everyone's holiday was canceled. But our paranoid optimism paid off: We got favorable out-comes from most of these small details, which when taken all together became very meaningful.

Thousands of Details

What resulted wasn't a single agreement but hundreds of contracts covering not just the sale of the handset business, but also patents, trademarks, mapping licenses, real estate, and scores of other ele-ments, each of which needed to be created, negotiated, reviewed, and finalized before September 3.

To sign the thousands of contract pages, we reserved a double-sized conference room at our lawyers' office in New York. Three rows of tables were lined up lengthwise along the walls and down the middle. The agreements were stacked vertically in two rows down the center table and in a single row down the tables against the wall. Every stack represented a unique agreement. If Nokia had stayed in the paper busi-ness, we could have made a tidy profit.

While the contract work was time-consuming, the hours paled in comparison with the amount of due diligence–related work. During the due diligence process, Microsoft's subcontractors sometimes focused on things that we thought were of secondary importance. It was unclear whether they were nitpicking for the sake of prudence or whether they just wanted to bill the maximum number of hours. There was plenty of frustration.

In addition to the multiple self-sacrificing overachievers on the Nokia team, one person who deserves a lot of credit was Brad Smith, Microsoft's chief legal officer. A calming presence, he focused on the end result and resolved many problematic situations.

Adding to the complications was the need to clarify Stephen Elop's role. He had been hired to run Nokia's handset business, so should he follow the business to Microsoft? If he stayed with Nokia, who would run the mobile phone business for Microsoft? And if he stayed, was he the right person to run a Nokia without mobile phones? Steve Ballmer wanted him to return, and Microsoft could have insisted that he come—they could have argued that there was no point buying an asset without its manager.

I asked Stephen what he wanted to do. It was his call, I told him. After thinking about it for a few days, Stephen decided to move with the business. The Windows Phone hadn't been a happy story so far, but he felt responsible for turning it into a happy ending. This was the right decision. Had he decided to stay, I was not at all sure that we would have had a role for him.

His decision influenced the other top leaders in Devices & Services. All except one agreed to move to Microsoft. That was good for Nokia— we didn't need D&S executives if we didn't have a D&S business—and good for Microsoft.

At the board meeting on August 11, we spent a long time exercising paranoid optimism and exploring what could go wrong. What were the legal risks for the transaction in Europe and the United States? Would antitrust regulations become an issue? We tried to identify all the significant threats that could kill the deal but couldn't really come up with any. The least theoretical threat was that our shareholders would vote down the deal.

For that reason, throughout this whole period, we were obsessed about the possibility of news leaks. By now, between 600 and 800 people were involved with the due diligence and contracts. If the press got a whiff of what was happening, the whole deal could have been derailed.

When rumors fly, a lot of things lurch into motion: the target company's investor base can shift significantly, with long-term shareholders selling and hedge funds and activists buying; these new shareholders may have their own agendas to push; the press will start speculating with all sorts of doomsday scenarios; the buyer's shareholders may become active and start to put pressure on the buyer's board and management; the theories invented by the press and analysts will also be read by the buyer and may have an impact on the buyer's conviction to buy. Because of all of the above and lots of other things impacting both the buyer and the seller—and their shareholders, boards, management teams, and employees—the risk of the deal becoming a dud shoots through the roof.

The Two-Week To-Do List

With just two weeks to go, the board meeting on August 18 reviewed the very, *very* long list of actions that had to take place before the announcement.

To begin with, different types of announcements in multiple languages needed to be provided to multiple spokespeople around the world, all of whom needed to be briefed and trained to deliver the message in the right way through various media: press releases, web pages, PowerPoint presentations, video clips, etc.

We tried to anticipate the reactions to our bombshell. If Nokia shares went up, the business press would discuss the deal in positive terms—except in Finland, where the news would be negative and the press would likely paint Stephen Elop as a Trojan horse. If the share price went down, we would face a perfect storm. Bearish analysts would have a field day, competitors would make snide remarks, and the media would foment a blizzard of half-truths, misconceptions, and false assumptions, all of which would instigate further misunderstandings and criticism. In either case, we knew the employee reaction would be deeply emotional, so we prepared for things we hoped wouldn't happen, including employee walkouts, strikes, bomb threats, and even suicides. (Fortunately, nothing like that occurred.)

We had a plan to pre-inform on a confidential basis the president and prime minister of Finland, as well as other key ministers and the labor unions, which are typically critical of this type of news, the day before the announcement.

And, of course, we still had a business to run. Second-quarter results showed that operating losses in Devices & Services were slightly less than expected and that Lumia sales continued to tick up slowly.[2] We had, in the end, narrowly escaped breaching the internal strategy change threshold in Q2, but the same could not be said about Q3.

According to our plan set earlier in the year, the profitability of Smart Devices would be –2.6 percent in Q3. Now the forecast was revised down to –15.7 percent. That was clearly below the –12.2 percent threshold we had set back in February to pull the trigger to exit the Windows Phone business. This was not news in any way, but it provided another data point to support our decision to sell.

One Week to Go

On August 23, barely a week before our joint announcement, Steve Ballmer made an announcement of his own: He was retiring from Microsoft within the next 12 months.[3] He had alerted me about a week earlier. He explained that it was important to him to announce his resignation before our announcement to avoid misperceptions that he was fired by his board as a result of the Nokia deal. In fact, he told me, after that fateful June board meeting in which the Microsoft board rejected the deal he and I had agreed on, his departure—voluntary or otherwise—had been just a question of time.

With one week to go, everyone was on edge. Our teams had been working flat out for the past five weeks, and on top of that, there was the stress caused by the six-month deal–no deal roller coaster *and* by the grinding negotiations of the NSN acquisition. There were a lot of unsung heroes on the Nokia team who did much more than anybody could have asked under tough conditions. It was both heartbreaking and heartwarming to witness people giving everything to get the transaction done with the customary Nokia quality.

We had board and committee meetings planned for August 25 and 27, two meetings scheduled for August 29 and another for September 2. And, of course, there was the announcement on September 3.

At the same time, Microsoft twisted the rope. By now, we had provided 59,000 pages of due diligence material. Microsoft had assigned a team of 150 people to comb through them. With one week to go before the announcement, Microsoft sent us 900 additional requests for clarification. It was enough to make you want to pull your hair out.

The due diligence exercise exemplified the differences between Microsoft and us. Our own people did as much of the work as was humanly possible. Microsoft did exactly the opposite: They outsourced as much as was humanly possible. As a result, the Microsoft management didn't always know a lot about the asset they were acquiring because they assigned the dirty work to outsiders and only read the summaries.

As it turned out, the dynamics worked perfectly for us, and the terms and conditions were almost exactly what we wanted. We just had to sweat a lot to get them.

Old Nokia's Last Day

On September 2, the board once more reviewed the deal with the latest details and voted unanimously to approve it. There was a sense of calm resolution, tinged with sadness.

One of our first steps was to officially terminate Stephen Elop as CEO of Nokia and appoint him to be executive vice president of Devices & Services, with the understanding that he would transfer to Microsoft at the deal's closing. According to the terms of his original agreement, Stephen had the right to terminate his contract with full compensation if we changed his role. With his permission, we amended the agreement so that he gave up that right. His compensation was kept unchanged.

Now *we* needed a CEO. When the board had earlier discussed potential candidates to replace Stephen, my colleagues had asked if I would become the interim CEO.

We didn't have too many choices. NSN's CEO Rajeev Suri was not a viable option. There was still a possibility of selling NSN, taking the company public in an IPO, or doing something else to cash in the value we had created through the Siemens transaction. Even if we did hold onto NSN, it made more sense for Rajeev to keep running the networking business and for me to focus on keeping the overall house together. I was already familiar with what was involved in getting the Microsoft transaction to close. If Rajeev had to take charge of that, even with my help as chairman, he would have had to ignore the networking business for a few months, and that wouldn't have been healthy.

My philosophy all along has been, if there's no significant benefit in rushing to make a long-reaching decision, then don't do it. Leave your options open to think things over. We had so much going on with the Microsoft deal and had just closed the deal with NSN, and we didn't even know what the new Nokia would look like. We didn't need to make a hasty decision about a CEO, so why should we?

I agreed to become the interim CEO on two conditions. One was that I would commit *only* to an interim role and everyone would support me in my decision not to be a candidate for the role permanently. The second was that Timo Ihamuotila would serve as the interim president. That way, we could divide the work—I could focus more on determining the new vision and strategy and finding the right people to run the new Nokia, and Timo could take care of much of the communications to shareholders and the administrative side of things.

And that's how we went forward. At the September 2 board meeting, I was appointed interim CEO and Timo was appointed interim president.

I called Finland's president and prime minister to alert them to the next day's announcement. (Steve Ballmer and I were scheduled to meet with the prime minister after the announcement.) Out of consideration, I also called Jorma Ollila, Nokia's former chairman. Our conversation followed the usual pattern: I tried to be polite; he exploded and yelled that I had ruined his legacy.

The long day was almost over. There were still a few contractual details to be settled, and our legal teams continued to negotiate through the night. The final items were closed a few hours before the 6 a.m. deadline.

I still had one more meeting to attend—one of the most important.

A Family Conference

I knew I would be held accountable throughout Finland for the fate of our country's flagship company. I was prepared to take whatever heat and abuse might be thrown at me—that was my responsibility. But, thinking like a paranoid optimist, I was concerned about how the public reaction to the sale might affect my family.

On the evening of Monday, September 2, I called a family meeting. I sat down at the kitchen table with my wife, our 15-year-old daughter, and our 9- and 10-year-old sons. I had no idea how the next weeks would turn out, and I felt I had to prepare them for the worst.

I told them that tomorrow we would announce a significant change in Nokia. "This will be big news," I explained. "Maybe some Finns will take it very badly. Maybe some of your friends' parents will take it very badly. They may talk about it at home and your friends will be listening. Maybe the next day in school, you'll hear some bad things being said about your father. But there's one thing you need to remember: I and the team at Nokia have worked very, very hard to look at all the possible ways forward. This is not something we have done carelessly. We have worked at it for months and months. We have given it our utmost, and I'm absolutely certain that we are doing the right thing. So even if you hear something bad, you can find comfort in the fact that over time, people will see that this was the right thing to do."

It was heartwarming to see our children's sober faces as they focused on what I was telling them. Then they started asking questions: "What kind of a change?" "Can people still buy Nokia phones?" "What should we do if our friends start talking badly about you?" "What can we say to tell them that they're wrong?"

I advised them that they shouldn't get into arguments or fights or feel the need to defend me. "Just say, 'I know my father. I know he's doing the best he can.'" It was one of the most memorable discussions I've ever had with my kids.

As it turned out, they weren't harassed by their schoolmates at all.

Making the Announcement

I didn't get much sleep the night before September 3—I had to be up early the next morning—but I slept the deep sleep of the well prepared. My day began with the international news wire services at 6 a.m. Helsinki time—the reporters had been wakened before dawn to alert them to the press call—and ended many hours later after a meeting with the prime minister and Steve Ballmer, numerous internal meetings, 14 interviews, a town hall, and a webcast press conference with Steve Ballmer, Stephen Elop, and Timo Ihamuotila.

I had put a lot of thought into what I would say at the press event as this was our opportunity to shape how the news would be told to the world.[4] My speech reflected what I truly felt, and I was satisfied with the outcome.

I introduced myself as an entrepreneur, and I noted that like most entrepreneurs, I had gone through a lot of different phases over the course of my career. "Being an entrepreneur means aspiring to build products that change the world," I said. "Selling businesses is not nearly as cool, but sometimes it *is* the right course of action."

Selling Nokia's Devices & Services business was, I said, the most complex decision I had ever been involved in making: "This transaction makes all the sense rationally, but emotionally it gets complicated."

I stressed that Nokia had done great work in creating innovative products in a market that was undergoing fundamental change. However, I explained, the smartphone industry had become a duopoly, with the leaders building significant financial momentum at a scale not seen before while many established players had disappeared or faced difficult choices.

The investments required to drive large numbers of people to try a new experience were now significantly higher than ever before, and Nokia alone didn't have the resources to fund them, I noted. Microsoft, however, did.

I explained that the Nokia board had spent over a year exhaustively evaluating and analyzing all imaginable strategic alternatives, ever since the introduction of the Surface tablet in June 2012 heralded a tectonic shift in the Windows ecosystem. I said that we had learned that in today's market, the best opportunity for the devices business to prosper was to be tightly aligned with the operating system and associated ecosystem and cloud services.

Through nearly 50 meetings over the course of eight months, I continued, the board concluded that this transaction was the right path forward, the path that would maximize value creation for Nokia shareholders. "It will clearly strengthen our financial position, and it will provide a solid basis for future investment in Nokia's continuing businesses. Our employees in Devices & Services who transfer to Microsoft will have a stronger financial backing to be successful in the mobile marketplace."

I concluded that as a result of today's agreement, "Instead of one Nokia, there will be two global technology companies in Finland, both financially stronger and capable of investing in the future. This can be an important accelerator in the broader Finnish economy." (This is a good example of trying to provide the press with a headline and an idea for the story. If one just lists facts, the reporters will create the story based on their various individual points of views. By coming up with core ideas, such as "Nokia reinvents itself—again" or "Instead of one Nokia, there will be two technology giants in Finland," we were trying to guide the press to take a favorable approach to the story.)

Steve Ballmer then took the stage. I had tried to prompt Steve into making an oral commitment to setting up a data center in Finland. "It would be good PR for our deal if you could include that in your announcement," I suggested. Steve is a smart guy and didn't fall for that. He just said he would evaluate the idea, but he didn't make any promises in his speech.

Stephen Elop and Timo and I took questions for the next hour. Then we waited for the reactions.

The global press was generally positive, placing the deal in the context of Nokia's 150-year history of successful reinvention rather than "the end of Nokia." Even the Finnish media was more balanced than expected, with the "It's a new start for Nokia" theme tempering the expected Trojan horse comments.

As employees absorbed the news, there was shock and anger. Almost all were surprised by the announcement. Some felt betrayed by the deal, and many were sad that a company that had been such a dominant force was selling the entire business; but some were excited about the opportunity to fix the issues that had been hobbling our progress. As the days passed, frustration and resignation shifted to acceptance and even cautious optimism. "It's going to take some time to get my head around it, but there is no doubting the opportunity," one employee wrote in. And another wryly suggested, "Maybe we'll get employee discounts for Xboxes."

Thankfully, investors universally applauded the transaction. On Thursday, Nokia stock closed at €4.20 on the Helsinki Stock Exchange, up 41 percent.[5] Several investors who had been shorting Nokia stock for a long time immediately changed their position. A prominent analyst noted, "Nokia has in effect . . . created billions of dollars of equity value for NOK shareholders nearly out of thin air by utilizing the unique leverage it had in both relationships [with Siemens and Microsoft]. We believe Mr. Elop and the Nokia board are to be congratulated for a tremendously savvy re-thinking of the Nokia business that was built on an unbiased and unemotional assessment of its strengths and weaknesses and its leverage points with its partners."

The Backlash

We still needed to get approval from Nokia shareholders. We wanted—we needed—to put it to a vote, so no questions would remain.

We called an Extraordinary General Meeting (EGM) for November 19, 2013. In preparation, we published a proxy document—and inadvertently dropped a bombshell.

I played an unintentional role in creating the chaos. We knew there would be criticism of the value of Stephen Elop's contractual exit package. At one of our August board meetings, I had the "bright" idea of asking Microsoft to pay a portion of his compensation. I was naïve enough to believe this would mollify people, since the money would now come from Microsoft instead of from Nokia. Steve Ballmer believed my rationale and expected Microsoft to get some brownie points from the Finnish public.

We were both dead wrong.

Anyone who has ever read the compensation disclosure statements of large public companies frequently has only one clear takeaway: that they are extremely complicated and very hard to understand. This is partially because the regulators insist on a certain structure and partially because the lawyers are writing the text for other lawyers, not for laypeople. The objective is to describe the topic so that the company will not get sued, and if it is sued, it will win. That's a completely different objective than making things clear to shareholders.

The way that these documents are written serves one purpose and one audience but does a disservice to everyone else. I said, "*Nobody can understand this text.* I know all the data and *I* can barely understand it, so the typical shareholder certainly won't understand it. Some parties do not even *want* to understand, and this document gives them a perfect excuse to misunderstand in a way of their own choosing. We have to publish a Q&A that will address the questions people will ask when they see the payments we're making, answer them in simple language, and cover our legal risks by referring them to the full proxy statement for more details."

I suggested that we publish answers to questions such as "Was Stephen Elop a Trojan horse?" and "Did the board change Stephen Elop's compensation during the Microsoft negotiations?" By proactively articulating the negative interpretation and explaining the facts behind the events and decisions, it's much more difficult for journalists or the public to twist the narrative into hyperspace.

I blame myself for not following through. I was flying around the world meeting employees, customers, shareholders, and regulators in different countries. Our people were also extremely busy juggling lots of balls. The Q&A fell through the cracks.

The media pounced on Stephen Elop's compensation agreement and went wild.

Stephen was to receive what later turned out to be €18.8 million (about $25.4 million) in a package comprising an equity compensation worth about €14.6 million (the actual payment was based on the share price at the time Stephen eventually left the company eight months later) and an additional €4.2 million in salary and variable compensation, upon the closing of the sale of Nokia's Devices & Services unit.[6]

The committee that had hired Stephen in 2010 had signed off on a contract that included a "change of control" (CoC) clause. That's a fairly standard provision in a CEO's contract. The idea is that CEOs may resist selling the company, even when it would be clearly in the shareholders' interests, because they would lose their jobs and their share-based incentives would not have time to vest. CoC agreements try to neutralize the impact on the executive's compensation to remove the incentive to act against shareholders' interests.

What touched off the firestorm was that according to Stephen's CoC clause, all his shares in Nokia would immediately vest upon closing the deal. Since the share price had ballooned as a result of a beneficial deal, his equity was worth a lot. And this was on top of the normal termination payment.

This was all laid out in the proxy statement. But the press was out for blood. The issue wasn't whether Nokia was or wasn't footing the bill; it was the interpretation that Stephen was getting "rewarded" for what some newspaper articles were calling the "Elopcalypse."[7] The fact that Microsoft contributed to his compensation only confirmed suspicions that Stephen had been grooming Nokia for an eventual sale to Microsoft from the very beginning and had been biding his time to triumphantly return to Redmond with his plunder and step into Steve Ballmer's shoes.[8] Rumors started flying that Stephen had blackmailed the board, the board was paying him off, and a host of other conspiracy theories.[9]

We helped open the door for that by not preempting the sentiments with a Q&A.

At one point, I was flying back to Finland, and when I landed late in the evening, I saw a "Please call immediately" text message from a member of our communications team. No one ever likes to see those words. She told me that some of the Finnish media had claimed that Stephen was the only CEO in Nokia's history who had a CoC agreement. "That's not true," she said. "The two previous CEOs also had CoCs."

We needed to respond immediately, so that the rumor wouldn't blow out of proportion. We agreed over the phone to issue a statement in my name saying that Olli-Pekka Kallasvuo and Jorma Ollila also had a CoC agreement. The mistake was that we added the phrase, "A substantially similar change of control agreement." Our communications department checked the statement with our legal team, but they were both in a hurry.

A couple of days later, a journalist with *Helsingin Sanomat*, the largest newspaper in Finland, called to tell me, "You have lied." I asked how? By claiming that the two previous CEOs had "a substantially similar change of control agreement," he said. It turned out that Olli-Pekka Kallasvuo, Stephen's predecessor, had a CoC that paid out 18 months of salary and bonuses but no stock awards.[10] The journalist was right. We had issued an erroneous statement. And it was in my name.

But he was not interested that we had made a careless mistake late at night and under pressure. "You have lied" was the big news. *Helsingin Sanomat* published it, and the story spread to the main Finnish business paper, as well as the *Financial Times*[11] and blogs,[12] that the Nokia board had gifted Stephen Elop €18.8 million to sell out the company and had been less than honest about it.

Our comms team assured me that the furor would die down in a few days. It didn't. We were bombarded with interview requests from every possible channel. We finally decided to provide key media an equal opportunity to find out the facts, and our comms department scheduled a series of 45-minute interview slots with me over the course of one day. Our media team allowed the press to record the interviews, but TV cameras were out. The media team probably thought that a complex compensation topic offered irresistible opportunities to take a sentence out of context, and it tried to protect against that.

The interviews went well, and I believe I was able to convince the journalists by answering all their questions in detail. At the end of the interviews, they all seemed happy, including the team from Finland's public broadcasting company YLE, the country's main TV news outlet.

That evening I got a lesson on what to expect from the media when it is in a frenzy about a particular subject. The opening story for YLE was Nokia, but not in the way I thought. YLE had chosen to focus on the fact that Nokia did not allow TV cameras in the interview and tried to link that with the crazy compensation rumors. The actual facts of the interview itself were a side topic.

Luckily, YLE was an outlier, and only the main business daily *Kauppalehti* took a similar yellow press approach. All the other media outlets were more or less fact-based. As proof of the calming effect of providing the facts to the journalists, the whole topic died down in a couple of weeks.

I remember going through the Helsinki airport at this time and feeling that everyone was staring at me with anger in their eyes. Of course, they weren't, at least not all of them. But it felt really ugly. And it felt unfair. In hindsight, a great lesson!

An Extraordinary EGM

The Extraordinary General Meeting on November 19, 2013, was extraordinary in more than one sense. Some 5,000 people came to the Ice Hall, home of Helsinki's stellar ice hockey team HIFK—some to offer approval, some to voice their shock, sadness, and, in some cases, anger.

We tried to prepare for every contingency so that nothing could come back to haunt us. If the EGM failed, the whole Microsoft transaction could collapse, so it was of life-and-death importance to cross all the *t*'s and dot every *i*.

For example, we had originally booked an ice hockey arena in Espoo, the city right next to Helsinki that's home to Nokia's headquarters. Then our board secretary noticed that our bylaws stated that our Annual General Meetings must take place in Helsinki. Even though this was not the annual meeting but an extraordinary one, we moved the venue. That way, nobody could claim the meeting was invalid just because it was held 10 kilometers too far to the west.

I presented the board's proposal for the shareholders to authorize Nokia to sell Devices & Services to Microsoft at the agreed price. I explained the rationale for the transaction.

And then we opened the floor to questions from shareholders.

For the next four hours, I stood on stage and, aside from a brief interlude when Timo stepped in, I kept on answering questions as long as they kept coming.

Some were aggressive. "How is such a road to ruin possible?" one demanded. Another compared the sale of D&S to the theft of the magical Sampo mill in Finland's great epic, *Kalevala*. Still another insinuated that the sale was a conspiracy orchestrated by the CIA.[13] Others railed against Stephen Elop, calling him a "triple-A flop" who "drove the company to ruin."[14]

I tried to be polite, even when the person speaking was rude—and quite a few were in the first part of the meeting. I thanked them for their concern and complimented them when they actually asked a question. After a couple of hours, the audience exhausted its hostility and the mood started to change. More and more of the questions were real questions rather than irate statements. Some comments were even openly positive. Toward the end, the positive comments even began to get applause.

This was a good lesson in how to change the crowd's mood by being respectful and by answering as well as you possibly can, even when the questions are hostile or a little silly.

When every last question had been answered, we asked for a vote. That surprised the audience, because typically in these meetings, a vote is a waste of time. In most cases, the vast majority of the shares are held by institutional owners who vote in advance. Even if every single share physically present opposes the board's proposal, the chair could say, "Unfortunately, we only have 25 percent of shares represented here. Since we know that over 70 percent of the shares support the proposal, there's no need to vote." But we wanted a vote. We didn't want anyone to claim we had squelched any opposition. We wanted public endorsement of the deal.

When the votes were tallied, 99.52 percent approved the deal.[15]

• •

Be Diligent About Details

When you're crunched for time or dealing with an enormous project, it's always tempting to gloss over the details, promise that you'll check them on a future pass, or, worse, delegate them to someone else. I can't tell you how many times being paranoid about missing something led us to comb through documents until we were almost cross-eyed—and how those efforts often turned up items we could use to our advantage. In just one example, as I'll describe in Chapter 18, debating a single sentence within our team ended up saving us over €100 million. Or moving the EGM site to a different city just because somebody might claim that an EGM is the same as an AGM and have grounds to annul the meeting.

There's an old proverb that shows up across different centuries and cultures: "For want of a nail, the shoe was lost; for want of a shoe, the horse was lost; for want of a horse, the battle was lost; for the failure of battle, the kingdom was lost—all for the want of a horseshoe nail." A paranoid optimist imagines this scenario and digs into the details to ensure the right nails are in place.

. . . .

16

A RECIPE FOR REINVENTION

SEPTEMBER 2013–DECEMBER 2013

. . . .

We knew it was important that the new Nokia should do
something meaningful: be a good business *and* have
a positive impact on people's lives.

. . . .

NOW WHAT? THAT was the question on everyone's mind in the
days and weeks after September 3, 2013, as the news of our deal with
Microsoft reverberated across the company, the country, and the global
financial markets.

Even with Nokia's 150 years of history spanning many industries
from paper and pulp to cables, car tires, rubber boots, TVs, and PCs,
it was nearly impossible to imagine Nokia as anything other than a
mobile phone company. Since the early 1990s, the entire enterprise
had been centered on mobile phones and related devices and services: doing R&D for phones, developing their operating systems
and software, manufacturing them, selling them, and servicing them.
Everything else—the HERE mapping business, NSN's wireless infrastructure business and Advanced Technologies, the valuable portfolio
of crucial patents on which the mobile industry relied and paid royalties—was basically an outgrowth of our mobile phone identity.

Now we were excising Nokia's heart and seeking to transplant it into another host. We were dismantling the systems and moving almost all of the people who operated them to a new owner. Microsoft would acquire some 25,000 Nokia employees in 50 countries, including 4,700 people in Finland. Out of the 60,000 employees in 2008, some 32,000 people were still employed by Nokia just prior to the deal. After closing the deal, we would have about 7,000 employees left, almost all of whom worked for HERE (and the folks in NSN, of course).[1]

Over the course of our 150-year history, we had come close to bankruptcy more than once. Did we still have what it took to be successful in yet another radical transformation? And if so, what would we become? What would be the new Nokia?

A New Chess Game

While I had already had numerous discussions with Timo Ihamuotila, Henry Tirri, Juha Akras, and many others during the Microsoft negotiations, as a team we had not had nearly enough time to map out our alternatives for a new Nokia.

The board and our leadership team began to seriously frame our future in mid-August, devoting an entire meeting to the strategy and structure of a new Nokia. It was as if, in mid-game, we were switching to a new game of chess with a different set of pieces on different squares while losing many key pieces altogether. And all of this was happening while still continuing to play the old game as well.

Up to that point, all strategic planning had been dominated by the demands of the mobile handset business. There had been no point in hypothesizing alternative approaches with the other businesses that might hurt handsets. We just wouldn't do it, so why waste time thinking about it? But now the handset business would, we hoped, be moving over to Microsoft, and the strictures we had lived under would disappear with it.

We needed to make sure our thinking was no longer constrained by limits that were no longer relevant.

By September, we created a New Nokia Steering Group for strategy work. It was composed of myself, Timo Ihamuotila (our interim president and CFO), Kai Öistämö, Tuukka Seppä (a partner from Boston Consulting Group), and the heads of each of our businesses—Rajeev Suri of NSN, Michael Halbherr of HERE, and Henri Tirri (Nokia's chief technology officer). We met monthly. We also had a smaller working group, composed of myself, Kai, Timo, and Tuukka, which met on a weekly basis.

We began by analyzing the three businesses we had left from the perspective of planning strategy for each, independent of what the other businesses would need.

HERE's strength was that it was the industry's only high-quality independent source for digital maps. One attractive opportunity was to service the large ecosystems that didn't have a mapping asset: Amazon, Facebook, Microsoft, and Apple, as well as the new players expanding out of China.

HERE also had an opportunity in the business-to-business market, where it held a 90 percent share for in-dash navigation systems. We licensed automotive companies with our turn-by-turn navigation tools and other services, such as finding the cheapest gas station within the range allowed by the remaining fuel in the tank or finding the best parking space at the desired destination. HERE was also offered directly to consumers through free online services, which basically meant an advertising-based business model.

Then there was Nokia's Chief Technology Office, renamed Advanced Technologies (and later again renamed Nokia Technologies). Its only revenues derived from licensing our patent portfolio, but as home to our research efforts, it also developed key future technologies for the devices business and created new patent applications.

People may misunderstand the definition of a patent. A patent basically gives the patent holder the right to prevent other people or companies from doing what is covered by your patent. And nothing more. When we license a company to use our technology, they're paying to secure our promise not to sue them.

Advanced Technologies had a portfolio of about 30,000 patents, or 10,000 patent families with multiple patents covering different aspects of a particular invention. We had invented many of the core technologies in mobile phone user interfaces—for example, we had invented the app store. Patent licensing had brought in about €500 million in 2012,[2] and a large part of it was profit—there's very little cost involved in patent licensing. On the other hand, Nokia had spent tens of billions in R&D over the previous decades. That investment had created the inventions behind the patent applications.

Back when we had the mobile handset business, the value of our patents was often offset by our use of other mobile phone companies' patented technologies, for which we needed to compensate those companies. But now that the offset from our handsets was no longer part of the equation, the full value of our patents would become visible. How should we structure Nokia to maximize its value?

Licensing accounted for one-third of our profits and had a strong potential to grow. Advanced Technologies' research produced about 60 percent of our new patents. The rest was done by regular R&D, and as that was moving to Microsoft, new patent creation would be a challenge.

We had insisted that we keep most of our Nokia Labs personnel, but what would they work on? (Just to clarify: Nokia Labs was engaged in long-term, high-risk fundamental research, like Bell Labs; regular R&D work was more short term and customer driven.)

Engineers typically don't get excited about working on inventions just to file a piece of paper. They get more excited about creating something that will be used to improve people's lives. For that to happen, the company needs to come up with products incorporating an innovation that people can use. Our mobile phones had been a platform for all these great innovations. Without a consumer product business, what would motivate our researchers?

Then there was NSN. Even though NSN's profitability had mostly been in the red and we'd have been thrilled if it ever notched north of 10 percent, NSN post-sale would account for about 80 percent of Nokia's head count, 80 percent of our operating expenses, and 80 percent of revenues. How could we maximize the opportunity to create value through NSN, especially now that it wasn't encumbered by such external constraints as lack of funding and its owners fighting with each other?

NSN was kind of a one-trick pony, comprising only mobile broadband technology and associated services. A complete operator network is composed of a lot of additional technologies, such as routers or optical equipment. There was a clear opportunity in trying to buy Alcatel-Lucent, whose economies of scope—the company covered all the technologies of a complex network—were attractive.

When we first considered a merger with Alcatel-Lucent, the idea was that in the end Nokia would not own the combined business but would rather be able to exit the business in a positive way. Now that we were considering keeping NSN, the Alcatel-Lucent deal still made sense: Just as we had bought NSN for a discount and created value, maybe we could do the same with ALu.

But I have to admit, we were battle weary. The idea of doing something major like trying to acquire Alcatel-Lucent on the heels of the NSN buyout from Siemens and before the Microsoft deal had even closed was exhausting to even contemplate, not even considering how risky it would be to juggle so many balls at the same time.

Nokia's remaining three businesses were very different, their only common denominator being that they were part of Nokia. NSN was a network infrastructure player in an industry defined by intense price competition. Advanced Technologies was a research, incubation and licensing platform. HERE was a cloud-based business trying to answer the question "Where?" the same way Google answered "What?" and Facebook answered "Who?"

Each business demanded a leader with a different type of management experience. Each had a different business model with different customers. Each had a different go-to-market model. None really seemed to have much to do with the others. Was it worth holding on to them or preparing them to be spun off on their own?

We were leaning toward stabilizing the situation first. Our patent portfolio was still quite young, so while the old patents would eventually expire, we had plenty of runway. As a fallback, we believed we could make HERE and NSN IPO-ready in one to two years.

Having sketched out the pieces on the chessboard, there was no need to make a move quite yet. I was appointed interim CEO on September 2. The next day, we announced the sale of the handset business, and for the next few weeks, we had our hands full finalizing and announcing the Microsoft deal.

Five Objectives as the CEO

The board returned to shaping our future in mid-September. With the strategy teams, we dug in to identify the key issues and hone our solutions through iteration after iteration.

As I saw it, my goal as chairman and interim CEO was to achieve five distinct objectives:

1. Create a new vision for Nokia.
2. Build a strategy to implement the vision.
3. Choose the right organizational structure to drive the execution of the strategy.
4. Pick the best CEO and management team to lead the organization.
5. Decide what kind of balance sheet we would need.

Although these tasks would seem to be sequential, there is a lot you can prepare in parallel. I believe in making decisions in a certain order but through an iterative process; since all the parts interlock and affect each other, you need to touch each of them several times so that you can see how each evolves during each phase and what the ramifications are for the whole. Instead of marching forward in a straight line, we circled our target in a series of tightening spirals, revisiting each objective, asking questions, examining the pros and cons, and further developing our thoughts on each pass as we gradually homed in on our ultimate goal.

We had a number of months in which to plan. For paranoid optimism to be effective, it was best to give everyone as much time as possible to think through all the different scenarios, face their fears, and articulate their hopes. People had multiple opportunities to state their opinions, voice their doubts, and revise their thoughts. Nobody felt forced to accept something he or she didn't want.

We structured the process according to three phases, each with a series of key questions to answer within a certain period of time. We wanted to imagine different scenarios and explore all possible options. We started diving into those questions with the board and the management team at the board meeting in mid-September.

Phase I focused on the roles of NSN and HERE and whether we wanted to keep our options open about divesting them. The key questions were:

- Do we have a valid reason to continue keeping NSN "for sale"?
- Do we have a valid reason not to structure the new Nokia around NSN?
- Are there strong synergies between HERE and the other businesses; i.e., do we have a long-term reason to integrate HERE?
- What are the principles for setting up the "Level 1" structure, i.e., the structure of how the functions and businesses report to the CEO?

As open-ended discussions should, the last question raised another series of issues about the structure of the new Nokia. Two models were considered:

- Nokia could be a holding company incorporating three separate and independent operating companies, each with its own CEO and its own corporate functions, such as finance, HR, legal affairs, etc. In that model, a group CEO or the board would oversee the companies. However, the value of a holding company is not the sum of its parts; it's actually less, because the market assumes that the company cannot be led in an optimal way when it's involved in a number of different and unaligned businesses. Keeping NSN as a separate business within a Nokia holding company would discount both its value and Nokia's share price. That seemed counterproductive after all of NSN's sweat and tears to increase its value.

- Nokia could become a portfolio company. The three operating companies would share some corporate functions under the leadership of one CEO. If there were synergies between the businesses, there would be little discount in the overall value. However, if there were no synergies, then the value would drop.

By the end of October, we came to the conclusion that we wouldn't sell NSN. Because NSN was the biggest business we had, and Nokia and networks went back a long way, it felt natural for it to become the core of the new Nokia. We were also discussing a potential Alcatel-Lucent deal quite actively.

That led to a showdown at the October 31 board meeting.

Searching for a Happy Medium

The board was divided into two camps. One faction felt that being an infrastructure player was not the identity Nokia was known for: It wasn't disruptive, it wasn't exciting, and it wasn't a growth industry. This group felt that we should bet on Advanced Technologies and HERE, and retain the possibility of selling NSN if we got a good offer. The other camp believed that infrastructure was a slow-growth business, but it could provide a stable platform on top of which we could build some very exciting new opportunities.

We had people who said, "We *have* to become a holding company so that we have sufficient independence for HERE and Advanced Technologies." NSN was—and is—a very disciplined operation; it had to be, because it's quite big and it had been squeezed like a lemon to extract every possible ounce of productivity. You can imagine how the members of a loosey-goosey research community would react if they were forced to live under similar strict rules. It just wouldn't fly.

That faction was opposed by people who said, "Over my dead body"—and that's an exact quote. They felt that a holding company discount imposed on our share price would destroy our shareholders' money. We would become slow, inefficient, and hierarchical, with the group leadership confined to an ivory tower. Those people wanted a fully integrated organization with no extra layers; there would be one CEO, and all the functions and business leaders would report to him or her.

The management team was divided as well.

We started the board meeting without much common ground between these two camps. I had been very careful to stay outside this fight so that I wouldn't influence people to move in a particular direction too early. I strongly believed that before we had to make a decision, it was important to give people the maximum latitude to think with an open mind. And I honestly didn't have a strong opinion: I could see the benefits of both points of view.

I had structured the meeting so that both camps could present their opinions. I invited Rajeev, Michael, and Henri to come in, one at a time, and explain how they would like the whole company to be structured. Not surprisingly, Rajeev suggested an NSN-centric model, Michael advocated for maximum independence for HERE and Henry recommended investing in an independent Advanced Technologies.

After they had all said their piece, I asked them to leave so that the board could continue on its own. We debated and discussed and brainstormed for a couple hours. A long day was dragging on toward evening, and everyone was tired and hungry and cranky.

That's when it struck me that there was a way to do all of the above.

With the debate still roiling behind me, I went to the flipchart at the front of the room, turned it away from the board members, and started drawing. I sketched a very simple picture. HERE was on the left and Advanced Technologies on the right, each in its own box. NSN was in the middle, also in its own box. Above NSN, I put a box labeled "CEO and support functions," with a big oval encircling the CEO and NSN boxes, leaving HERE and AT outside.

Turning the easel to face the room, I asked for everyone's attention. "We could actually achieve a good balance of a holding company and an integrated organization," I said.

I first addressed the party that wanted efficiency without the overhead of multiple CEOs and overlapping functions: "We can run the business in an integrated fashion with one CEO and one set of corporate support functions. We'll take them from NSN, because NSN is the biggest business and has the most disciplined setup. NSN will not have independent corporate functions; its support functions will support the entire group. NSN will be run directly by the Nokia group CEO; basically the centralized part of Nokia will comprise NSN, and whoever is the NSN CEO will also be the group CEO. HERE and AT will be two relatively independent businesses, each of which will have a president who will report to the Nokia group CEO, so there's very little overlap."

Then I turned to the other camp to show how, under this model, both HERE and AT could preserve sufficient independence to have the operating cultures they needed to be successful.

There would be little or no holding company discounts and no leaders walled up in ivory towers. What there *would* be were the efficiencies of a single CEO and shared corporate support functions as well as a necessary level of independence.

This integrated organizational model met the critical criteria for both parties, so it was easy for each camp to support. In the end, this was what we agreed on. And with that, the hot air simply whooshed out of the room. We all took a deep breath and regained our equilibrium.

In retrospect, the solution seemed so obvious. But it had been eclipsed in the heat of the debate and the deluge of analytical details.

Our decision about the structure of the new Nokia—unanimously agreed upon—determined our approach to Phase II and Phase III. While Phase I was more about NSN and HERE, Phase II, which was the focus of discussion in mid-November, examined the key value drivers and long-term trends over the next few years for Advanced Technologies: What was its business scope and operating logic? How would we attract and retain talent and manage R&D? We had a number of new research projects that we had not mentioned to Microsoft. Which should we nurture, and what would we do with them?

Phase III discussions took place in mid-December. We sharpened our focus to come up with detailed recommendations about the direction of the portfolio, the right governance model, and the high-level implementation steps and timing for the transformation into the new Nokia.

By that time, we had a clear vision of our future.

The Programmable World

From the beginning of this process, we knew it was important that the new Nokia should do something meaningful: be a good business *and* have a positive impact on people's lives. On a more mundane level, we needed an overarching common story line that could connect and carry the individual strategies of the three disparate businesses and create faith in our future.

Henry Tirri, our chief technology officer, first proposed the concept of the "Programmable World" as Nokia's vision of the future world in September. The term had been percolating for a few months: A feature with that title had run in *Wired* magazine in May,[3] followed by an article in *Scientific American*[4] and one in *Fortune*, which declared, "Businesses must embrace the programmable world. Or die."[5]

The idea behind the Programmable World is the ability to continuously analyze the real world through billions of miniature sensors, making sense of what is happening based on the data collected and weaving a web that transforms our everyday world into a designable environment. Some people call this phenomenon the Internet of Things (IoT) or the Internet of Everything. It's at the heart of the burgeoning universe of artificial intelligence and machine learning.

As a concept, the Programmable World was intriguing. You think of the world as something you can program; you can create rules that the world will follow. It's a slightly scary thought, but on a purely pragmatic level, it means that as more things will be automated—from driverless cars to asthma inhalers whose sensors continuously analyze your physical signs and combine those with past data to map when asthma attacks are most likely to occur—our lives can be safer and more productive.

We became more and more convinced that the Programmable World was the vision of the future that we expected to happen and that it was a future in which Nokia could play a meaningful role.

In retrospect, it's beautiful how nicely it tied everything together: NSN would create the digital nervous system that connects everything; HERE would provide the crucial context denoting "where" things were happening that the digital nervous system needed to know about; and AT had a huge patent portfolio covering lots of the technologies that would make the Programmable World work, plus AT was doing research to create further inventions that would be necessary as the Programmable World developed.

We didn't want to lock ourselves into anything too early. But the Programmable World was often part of our discussions as our thoughts about the new Nokia evolved, and it was the subject of many of my presentations, both internal and external. Our people began to get the point that this was important to our future.

Meanwhile, the concept of the Programmable World provided high-level guidance about which direction we should follow and the strategy that would enable us to get there.

Be Brave Enough to Dream Big

When we started doing the work, I asked the leaders of the different business groups to come up with an internal strategy to maximize value creation for each business: What kind of a world did they envision in the next 10 years? What would they like to do in that world, and how would they like to shape it? What kind of position would they like to achieve in that world?

I expected differences between the businesses. What I didn't expect was lack of aspiration. To my surprise, the vision and strategies laid out by both NSN and HERE were not ambitious at all, although for different reasons. For NSN, that probably had to do with the very hard times the company had endured for seven years—suffering through cost cutting, undergoing restructuring, being reduced to such a tight-fisted survival mode that employees had to pay for their own coffee. It's hard to break out of that austerity thinking, especially since NSN's ability to make a profit was so new. HERE and the remnants of Nokia, on the other hand, were suffering from an existential crisis. They were moving into a very different business universe and didn't know what they were allowed to aspire to be.

Essentially, one group had talent but had forgotten how to dream big; the other group also had lots of talent but had been so demoralized that they no longer believed they had the right to redefine the game.

I raised my concerns to the board. I told them that the groups had no vision: They just proposed incremental improvements from where we were at the present. What they proposed wasn't good enough to build what we wanted or what we needed. It wasn't exciting enough to capture people's imagination. It wasn't ambitious enough to create a new future for a new Nokia.

Bruce Brown, the chief technology officer of P&G, suggested a process called "Future Back."[6] It's a way of thinking about strategy that asks you to imagine a moonshot future scenario and then work backward to articulate the steps necessary to achieve it.

I thought it was the perfect tool to force the leaders of NSN and HERE to break out of the prison of conventional thinking and have the courage to imagine the implausible. Their minds were free to dream about the world 10 years from now; what bogged them down was getting there. By starting at a point in the future and then backing up one year at a time, the Future Back exercise creates a tangible road map to tomorrow.

We asked all the businesses to redo their strategy work based on the Future Back model. They consequently came up with many new ideas and alternatives.

That's what strategy work should be: to imagine alternatives, so that we can identify the ones we want to pursue and plan how to achieve them, as well as naming the negative options and preventing them from becoming reality. Future Back eventually led to our acquisition of Alcatel-Lucent.

Who's in Charge?

Deciding on the vision, the strategy, and the organizational structure weighed on the selection of the CEO. Some companies select a new CEO and say, "Now you devise a strategy for us." I think that's just an easy way out for the board. You can predict what kind of strategy a particular type of CEO with a particular type of background will pick. For example, if you want a software-centric strategy, pick a software executive. If you want a services-centric strategy, pick a services expert. If you want something very aspirational, pick an entrepreneurial type, someone who has already done it.

We said, "No, it's our responsibility to choose the vision and strategy and then create an organization that's best structured to implement the strategy. Only after we have the right vision, strategy, and structure will we find the right people for the roles." It's better that way than to change the roles to fit the people we get.

I was in charge of finding the next CEO from the outset. A headhunter had come up with about thirty external candidates, of whom I interviewed six over the course of the fall, and some more than once. We wanted a large list because we weren't sure what kind of CEO we would need. When recruiting, I always aim to find three candidates, all of whom could do the job. Choosing between them is a pain, but it is a luxury to get to choose from three great candidates. You cannot go badly wrong.

I was looking both at CEOs who could run a holding company and at CEOs who could run a company centered on the network infrastructure business. Another sieve was filtering for someone who would be at home leading a very innovative consumer company or someone who would be comfortable in an infrastructure-centered business. We had a number of good external candidates as well as Rajeev Suri and some other internal candidates.

The board debated all the names a number of times. We didn't rush into a choice; we would make a decision only when we were at the right stage of the process. The ultimate choice of CEO would be linked to the organizational model we chose.

. . . .

"Credibility Is a Currency Grounded in Actions"

What do you say when you can't say anything?

One of the most painful aspects of this period was not being able to give our people details about Nokia's future. Our people wanted to know what we would do. We did not know, and what we knew we could not tell. (If we had been a private company, things would have been completely different.)

Leaders at every level regularly face this dilemma, especially so during a time of change. Rumors percolate; speculation escalates. Discord becomes inevitable.

I said in Chapter 10 that trust both greases the gears and glues everything together. It's also the oil that calms the raging waters. But merely to say, "Trust me, it will all work out," is naïve on your part and insults your audience's intelligence. This is especially true when a company announces bad news.

My advice is:

- Never lie.
- When you can, it's best to admit openly that you cannot talk about the topic.
- If you can, explain *why* you cannot talk about it.
- When you talk with your own people, say the maximum you can, and do your best to help them understand that you *are* doing your best.
- If you cannot talk about the outcomes, discuss the process that will lead to eventual choices.

Credibility is a currency grounded in actions. There is no shame or embarrassment in admitting that you don't have answers but that you are working hard to provide them—as long as people can see that you are, in fact, doing what you say.

I have always believed that difficulties create opportunities to build trust, whether it's trust between individuals or teams or even companies. Every obstacle is a chance to do the right thing at the moment—and to build a piece of something permanent. Investing in trust pays dividends for a long time.

. . . .

17

LEADING WITH A FOOT
IN TWO WORLDS

JANUARY 2014–APRIL 2014

. . . .

It was as if the arm had cut itself off from the body,
and while the body moved over to Microsoft,
the arm was left behind to run things.

. . . .

DESPITE WINNING THE approval of 99 percent of shareholders at
the Extraordinary General Meeting in November, the sale to Microsoft
wouldn't be officially completed until we obtained regulatory approval
from each major country in which we operated.

There was no question that we had made the right decision in selling the handset business. We had definitively breached the strategy
trigger in the third quarter. Furthermore, our November 2013 forecast
for smart devices' fourth-quarter operating margin was down to –27.5
percent, and in December it sagged even further to –29.6 percent.
Market share for high-end Lumia smart devices was an infinitesimal 1
percent. (Yes, that's 1 percent.)

At the same time, the stock market applauded our actions. We had
seen almost unprecedented investor interest during the three months
since the September announcement of the transaction. Our share price
had more than doubled by early January 2014 as investors anticipated a
change in our fortunes.

But for now, we were essentially a caretaker, responsible for running Devices & Services for its new owner and, especially important, responsible for handing over the business in the best possible condition.

It was a strange and anxious period.

Wrestling with Regulatory Approval

Our number one priority was to close the deal, and to do it as fast as possible. Assuming we'd be lucky and speed through the regulatory approvals, we set January 31 as the tentative closing date.

Many big transactions stall over antitrust regulations. Here's why: Let's say there is a country with only two subsidiaries of two global vendors providing a given product or service. If one company acquires the other, there would be a monopoly in that country. There may be additional vendors worldwide, but if there's only one left in that country, then the local authorities would impose conditions. They might decide that while the deal can close globally, in their country there have to be two independent players and the conditions for closing are that the acquired subsidiary has to be sold to a new owner, thereby preserving the competitive situation.

We didn't anticipate that the Nokia-Microsoft transaction would trigger any antitrust alarms. If anything, our deal would enhance competition. The company that had provided the products, i.e, Nokia, was running out of fuel, which had already decreased competition. By buying the business, Microsoft was entering a new business (for Microsoft) while leveraging its financial muscle to offer consumers an alternative in a market dominated by Apple and Samsung. At the same time, Microsoft's boost to Nokia's finances enabled Nokia to be a stronger player in the infrastructure industry. Competition would increase all around while the number of players remained unchanged. There should be no reason for any regulator anywhere in the world to delay in approving the deal.

Or so we thought.

The transaction sailed through the regulatory antitrust process in the United States and the European Union. In the wake of these two approvals, most other countries followed suit. Then China and South Korea slammed on the brakes.

We had major competitors in China (Huawei, ZTE, Xiaomi, etc.) and South Korea (Samsung, LG, etc.), which used the opportunity to delay the regulatory process. In China, especially, Nokia's local competitors were worried that once we sold our handset business, we would force them to pay for our patents. They used this opportunity to aggressively lobby their authorities to make access to our patents part of the conditions to closing the deal.

China has a three-stage regulatory approval process. Nokia had a very good track record in China: We were a strong brand and had good connections. We expected to get approval in the second stage by mid-February at the latest and maybe even by January 20, so that we could close at the end of the month.

But nothing happened.

If a smaller country delayed or denied approval, we could simply close the deal without including it, which meant that whatever assets we owned in that country would not move to Microsoft. (In fact, that's what happened with South Korea; it didn't give regulatory approval until August 24, 2015—nearly two years after the announcement of the transaction.[1]) But China was such a huge market that if the approval didn't go through, the deal would be sunk.

The closing date was rescheduled to February 28, 2014; then it slipped again. And again. As the process moved into the third stage, we had to consider the possibility that approval might be denied. If that happened, we could reapply, but then we'd have to repeat the entire process, which might delay us another eight or nine months. Meanwhile, the market for the Windows Phone was withering before our eyes.

Creating Our New Capital Structure

Despite the desire to close in January, to be honest, the initial delay was a bit of a relief. We weren't ready.

By our mid-February board meeting, we had a vision statement, a high-level strategy, a structure for the new Nokia, and a management team in place and a good idea of whom we wanted as CEO. That was four items checked off my list of five objectives.

We were still working on the capital structure.

Following the precepts of paranoid optimism, we went through a holistic analysis of our capital needs in good times and especially in bad ones. For instance, we calculated the cash buffer we would need should the bursting of the tech bubble in 2001 repeat or the 2008 financial crisis reoccur. We examined the hits we had taken during the handset disaster and did Monte Carlo simulations to see the effects should a downturn of similar magnitude happen again.

Like preparing for a bad winter, we worked out the kind of balance sheet we would need to weather each of these storms. What kind of acquisitions might we make? How much funding would be available— either from the equity markets or from other sources—depending on the different scenarios?

Our goal was to climb out of the junk bond basement and return Nokia to investment-grade status. Different rating agencies use different formulas to evaluate the balance sheet. Their conditions gave us a good spot from which to triangulate our position and come to an understanding of what the balance sheet needed to be.

In the end, we decided on a €5 billion capital structure optimization program focused on recommencing dividend payments, doing share buybacks, and reducing interest-bearing debt.[2] This was announced at the end of April. By mid-May, Nokia's credit rating was upgraded by both Moody's and Standard & Poor's.[3]

But that was three months away.

Leading in Limbo

There's a Finnish saying about "hanging loosely in the hangman's tree"—you feel as though you're slowly strangling. As the calendar inched into the spring of 2014, many people felt they were twisting in the wind, barely able to breathe.

Along with the vast majority of Nokia employees, almost all of the senior D&S managers were moving to Microsoft: the head of mobile phones, the head of smart devices, the guy in charge of sales, the lady in charge of marketing, the supply chain and manufacturing leaders. Our chief legal officer was leaving. Our head of HR had delayed his departure a few times because we needed him, but he, too, was planning to go. Of our top management, only Timo Ihamuotila stayed on as CFO and interim president.

It was as if the arm had cut itself off from its body, and while the body moved over to Microsoft, the arm was left behind to run things. No one knew how to deal with this situation. We had to make up the rules as we went along.

Everyone was anxious about the future. One group of employees would be moving to Microsoft when the deal closed: They were anxious about their future working environment and how the decisions they took now might be viewed when they were on the other side of the fence. There were people who suspected or knew they would be laid off when the deal closed: They were anxious about their next job. Then there were the people—the smallest group—who would stay and continue to work at Nokia: They were anxious about what that work might be.

With everyone working closely in teams, you can imagine the dynamics we were facing every day, especially when we all got revved up for the final closing and it was postponed *four times.*

During these months in limbo, nobody knew what the new Nokia would be like, what new strategy would be set, and when the new management team would be formed and who would be on it. All this uncertainty took the sharp edge away from people's ability to think about new ideas and dulled their motivation to try new big things. I can't emphasize strongly enough how emotionally challenging this period was.

As a leader, you have to pay attention to what's going on and try to reduce uncertainty.

Even very senior people—*even* stoic Finns—get stressed out. Some needed to vent; some needed to cry. There were some people who didn't see a role for themselves in the new Nokia but didn't want to leave. As we talked it over and it was clear that they should leave, what was especially painful for them was the thought of saying good-bye to a company that had been their life. Their professional identity was rooted in Nokia; their entire career had blossomed at Nokia; their friends and family were part of Nokia.

Some people suffered from the fact that their compensation had been completely out of sync with how hard they had worked. We linked executive compensation very tightly to the performance of the company, not the individual. Bonuses had been low since 2001 as the company consistently missed its own targets (with the exception of 2006 and 2007). Since Nokia had done so poorly financially since 2008, even people who had reasonably good salaries felt they had missed out compared with their counterparts in other companies whose soaring stock enabled them to earn five times more. Even when they knew the facts, they got mired in this emotional swamp and naturally felt unfairly treated and angry.

In this sort of situation, you just have to listen and not say much until they have gotten everything off their chest. Then you start piecing things back together. What I always think, and what we often say to each other when we have to make a tough decision, is, "We just need to do the right thing."

What was the right thing to do?

The right thing comes down to fairness. It's about simple human decency and treating people the same way every time. Often it's very difficult to figure out the right answer: You know how to assess your alternatives, but sometimes none of them are good enough, and getting to the action may not be clear.

I have found if I hold tight to the principles of entrepreneurial leadership and let them be my guide, the right action *will* eventually reveal itself. For instance, in the case of compensation, it would have been wrong to start correcting the past. There was nothing broken in our compensation models; the problem was that the company did not perform. What we could do, however, was make sure that the model for future compensation felt fair and motivating.

Meanwhile, the closing date was rescheduled again. February came and went, and we still did not have approval from China. Negotiations were ongoing, which gave us hope. As March 20 approached, we thought we might close at the end of March—only to be disappointed again. New target dates were set: April 1, April 4, April 11, and April 25.

Between the uncertainty and the frustration of trying to get the deal closed, everyone's emotions were sizzling like high-voltage wires. They had metamorphosed from fear ("We have no idea what will happen to us!") to acceptance ("We understand why and what and how. We're ready to move forward.") to impatience ("Why isn't something happening? Can you please close already?"). One of the senior managers said to me, "If the closing drags to the middle of the year, we'll kill each other."

We just wanted to get on with our lives.

An Intriguing Opportunity

Just because we were in limbo about the closing didn't mean we sat out on the sidelines. The business world moved on. One of those changes offered an intriguing possibility: getting back into mobile phones.

We guessed Microsoft was thinking of divesting the low-end mobile phone business that it had bought from us just months earlier. We owned the Nokia brand, and while we had licensed it to Microsoft for a period of time, Microsoft did not have the right to transfer the brand to a third party without our approval. We essentially had veto power over any possible sale. At the January 2014 board meeting, we raised the question: Should we buy back the business ourselves?

The opportunity was intriguing. We had sold the business for a very good price, and now we might have a chance to buy back the part that made a profit at a fire-sale discount. We could finally start the Android program we had often talked about.

Over the course of the next six months, we identified three alternatives: we could go for full ownership of the business; we could do a joint venture with a contract manufacturer, like Foxconn; or we could license our brand and intellectual property rights to a third party for a hefty fee. I had a slight preference for buying back the business, but the majority of the board and the management team thought it was too risky. They felt it would be safer to go with the third option. I understood the risk and did not resist.

It took a long time to find the right party, but eventually an arrangement was concluded between Microsoft and HMD, a newly established Finnish company. HMD did exactly what we would have done: It partnered with Foxconn so it wouldn't have to tie up capital in factories. The first Android-based Nokia phone was released in early 2017.[4] HMD shipped nearly 60 million feature phones and became the second-largest maker in this market segment in its first 12 months of operations.[5] Its business in the smartphone segment also got off to a great start, and it did well in the markets it focused on. For instance, it was number three in the highly competitive U.K. smartphone market after the first year.

The New Nokia—at Last!

On April 25, 2014, we completed the sale of substantially all of our Devices & Services business to Microsoft. (In the end, the Chinese authorities resisted the selfish efforts of our Chinese competitors to subvert the regulatory approval process. The government followed the established international practice. It just took some time to work out.) Just shy of eight months after the original announcement, we finally closed the deal. Thanks to the reverse price adjustment in our contract, it now looked as though Microsoft would pay us an additional €140 million.

The closing itself wasn't much of a spectacle. Each company authorized its chief legal officer to sign the necessary documents, and that was that.

But for our company and our colleagues and employees, the event was a huge milestone. We had *finally* closed. While many mourned the end of a very special era, the past was now the past. We were a new company and were moving forward.

We had agreed with Microsoft on a basic rule about real estate. If more than half of the people in any Nokia building were moving to Microsoft, then the building would belong to Microsoft. Because the majority of the people employed at our headquarters worked for Devices & Services, that meant that Nokia House would be transferred to Microsoft. The headquarters for the new Nokia would be at the NSN campus.

This was a big deal. Media stories on Nokia routinely showed the massive glass structure overlooking the Gulf of Finland. Nokia House was an icon, not just for Nokia but for Finland.

The new Nokia would officially commence on Tuesday, April 29, 2014. We unfurled a huge banner on Nokia House proclaiming, "Nokia on the Move." Then we hoisted an equally large banner on the outside of the new Nokia headquarters building on the NSN campus announcing, "Welcome, Nokia."

This was also Stephen Elop's last day at Nokia before he transitioned to Microsoft. He had come to Nokia at a time when the company was already in a steep downward spiral. Symbian was already beyond redemption.

As the first non-Finnish Nokia CEO, Stephen had to bear an unprecedented amount of curiosity that sometimes turned into hostility. After the domestic press turned against him, his working conditions became less than ideal. Savagely criticized for his mistakes, he never got the credit for the things he did extremely well under the most difficult circumstances. The fact that Nokia's organizational health continued to improve throughout Stephen's tenure is testament to the good leadership he brought to the company.

A New CEO

We had another announcement: Nokia had a new CEO.

I became better acquainted with Rajeev Suri, the CEO of NSN, when I became chairman and the board started our deep dive into its business. Over the course of two years, Rajeev and I had worked closely together during NSN's massive effort to become profitable and the soul-searching we did as we sought to create a new Nokia. In hindsight, it was a prolonged job interview under many different and difficult circumstances.

Throughout the process, my board colleagues suggested more than once that perhaps I would change my mind and remain as CEO. It would be wrong to say that I wasn't attracted to the idea. I had been the CEO of F-Secure for 18 years before becoming chairman, and the experience of being Nokia's CEO—in spite of the intensity or maybe because of it—reminded me how much I loved the CEO role. You are the absolute center of what's going on. It's exhilarating. It's intoxicating. It's addictive. It's exhausting. And it's a lot of fun.

But when I took the role, I had promised that I would *only* serve in an interim capacity. I had promised not just myself, but I had said it aloud, both to the board and to my family. I felt bound to honor my commitment.

My chief priority was to pick the best possible CEO for the company. On April 4, 2014, Rajeev Suri was appointed as the CEO of Nokia.

Three weeks later, he was tossed into his first board meeting as Nokia's CEO. It could not have been comfortable for him. After all that the board and I had gone through together, we were a tight-knit bunch, and Rajeev was a bit of an outsider. And it was natural for him to question whether, as his predecessor who was now his chairman, I would try to micromanage or whether I would truly step down.

But as I said earlier, difficult situations are opportunities to create trust. I deliberately tried to give Rajeev breathing space so that he could find his own way. And as Rajeev saw that I truly meant what I had said, his confidence grew quickly.

I have to confess that I suffered a bit of emotional whiplash. I was no longer on point from early morning to late at night, going from meeting to meeting here, there, and everywhere. I could relax a little. On the other hand, I had done a lot of heavy lifting and naturally felt accountable, especially now that Nokia was becoming a very interesting company to lead.

But within two weeks of my first board meeting as chairman only, I realized again why I had promised to step down. The fact is, there's no role where you can have all of the positives and none of the negatives. While there are certain aspects of the CEO role that I love, for me there are more positives in the chairman role. You don't need to spend all your time putting out the everyday fires. You can explore bigger issues and focus on the long term. You can even spend time acquiring completely new skills.

If I were the CEO, I wouldn't have been able to spend time studying artificial intelligence and machine learning, and my life would be poorer without that—not to mention spending more time with my family. People often say that they only find out what they had after they lost it. For me, it was slightly different: I found out what I had when I moved on.

And Nokia has a great CEO.

Bridging the Culture Chasm

In the days and weeks after the closing, everyone had a bit of a hangover. People were exhausted, both physically and emotionally. The board and board committees had met over 100 times in less than two years; in 2013 alone, we had 64 board and board committee meetings. It took time for everyone to start to feel energized again.

We also had to build trust and respect between two clashing cultures. NSN's culture had been strongly influenced by the hardships it had endured. It was frugal and disciplined but at the same time was perceived to be heavy on process and light on individual empowerment. The handset culture (which encompassed everything affiliated with Devices & Services) was the opposite: loosely organized and more accustomed to betting on big risks and reaping the rewards of an adoring public.

There had for some time been a feeling of superiority among the handset people compared with the networks folks, because the handset business had soared while the networks floundered. Then the tables turned. Suddenly, the handset business was hemorrhaging money while the former stepchild had become the savior. There was a sense among some of the networks people that it was payback time for "those arrogant handset people." And the folks at what had been renamed Nokia Technologies were now rudderless and probably hated the idea that their innovations would now focus on "boring network stuff" instead of "cutting-edge consumer products."

If we wanted to survive and succeed, we would need everyone to pull together.

We went back to the old Nokia values—not the values of 10 years ago but the core values that had saved the company from bankruptcy in the early 1990s. They had pulled Nokia out of its tailspin and created the Nokia we all loved. We had faith that they would steer us through our reinvention and propel our revival.

Interestingly, these four values almost exactly reflect the precepts of entrepreneurial leadership:

- **Respect.** Act with uncompromising integrity. Treating people with respect is the basis for building trust.
- **Achievement.** Be accountable—not just for setting high standards but for making continuous improvements that constantly raise the bar higher for yourself and your colleagues.
- **Challenge.** Never be complacent. In other words, explore alternative scenarios, embrace bad news, and leverage the power of paranoid optimism.
- **Renewal.** Always be willing to listen and learn, to refine your skills, adapt your habits, and master the ability to change with a changing business environment.

These four simple words struck a chord with everyone. They reminded us of what we had been and what we could be. They provided a foundation for the right way to behave, to make decisions, and to take action.

Melding the two different cultures into a unified company is a road we're still traveling. People change slowly. But being very clear about what you want, walking the talk, rewarding the right behavior, and promoting and hiring the people who embody those values sends a powerful signal about the kind of company we want to become. And perhaps most importantly, making every new recruitment count. When you have a clear understanding of the target culture you aim for, you can look for people who naturally live that culture.

We had already done something similar on a smaller scale with the board of directors when we articulated and agreed on the Golden Rules for board behavior, which I described in Chapter 10. We saw the benefits in the close working relationship between the board and the leadership team. We reaped the results in accomplishing the Microsoft and NSN transactions, in providing Nokia with a future, and in launching our transformation.

We weren't the only ones who observed this. I can say, based on the feedback we got from the ranks, that it was noticed and felt by people everywhere in the company. They saw that the board and leadership team were equally dedicated and were pulling together.

After years of confusion and disappointment, they felt a new confidence in their future.

. . . .

Building the Right Habits

Despite the extreme tension and turmoil, we had to maintain the good practices, intelligent behavior, and esprit de corps that kept the company running while instilling the habits and capabilities that would build the new Nokia.

The way to create a culture is by being a role model. Oftentimes, you don't need to "lead." You just *do*, and people will do what you do. Talk is cheap. Taking actions that people can see and are motivated to copy and repeat is better than any high-toned speech. It's the simplest way to lead: lead by example.

I have found that the role of the leader is actually the easiest role during a crisis. Leading keeps you busy; it keeps you motivated and gives you strength to persevere. When you feel accountable, you draw energy from that because as a leader you cannot collapse or be seen as losing control.

When you know you can't stop, it's actually much easier to keep going. The worst thing is to waste time wondering whether you can go on or whether people will understand if you stop. If that option is out of the question, then you can focus all your energies on moving forward.

Of course, there's a difference between moving forward mindlessly and moving forward with intent, between ordering your team to keep going and inspiring them to follow.

The following precepts helped us become a cohesive unit, draw strength from one another, and set a model that others could learn from and apply to their own teams:

- **Be a paranoid optimist.** Openly and honestly address the worst that could happen. That removed part of the fear for us, and it allowed us to recognize that we had alternatives. As long as we had alternatives, we could influence the ones we wanted to have happen to us. That created optimism. And if the leaders sincerely radiate optimism, it's infectious.
- **Encourage accountability.** We wanted everyone to think like a leader, so we gave people a lot of autonomy. We tried to maximize the number of people who felt they had the license to say, "I will do it" or "I will decide it" when needed, in order to minimize what had to be escalated.
- **Promote scenario-based thinking.** We wanted every single person in the company to always be thinking of alternatives. That meant not just identifying existing alternatives but constantly imagining and even manufacturing different options, both negative and positive, as well as the actions associated with them.
- **Build trust.** As I've said before, trust is the grease that makes things run smoothly. In our constantly shifting environment where problems seemed to crop up out of nowhere, trust was also the fuel that kept us going. That meant people had to operate openly, colleagues had to be treated with respect, and bad news had to be shared quickly.
- **Never lose your calm.** The more tense the situation, the calmer you should become. The more scared you are, the cooler you should be. When you know that you cannot afford to get angry,

it's actually pretty easy not to get angry. You only get angry when you think you have that luxury.

- **Laughter**—or just a few smiles—can do wonders to reduce tension, clear the air of anxiety, and enable people to start thinking productively.

Inculcating these habits made us very quick and flexible—and helped a huge amount during this period. At their core, like a reassuring heartbeat, was the constant reminder of the power of paranoid optimism to enable us to shape our future.

. . . .

18

THE FOUNDATION
FOR OUR FUTURE

OCTOBER 2013–JANUARY 2016

. . . .

*Alcatel-Lucent and Nokia complemented each other perfectly,
like the pieces of a jigsaw puzzle fitting neatly into place.*

. . . .

BACK IN THE fall of 2013, Jesper Ovesen, the executive chairman of NSN, capped a routine presentation to the board with a surprising demand: Merge with Alcatel-Lucent within the next three weeks. I have rarely been as surprised at a board meeting—not by the idea, but by the proposed timeline.

Merging with Alcatel-Lucent would increase NSN's market share in the global wireless infrastructure market from 18 percent to more than 30 percent, leapfrogging over Huawei and closing in on market leader Ericsson.[1]

But at the time, it was the last thing we wanted to consider. The board was exhausted. We had bought out Siemens's share of NSN just a few months earlier and clawed ourselves back from the edge of the abyss with the Microsoft transaction, which still needed to close successfully and therefore could still fail. We didn't have a permanent management team, vision, or strategy as a company. There was little appetite for another enormous deal—certainly not a 50-50 merger of Nokia and Alcatel-Lucent.

Even if NSN's troubles hadn't provided us with a front-row seat to the flaws in a so-called merger of equals, the messy 2006 merger between France's Alcatel and the U.S.'s Lucent would have been a classic case study of what could go wrong. In political mergers like these, turf wars often take precedence over basic business: People wrangle over which national flag will fly higher, which party has the chairman's role and which the CEO's role, where the headquarters will be located, how many representatives of which nationalities will be in leadership positions or on the board, and so on. It's a recipe for disaster or, at the least, value loss, and had been conclusively proved so by Alcatel-Lucent, and, to some extent, by Nokia and Siemens as well.

In addition, as one of our board members declared, "Over my dead body will we acquire a French company." There's a fairly extreme stereotype of a French company: The French government intervenes in ways big and small, the company is hugely expensive and problematic to restructure—hostile unions have been known to kidnap company leaders and hold them hostage[2]—and the culture rejects anyone who isn't French. Of course, many of these declarations came from people who knew very little about French companies and even less about Alcatel-Lucent.

Furthermore, even though it seems so obvious now that our vision of the Programmable World required us to deliver an end-to-end solution, at that time we had not yet decided on that course of action. It was one of various alternatives, not a predestined outcome.

Under the circumstances, Jesper's suggestion—and the urgency he put behind it—seemed a real outlier. And since one doesn't negotiate a complicated deal in three weeks, the irrationality of the suggested timeline reduced the credibility of the idea itself.

Moving Forward—Cautiously

Still, the fundamental idea made sense. Nokia was a one-trick pony. We were perhaps the best mobile broadband company in the world, but that is just one link in the overall chain that creates a comprehensive global communications infrastructure. While Nokia had the global scale in mobile broadband, we did not have the scope of capabilities to support our emerging vision of the Programmable World, where everything and everyone will be connected.

Acquiring part or all of Alcatel-Lucent could provide an ideal solution.

To launch a truly successful M&A process, one of the first questions to answer is how time will affect the relative strengths of the two parties.

Alcatel-Lucent was in the early phase of the restructuring that NSN had already undergone. If the restructuring didn't work for them—a distinct possibility—our competitive position would be even stronger. We had several positive business irons in the fire; if they worked out, there was a good chance of our share price going up, enhancing our leverage if we opted for a full merger. We could afford to watch, analyze, and plan to be at maximum readiness when it came time to move, if ever.

On the other hand, we weren't the only ones interested in Alcatel-Lucent. There were rumors that Samsung wanted to snap them up. We were also concerned that Ericsson might buy ALu and then break them up. If Ericsson did that, we could pick up some pieces, but they might not be the pieces we wanted.

We decided to move forward—cautiously.

Over the course of the fall of 2013, I had a couple of opportunities to talk with Alcatel-Lucent CEO Michel Combes at, among other places, the European Roundtable of Industrialists, a forum of 50 chief executives and chairmen of some of the largest European companies. We each put out feelers and hinted at the eventual possibility of something more serious, although I had to tell Michel pretty bluntly that for now we had our hands full trying to close the Microsoft deal.

Rajeev also had engagements with Michel. After those meetings, we always compared notes and kept the board up to date on any insights. As part of our getting-to-know-ALu approach, we revisited the subject at every board meeting and delved deeper each time. By our board meeting at the end of March 2014, we had identified five different ways of moving forward on some sort of ALu deal, ranging from buying their wireless business—the easiest option—to acquiring the entire company. These were in addition to our broader strategic alternatives.

But the timing wasn't yet right. In separate conversations with me and with Timo Ihamuotila, Michel Combes made it clear that carving out ALu's wireless business was not an option. We didn't know ALu well enough and were simply not ready to make a move for the whole company. Regardless of what ALu might have proposed, we probably would have said no.

Introducing Project Maine

We held our September board meeting in Silicon Valley that year. We invited speakers from the venture capital community, infrastructure players, and our customers to broaden our thinking. The aim was to give the board members and management team a new perspective on strategic alternatives—specifically, how to ensure our competitiveness in the networks business. I wasn't sure myself and was looking forward to learning something new.

Alcatel-Lucent, meanwhile, had shifted their position. As we had predicted, ALu had not had a good year. While their massive restructuring effort was successfully cutting costs, they were still bleeding cash, especially in mobile broadband.[3] We could sympathize—even though we hoped to profit from their pain.

On September 15, a Nokia team led by Timo Ihamuotila met with an ALu team led by Jean Raby, their CFO. We had earlier declined an invitation to create a joint venture between ALu's wireless business and our wireless business. Now they declared that they not only were willing to sell the division but wanted to fast-track the process so they could approve it at their September 28 board meeting and announce a deal before their Capital Markets Day in November.

Things were getting serious enough that for the first time, we gave the topic a code name. From now on, all things ALu would be referred to as Project Maine. In Nokia project codespeak, ALu was dubbed "Alabama." We were called "Nebraska."

At our board meeting, we focused on two out of the five alternative ways forward:

Plan A: Acquire ALu's wireless business. This was the low-hanging fruit in ALu's portfolio: ALu was too small to both invest sufficiently in R&D and be profitable at the same time. We knew mobile broadband inside and out and, more important, were big enough to make a profit from it. Of course, we would be buying a lot of trouble because we would need to integrate our two businesses, which would mean both cutting costs and undergoing a painful integration of the overlapping product lines. But that was well understood.

There was, however, a kink in ALu's mobile broadband business: their Chinese joint venture. Alcatel Shanghai Bell (ASB), a 50-50–owned company with the Chinese state, was not just the exclusive outlet for Alcatel-Lucent's business in the enormous Chinese market, but also a significant R&D operation. Simply swapping out a French company for a Finnish one and continuing as before would not have been smart. We would want to change things to bring fully westernized governance into the ASB. This was one of the topics that the Nokia board and management dove into deeply to understand better.

Plan B: Acquire all of ALu. Alcatel's vast portfolio included their fixed-line business, which is basically how consumer households and companies' offices are connected to the internet; the routing business, through which large and very efficient routers are sold to network service operators; the business that manufactures, sells, and services fiber-optic equipment; the software required to run the networks and service customers; and a submarine business, which built and serviced the long-haul undersea optical cable connections between continents.

We'd been involved earlier in some of these business areas but not all. I had recruited new board members with experience in network infrastructure, but both our management and overall board had some learning to do.

Complicating an already complicated proposition were three requirements we suspected the French government would demand in an acquisition. It would want the French side to be allowed to nominate possibly up to half of the board of directors of the new entity; it would want the ALu brand to continue, i.e., naming the new company Nokia Alcatel-Lucent; and it would want a minimum number of jobs to be kept in France.

Plan B was intriguing, but we were still gun-shy. Plan B carried all the hair in Plan A plus some. For example, we knew that ALu had a pension liability of close to €30 billion and a huge pension fund to cover it. (Some people joked that ALu was actually a pension fund with an attached networking business.) It was simplest and safest to start negotiating on the smaller perimeter.

But we didn't stop thinking about the whole picture.

Shifting from Plan A to Plan B

We took the paranoid optimist's approach that had served us so well: coming up with alternative scenarios, analyzing the pros and cons of each option, asking lots of questions, getting answers, then repeating the cycle. With each iteration, you go both deeper and wider, and your understanding improves.

That autumn of 2014, we proceeded negotiating on Plan A but stalled on a big price difference. We had proposed a €1.15 billion for Alcatel's wireless business; they asked for €1.5 billion. They later lowered their ask to €1.25 billion, but we did not believe we should pay more than €1.15 billion. Furthermore, our closer scrutiny raised concerns that Plan A would be a difficult carve-out and riskier than we originally assumed.

Plan B was becoming more attractive. Our cycle of iterations had clarified our thinking about the networks business. We believed we especially needed to get hold of IP routing technology. There were two large entities that seemed likely candidates: Alcatel-Lucent and Silicon Valley–based Juniper Networks. We also reviewed a number of smaller players, but buying a subscale player would have been risky.

Come December 2014, we had learned much more, but we still worried about unpleasant surprises in the ALu businesses that were new to us. It is quite difficult to gain expertise in a business you are not engaged in yourself and have to study from the outside.

We decided to continue the discussions around Plan A but simultaneously begin to investigate the possibility of Plan B by arranging meetings across the board. Rajeev and Timo met with their counterparts at Alcatel-Lucent, CEO Michel Combes and CFO Jean Raby. I started creating some personal connections of my own by inviting myself to dinner with ALu chairman Philippe Camus.

We met on January 16 at Restaurant Laurent in Paris. A former hunting lodge belonging to Louis XIV, the Michelin-starred restaurant is known for its secluded corners and intimate banquettes. Philippe had reserved a private dining room for the two of us. I expected this to be a careful dance, with both of us feeling the other out and being very selective with our choice of words. It was nothing like that. Philippe was honest, straightforward, and so outspoken that I felt I had to try to hush him when the waiter was in the room.

He leapfrogged over Plan A and calmly laid out how his team had already embraced the possibility of full acquisition. They had warned the French government that ALu was too small to continue alone. They had tapped Verizon and AT&T, their two biggest customers, for their reaction to a Nokia-ALu combination. The management team and the board supported an acquisition, he told me, and the two employee union representatives who served as observers to the board were also in favor.

We were still uncertain whether we wanted to do this, but Alcatel-Lucent was clearly convinced that they couldn't continue alone. They were pursuing other possible suitors—Philippe did not name them, although our guesses were Cisco, Ericsson, Samsung, and Huawei. But Nokia was the best fit, and we both knew it.

"The Time to Act Was Now"

At our first board meeting of 2015, held in mid-January, Plan A was still the default option. Plan B remained a controversial alternative. But I had come to a conclusion over the Christmas break, one that was reinforced by my meeting with Philippe Camus: We should make a serious effort to assess acquiring all of Alcatel-Lucent. I had discussed the topic with Rajeev, and we both agreed.

Our reasoning was as follows:

Our CSP (the term "communications service provider" had supplanted "teleoperator") customers were consolidating. Many countries were shrinking from four operators to three. Big operators like to buy from big vendors—and we weren't big enough as a pure mobile broadband specialist. Also, Nokia had a disproportionately high number of those fourth operators in our customer portfolio. As they were swallowed up, our market share would be under pressure.

We believed the whole world was moving toward a tendency for services: from buying tools to paying for an outcome, from selling products to providing services. Nokia was presently delivering only the mobile part of the network. It was an important part, but it was nowhere near a complete solution. And because it was just one part, we could not guarantee the outcomes that the operators would want because we could not guarantee how other companies' solutions would work. For example, security was clearly becoming more important, and as everyone knows, in security the chain is only as strong as the weakest link. If we could not deliver an end-to-end solution, we could not commit to any particular level of security.

While our operator customers would discuss the mobile network with us, they did not feel we were the right party to talk to when the topic was the future of their entire business or the entire network architecture. If we could not participate in that discussion, we would not be able to influence the direction being chosen. We wanted to get to that table.

The evolution of 5G would enable new business models, but it would also drive significant investments to network elements outside our traditional strength in radio. We wanted to be driving those new business models. We needed a seat at that table, too.

The pricing power of the CSPs was huge. The bigger our portfolio, the easier it would be for us to tactically price our solutions to a single customer. When the operators put a lot of pressure on the price of a certain technology, we could always attempt to have a higher margin on something else or increase our market share at the expense of a competitor in return for providing a lower price on the technology the customer wanted. Overall, a wide portfolio offered us protection and gave us options in the fiercely competitive price war.

These developments would not stop. The time to act was now.

All the Pieces in the Puzzle

Alcatel-Lucent's scope could provide many of the critical components we needed to complete our end-to-end portfolio, but success in the consolidating market also demanded scale. ALu could supply that, too. The two companies complemented each other perfectly, like the pieces of a jigsaw puzzle fitting neatly into place.

ALu's weakness was a subscale radio business that was dragging the rest of the company down. We had exactly the right medicine to fix it: Our mobile broadband business was well managed and big enough to be both competitive and quite profitable. Together these two businesses could support the required large investments in mobile networks R&D and generate a higher profit.

Nokia didn't have much of a presence in the enormous and influential U.S. mobile market. Our big customers were T-Mobile and Sprint, which together accounted for barely 30 percent of the U.S. wireless subscription market.[4] ALu's main customers were AT&T and Verizon, which together commanded 68 percent of the market.[5] These were two of the most demanding customers in the world, and it's often good to work with the most demanding customers because they help you to be more competitive.

ALu was also the global market leader in fixed-line access, was among the top three in routing, and had very interesting growing software assets. We didn't have routing or fixed networks businesses at all, so the lack of overlap would make integration easier.

To top it off, there was Bell Labs (a subsidiary of ALu), which invented many of the foundational technologies that underpin information and communications networks and all digital devices and systems, and whose research has resulted in eight Nobel Prizes, two Turing Awards, three Japan Prizes, and a plethora of National Medals of Science and Engineering, as well as an Oscar, two Grammys, and an Emmy for technical innovation.[6]

To have a seat at all the tables and a chance to be a dominant player in the future, we needed to acquire Alcatel-Lucent.

I strongly believe that one of the chairman's most sacred duties is to ensure that people can and will express their true opinions. This means that the chairman and, based on the same logic, any strong opinion leaders on the board should avoid expressing their opinions before the others have spoken. For many meetings, I had not had a strong opinion, and we had all had multiple chances to discuss the various angles.

I felt this was the time to explain my conclusions.

Some of my colleagues on the board were still in the "only over my dead body" camp, so I did something I almost never do. As I had pre-agreed with Rajeev Suri, I stepped in front of the board and explained my reasoning. I also drew a picture of a network architecture where I circled the components that we were presently delivering to highlight how far we were from being an end-to-end player. It was an embarrassingly bad sketch, but it made its point: Huawei was best positioned, Ericsson and ALu had a full offering with weak areas, and our menu was full of holes.

We had one major advantage. As we had forecast, the past 12 months had been more favorable to Nokia's stock price than to ALu's shares. Where their shares were down 12 percent, ours were up 12 percent. Instead of the dreaded merger of equals, we had moved to a clear acquisition model. We would own up to two-thirds of the combined company by value.

After a discussion, the board agreed that we should actively explore this avenue. That was all I wanted.

Operating Like a Well-Oiled Machine

So far, we had largely focused on Plan A. We all still had much to find out about the full company.

Everything we had learned over the past two years prepared us for the complexities of this deal. Soon after we completed the NSN acquisition, we had recruited new board members who were familiar with mobile broadband and related businesses, and we spent many board meetings moving up the learning curve. Our management team knew how to drive this type of integration successfully. Our experience with Microsoft had given us a tried-and-true approach to building trust and respect during negotiations. Thanks to living and breathing the Golden Rules for two years, we knew what to expect from and how to rely on each other. We operated like a well-oiled machine.

At our board meeting on February 27, we updated the initial five options for moving forward with Project Maine:

1. Seek organic growth and overinvest in our own R&D
2. Bolt on the necessary technology by acquiring smaller companies (our "string of pearls")
3. Plan A (acquire ALu's wireless business) plus the string of pearls
4. Plan A plus attempting to acquire Juniper to access its routing and switching expertise
5. Plan B (acquire all of ALu)

With our now-ingrained habit of planning for alternative scenarios, we took a deep dive into Plan A and Plan B. We decided to keep Plan A as a backup. If we could not agree on Plan B, we would go back to Plan A.

Having analyzed all the scenarios, the board approved the target of acquiring all of Alcatel-Lucent according to these parameters: acquiring 100 percent of the stock; ensuring 67 percent to 70 percent ownership by Nokia shareholders; appointing the chairman and CEO from Nokia; designating Helsinki as the headquarters of the combined company; and dividing the board of directors with seven members from Nokia and two from Alcatel-Lucent.

Earning Trust

We had our first official negotiation session with Alcatel-Lucent on March 5, 2015, in Paris. We drew on our experience with Microsoft and said that we should follow the 4 x 4 model that had worked so well in our previous transaction. It actually ended up being a 4 x 3 model, pairing Philippe Camus and me, Rajeev and ALu CEO Michel Combes, and Timo Ihamuotila and our chief legal officer Maria Varsellona with Jean Raby, who was serving as both CFO and CLO for ALu.

I opened the meeting by thanking the Alcatel-Lucent team for agreeing to meet us and repeating Philippe's and my shared view that combining the two companies would be the best thing for both of us. It would add the scope and scale we needed. And it would solve their problem with mobile networks and provide a chance to participate in creating a European counterforce to the Chinese juggernaut Huawei.

Then I said that there was one thing I had learned from the Microsoft deal. "We all know there will be tough moments in the process, and negative surprises and difficult decisions on both sides. The only way to get through them is to have trust in the other party. But that trust doesn't come for free—it has to be earned."

I told them that the way we had learned to create trust in this sort of transaction was to have small teams from each company—rather than an army of outside advisors—and very frank conversations. I reminded everyone that we would most likely be successful by driving toward a win-win for both parties, instead of treating the discussions as an adversarial process where one party needs to win and the other needs to lose. "We don't have to win every small skirmish," I pointed out. "We just have to win the war. And we can both win the war by being on the same side."

I finished by saying that our overriding objective was to conduct ourselves from the Nokia side in such a way that the negotiations would engender everlasting mutual respect, regardless of the outcome.

That's exactly what we did.

Of course, there were plenty of complications along the way. To begin with, there were the expected Finland versus France/Nokia versus Alcatel power struggles. The French side, almost as a required gesture, at the beginning of the discussion advocated a model for a merger of equals, while we were clear that we were only considering an acquisition. They proposed that their CEO would take on the CEO role of the new company. (Philippe Camus had announced his desire to step down, so ALu didn't push for a French chairman.) They suggested that the combined company have two headquarters: one in Helsinki and one in Paris.

Last but definitely not least, we were very aware that both the Alcatel-Lucent and Nokia-Siemens mergers had failed. How could we prevent history from repeating itself? We analyzed what had gone wrong in those mergers and tried to figure out what we could do to preempt the causes.

We hit a brick wall numerous times. What helped get us past it was the trust being built between the teams.

After our dinner in January, Philippe Camus and I had spoken a number of times by phone, but as the negotiations proceeded, we wanted to talk face-to-face. We were, of course, paranoid about confidentiality. I suggested that instead of meeting at a law firm somewhere, I would reserve a suite in a hotel where we could meet without anyone seeing us together.

For this to work it could not just be any hotel. The elevators at most modern hotels won't let you up without an electronic room keycard, which requires announcing yourself at the front desk. That was the last thing I wanted. I had someone call around London hotels and found out that the Savoy Hotel still has old-fashioned elevators. On March 10, Philippe strolled into the hotel and, without signing in at the front desk, walked right into the elevator and pressed the number for the second floor. Even if a banker lurking in the lobby recognized him and had seen me in the lobby a few hours earlier, there was no reason to be suspicious. It was altogether plausible that both of us could be staying there on separate business. And if there was a hint of a French-Finnish farce about the plan, who cared? This way was more secure than using a law firm and cheaper, too. Even more valuable was the opportunity for Philippe and me to get to know each other better.

Best and Final

We continued to haggle over the price and other headline terms.

At our first official meeting on March 5, we offered an exchange ratio of 0.491; i.e., ALu shareholders would get 0.491 Nokia shares for each ALu share. Alcatel-Lucent's counter-ask was 0.60 per share. We weren't on different planets, as we had been at the beginning of the Microsoft negotiations, but it was a very wide gap.

As we had done so successfully with Microsoft, we tried to triangulate the value in different ways and convince the other party by facts. It didn't work. This negotiation was not as logic-driven as the one with Microsoft had been.

We went through several rounds, making slow progress but no breakthroughs.

When I talked to Philippe by phone on March 22, our latest offer was 0.538. He said that he could come down on his ask, but the price reduction depended on ALu CEO Michel Combes becoming the CEO of the combined company. If Rajeev became the CEO, the exchange ratio would have to be higher. I rejected the proposal and told Philippe that Nokia needed to have the right to appoint the CEO. This was not a power game; I was truly convinced that Rajeev was the right CEO for the company.

On Friday, March 27, our teams met in the London offices of ALu's lawyers.

Philippe had made the last proposal. It was now up to Nokia to make the next offer. Instead, in a one-on-one meeting with Philippe, I said, "Philippe, it's impossible for me to make you any kind of a new offer because you will misunderstand its meaning, and if you don't, then your team members will. The way you will misunderstand is that you'll expect us to meet in the middle of our new offer and your existing proposal, and I'm telling you that is just impossible. If I give you a new offer, you'll think I have a reasonably big buffer to negotiate, and that's just not the case. I know you made the previous offer, but now I need you to make a significantly lower new offer."

He said he understood but needed time to discuss it with his team. After deliberating for half an hour, he came back with an offer of 0.564 per share, a big step down from the earlier indication.

At our board meeting earlier that week, I had been authorized to target an exchange ratio between 0.550 and 0.563. ALu's new offer was slightly above the upper range I was authorized for, but the goal was within reach. I was confident we would have a deal.

But we weren't quite done.

I thanked Philippe for his offer and for understanding and told him that now *I* needed 30 minutes to discuss it with my team. What I really needed was to ask the team, "Help me to find a way to express our 0.550 offer so that he will not negotiate further."

The choice of words can be critical. There's a phrase that is very powerful in M&A deals: "best and final." "Best and final" means "This is the best we can do. It's our final offer. Take it or leave it." The implication is that if the other side doesn't take it, we'll walk away. It's a big decision to use the phrase "best and final." If you don't mean it and the other party calls your bluff, you lose all credibility. I said to the team, "I don't want to say 'best and final,' but I want the same effect."

This is an example of how single words or a single sentence can be worth huge amounts of money. We spent close to 30 minutes struggling to come up with the perfect wording. Then Scott Simpson, our external lead counsel from Skadden Arps, suggested a very simple solution: "Why don't you just say, 'This is what I want you to take back to your board'?" That felt right. It was a very direct, personal request; it makes the other party want to do you a favor in a way. And it's hard for the other person to say, "I *don't want to* take this back to my board." It destroys the mood of the moment.

I returned to Philippe and made a counteroffer of 0.550. I explained why we thought it was a good offer, and then I said, "Philippe, this is what I want you to take back to your board."

Being a good negotiator, he wanted to haggle and suggested splitting the difference at 0.555. I just repeated, "Philippe, this is what I want you to take back to your board."

He agreed and stood up to leave. (I never learned what his lower limit was. It is well possible that he still had room to negotiate, but that does not matter. What matters is that we both were satisfied with the outcome.)

I asked him, "Can I trust you to recommend these terms to your board?" He answered, "I will."

We had a deal. The 30 minutes spent on finding the right words possibly saved us over €100 million. Time well spent. Words have power.

Getting to 95 Percent

We publicly announced our takeover offer on April 15, 2015: a €15.6 billion deal that would create a powerful rival to Ericsson and Huawei. The reception was quite promising. It was necessary to elicit positive remarks from key French ministers, and we did. Even though Emmanuel Macron, then France's economy minister, had been a tough negotiator, driving to protect French interests, in the end he declared, "It's a good move for Alcatel-Lucent because it is a move for the future."[7]

Our main concern was that some of the big ALu shareholders might oppose the deal—most likely not because they believed that the deal shouldn't be done, but rather because they hoped to force us to pay a higher price. A fusion of two companies can happen only after one of the companies completely owns the other one. If we could accumulate 95 percent of the shares, we could force the remaining shareholders to sell in what's called a squeeze-out.

This meant that anyone owning more than 5 percent could hold us hostage.

One of the best ways to destroy value in a deal like this is to be trapped in the limbo between having passed the last opportunity to back away and not yet reaching the point of being able to operate the companies as one. For us, that meant getting stuck between owning over 50 percent of Alcatel-Lucent, which we had agreed would be the closing condition, and owning below 95 percent, when we would have a quick path to take full control.

At worst, this could be a catastrophe. Imagine many months, or even one to two years, of the companies operating independently, competing against each other in the market, with everyone knowing that as soon as full ownership was reached, the companies would merge, and lots of people would be out of a job (we would not need two CFOs, or two customer account teams for Vodafone UK, or two headquarters, etc.), and lots of overlapping products would be killed. How do people react to that uncertainty? Many of the best people would look for a job elsewhere to get rid of the uncertainty. How do competitors react? They would go to our most important customers that used Alcatel equipment and tell them: "Nokia will discontinue the equipment you depend on. Why not speed up the inevitable and let us swap your equipment out?"

The pain would not stop there. Our own sales teams would be stalking the same customers and competing against each other. No matter what we said, there would be a strong incentive for the Nokia salesperson to whisper to the customer: "Don't buy the Alcatel solution. I know it will be discontinued after we take control." And the Alcatel salespeople would be advising the same customer: "Don't choose the Nokia solution. I heard from 'upstairs' that it will be discontinued after the merger finishes, and it will be our solution that will continue." It would be pretty difficult to meld these sales teams together when we finally could do it.

This limbo is an enticing opportunity for certain types of investors who buy into companies that are in the process of being acquired and then essentially blackmail the bidder into paying a higher price for their shares. They say, "If you don't pay me a premium, I won't sell my shares, which means you won't achieve the squeeze-out level and can't start restructuring."

Odey Asset Management, a London-based hedge fund that had bought more than 5 percent of Alcatel stock, opposed the deal soon after it was announced.[8] In June, the world-famous activist fund Elliott amassed a 1.3 percent stake and also came out against the transaction.[9]

I felt strongly that we couldn't wait for 95 percent to run the two companies as one. We had to do it as soon as we were over 50 percent, even if it was by just one share.

Early in the fall of 2015, I sat down for an update from Maria Varsellona, our CLO, and her team. I was actively coordinating with

Philippe Camus, just as Rajeev was coordinating with the COO of Alcatel-Lucent, to ensure that we completed the deal with the least possible amount of damage. (Michel Combes had resigned on short notice that summer, much to everyone's surprise.)

I asked Maria a simple question: "When is Day One?" (This referred to the first day of operations for the combined company.) She told me that it was planned to be the day when we reach 100 percent of ownership. Knowing all the value that could be destroyed, I responded that we just couldn't wait for 100 percent. We simply had to figure out a way to have Day One when we reached at least 50 percent of ALu shares or, alternatively, 66 percent of ownership. I believed the ALu team understood the risk of value destruction and would be ready to support us if we proposed a solution.

This was one of those moments when tradition needed to take a backseat and we needed to be innovative. Once again, I saw how the right challenge made people achieve something they might have thought impossible just a short while earlier.

Thanks to Maria and her talented team, we created a complicated legal structure that protected minority shareholders while enabling us to move ahead with the integration before becoming the sole owner of ALu. As a result, we could begin restructuring and integration efforts immediately after the first tender offer closed at above 50 percent of ownership. It was unorthodox and risky, but it was legal—and it was exactly what we needed.

(Once again, I was blessed to be working with a stellar CLO, just as I was during the Microsoft negotiations. And an exceptional CLO practically guarantees an excellent legal team. Our legal team has been second to none throughout my chairmanship.)

This could not have worked without active participation from the ALu team. They fully understood that this approach was by far the best for all shareholders. But it still required admirable courage from them to support this approach. They had to agree to give up control of the company while it was still an independent entity and turn that control over to the selected joint leadership of the future merged entity.

Jean-Cyril Spinetta chaired a committee of independent ALu board members formed to protect the minority shareholders' rights in whatever intercompany transactions we might do. For instance, as we decided to terminate certain ALu products in favor of competing Nokia products, Nokia compensated ALu financially for this. The committee approved each such transaction and verified that the compensation was fair.

Had the ALu management and board decided to play difficult or just play safe, this would not have worked. I have great respect for them because of what they did. This was also testament to the trust we had been able to establish between the two parties.

At the Nokia Extraordinary General Meeting on December 2, 2015, the resolution to approve the Alcatel-Lucent acquisition went through without a hitch. It was clear to our shareholders that this was a good deal.

Day One

Day One occurred on January 3, 2016. Our unorthodox arrangement enabled us to reach Day One a full year earlier than if we had to wait to reach 100 percent of ownership. (We achieved the necessary 95 percent on November 2, 2016.[10]) We did it without paying anything extra to the hedge funds or activists. And by avoiding a long waiting period, we protected shareholder value.

By the time of Day One, we had already appointed roughly 10,000 leaders in the nonexistent virtual combined company. We chose them based on merit and only counted afterward how many had come from Nokia and how many from Alcatel-Lucent. As it turned out, the breakdown was 52 percent from Alcatel-Lucent and 48 percent from Nokia.

We immediately started talking with the largest customers of both companies, and they responded extremely well to the scope of our new end-to-end portfolio. Just as we hoped, over the next few months, we started to see a clear increase in our credibility with major CSPs, which understand that network performance is based not just on the parts of the networks but also on how those parts work together. Our status opened doors to new customers that increasingly need the kind of mission-critical networking capability we provide.

We began to deliberately construct a common culture. The work we had begun in melding NSN and Nokia Technologies into a unified company gave us a foundation to build on and a pattern to follow. This time the task was much more complicated: Thanks to acquisitions by both Nokia and Alcatel-Lucent, we were a Finnish-German-Japanese-Chinese-American-French-Canadian miscellany with employees in a hundred other countries as well. We needed to transform a crazy kaleidoscope into a coherent picture. This is part of our ongoing reinvention.

"We Are a Company Reborn"

The Nokia that ended 2016 was a fundamentally different company from the Nokia of just one year earlier, let alone the Nokia of 2012. When I became Nokia's chairman, we were a struggling mobile phone maker. We had started 2016 primarily as a mobile networks and patent licensing company. We ended the year as one of the top three companies in the global telecom infrastructure industry, with a complete portfolio spanning mobile, fixed, cable, routing, optical, stand-alone software, services, digital health, and virtual reality, as well as licensing activities covering patents, brand technology, and more.

Soon after the Alcatel-Lucent deal closed, I was speaking at a panel in China with the famous Chinese entrepreneurs Jack Ma, Pony Ma, and Robin Li. I told the audience that among the present companies of Alibaba, Tencent, and Baidu, Nokia was at once the oldest and the youngest—the oldest because Nokia had recently celebrated its 150th anniversary and the youngest because, as a result of our reinvention, we were a newer start-up than they were.

If we can get our employees to feel that we are a combination of old and young, of experience and youthful courage, we may have a unique advantage.

Today, we are an almost entirely new Nokia. Out of some 100,000 employees, fewer than 1 percent held a Nokia badge in 2012.

We transformed ourselves from an enterprise on the edge of extinction to a company with the skills and strengths to fulfill our promise: to create the technology to connect the world. This transformation created tremendous value to our shareholders. Our enterprise value grew more than 20 times from 2012 to 2016. We have also paid a multiple of that enterprise value in dividends over the last few years.

We are a company reborn. Proud of it and humble because of it.

CREATING YOUR OWN LUCK

. . . .

Over the course of a year, we each have 365 daily
opportunities to boost the possibility of a positive scenario.

. . . .

WHEN GOLF LEGEND Jack Nicklaus hit his eighteenth hole-in-one,
the story goes, a fan congratulated him on his good luck. Nicklaus
thanked him and replied, "The more I practice, the luckier I get."

That saying applies to all of us. Like Nicklaus, we at Nokia prac-
ticed day and night for many months and years. We were immensely
lucky in our transformation, but it's hard for me today to differentiate
between what was real luck and how much we influenced that luck
because of smart people exercising paranoid optimism.

In 2012, we were locked into a Windows Phone partnership, where
only a breakthrough of the ecosystem would have made us successful.
Anything else seemed to lead to the end of Nokia.

Once it became clear that Windows Phone would not make it against
the early mover advantage of Apple and Google, we had to come up
with a way to change the game we were playing. With Microsoft's help,
we managed to detach ourselves from the old game and with assistance
from Siemens, we found our new game. Acquiring Alcatel-Lucent was
necessary to equip us to be a strong player in our new business.

The most challenging part of the exercise was managing the multitude of simultaneous dimensions and the number of alternative

scenarios in each dimension. The uncertainty created by all those moving wheels within wheels, the worry about their own future felt by the tens of thousands of employees and all the negativity multiplied by the media and stock markets made the human element the critical aspect of our story.

The key requirement that enabled us to navigate through the journey was the ability to create trust. I cannot sufficiently emphasize how critical it is to view all actions through the analytical lens of trust: What impact does each action have on trust and how do we implement those actions in a way designed to have the optimal impact on trust, both internally in the company as well as externally with our partners and customers.

I believe you can create your own luck. By doing the right things, you definitely shift the probability curve in your favor. Identify your alternative futures and exercise scenario-based thinking. Think about the everyday actions you can take to increase the likelihood that things will tilt your way and decrease the probability of a scenario in which there's a negative outcome. Those add up: Over the course of a year, we each have 365 daily opportunities to boost the possibility of a positive scenario.

What's an example? There were many during Nokia's transformation, but let me give you one from 2017.

I am both paranoid and extremely optimistic about machine learning and artificial intelligence and their ability to disrupt—well, almost everything. In early 2017, I was struck by how fast machine learning was developing, and I was concerned that Nokia had been a little slow on the uptake. What could I do to help the company along?

I was fortunate to leverage my position as chairman of Nokia to worm my way onto the calendars of several of the world's top AI researchers. But I only understood bits and pieces of what they told me, and I became frustrated when some of my discussion partners seemed more intent on showing off their own advanced knowledge of the topic than truly wanting me to understand "how it really works."

I spent some time complaining. Then I remembered that for an entrepreneur, a problem is always an opportunity. Don't wait for other people to do what you could do yourself—and *do* act in such a way that you not only solve your problem but solve it for other people as well.

As a longtime CEO and chairman, I had fallen into the trap of being defined by my role: I had grown accustomed to having things explained to me. Instead of trying to figure out the nuts and bolts of a seemingly complicated technology, I had gotten used to someone else doing the hard work.

Why not study machine learning myself and then explain what I learned to others who are struggling with the same questions? After a quick internet search, I found and signed up for a series of online courses. I started programming again after a break of almost 20 years.

After three months and six university courses, I had covered the simple algorithms as well as many of the more complicated architectures, doing one project with each to gain a hands-on understanding. Then I dug in to figure out the most difficult part: how to explain the essence of machine learning in the simplest possible way, but without dumbing it down. My target audience was CEOs, politicians, academics in other fields, and, frankly, any decision maker.

I created a presentation that I wish someone had given me. Then I posted a blog about my journey (https://blog.networks.nokia.com/innovation/2017/11/09/study-ai-machine-learning/), which includes a presentation I gave at Nokia explaining what I learned. (It's also on YouTube, where it's been watched by over 42,000 people so far.)

Thousands of our employees have seen the video. Many of our R&D folks have come to me to confess how they were a bit ashamed that their chairman was coding machine-learning systems whereas they had not even started. But, they said, now they were devoting their own free time to studying machine learning and were working on the first Nokia projects as well. Music to my ears.

With that work, the probability curve shifted in Nokia's favor.

I could have just supported the Nokia CEO and management team in talking about the need to kick-start a fast catch-up. The fact that I took the threats and promises of machine learning seriously enough to go back to school was much more powerful. The idea that the chairman of a global company could start programming to learn a critical piece of technology was novel enough to get people's attention and encourage them to act on their own. My actions made it easier for our management to take Nokia to the leading edge in our industry in utilizing machine learning and AI.

We do a regular cultural survey in Nokia. Some of our smart HR people added a new question to it recently. They asked, "Do you feel you truly understand how machine learning works?" The fact that roughly half of our employees answered yes is a pretty good start to giving everyone that understanding.

Much more interesting, though, was to compare the results for the other questions between the half of our employees who felt they truly do understand and the half who felt they don't.

There was a huge difference between the two groups. Those who felt they truly understand machine learning were significantly more positive about our culture in all areas. For instance, one of the more challenging areas for large companies is entrepreneurial behavior. This group of employees gave Nokia more than 40 percent higher grades in entrepreneurial behavior than the other half. Perhaps our drive to bring everyone along to the world of machine learning is paying unexpected dividends.

The attention to machine learning hasn't been limited to Nokia. I have since given this presentation to, among numerous others, the full Finnish cabinet, many of the commissioners of the European Union, a group of United Nations ambassadors, and 200 teenage schoolgirls to get them interested in science. Many companies have made watching my introduction to machine learning mandatory for their management.

All of this helps Nokia's brand as a leading-edge technology company. Introducing people to AI is a start. But I hope I have done something more.

You don't often get the chance to reinvent a 150-year-old company. By doing my best to set an example for others about entrepreneurial leadership—by modeling personal accountability, focusing on the fundamentals, refusing to be trapped by convention, and, above all, being a paranoid optimist—I'm trying to maximize the odds that Nokia will continue to be lucky for a long time to come.

A good book should have a proper ending. But Nokia's story goes on and there is no end. There are only new beginnings. Someday, I'd like to read a story about Nokia's next transformation—but preferably not too soon. We have good plans for the foreseeable future. And if they don't work out, we always have a Plan B. And Plan C.

I hope this book helps you find the paranoid optimist in you.

NOTES

Introduction

1. http://www.wired.co.uk/article/finland-and-nokia.
2. http://www1.american.edu/TED/nokia.htm#r24.
3. http://www.corporate-eye.com/main/interbrand-announces-100-best
   -global-brands-2008/.
4. https://www.cnet.com/news/farewell-nokia-the-rise-and-fall-of-a
   -mobile-pioneer/.
5. http://content.time.com/time/specials/packages/article/0,28804,1993621
   _1994046_1993982,00.html.
6. Ibid.
7. http://www.managementtoday.co.uk/finnish-miracle/article/555753.
8. https://www.amazon.co.uk/Business-Nokia-Way-Secrets-Fastest/dp/
   1841121045.
9. https://www.statista.com/statistics/263438/
   market-share-held-by-nokia-smartphones-since-2007/.
10. https://finance.yahoo.com/quote/NOK/history?period1=1210392000&
    period2=1213070400&interval=1d&filter=history&frequency=1d.
11. "Nokia's Next Chapter," *McKinsey Quarterly*, December 2016;
    http://www.businessinsider.com/nokia-bankrupt-2012-4.

Chapter 2

1. http://www.eweek.com/mobile/nine-ways-the-apple-iphone-redefined
   -the-smartphone-in-2007.
2. "According to figures from analyst firm Gartner, Nokia's smartphone
   market share in 2007 was a dominant 49.4 percent," http://
   www.bbc.com/news/technology-23947212; Statista calculates
   2007: 50.9 percent, https://www.statista.com/statistics/263438/
   market-share-held-by-nokia-smartphones-since-2007/.
3. https://en.wikipedia.org/wiki/List_of_Nokia_products.
4. Cited in *The Decline and Fall of Nokia* by David J. Cord, Schildts &
   Söderströms, 2014, p. 88, http://archive.fortune.com/2007/10/04/
   technology/nokia_N95.fortune/index.htm.

5. http://www.knowyourmobile.com/nokia/2792/nokia-takes-40-share -world-mobile-market.

6. https://arstechnica.com/gadgets/2009/11/apple-grabs-17-of-smartphone -market-in-latest-quarter/?comments=1.

7. https://www.statista.com/statistics/216459/global-market-share-of -apple-iphone/.

8. https://www.wired.com/2012/06/mark-zuckerberg-is-worth-more-than -nokia/.

9. Yves Doz and Keeley Wilson, *Ringtone*, Oxford University Press, 2018, pp. 73–74.

10. https://www.macworld.com/article/1133988/smartphones/iphone 3gfaqs.html.

11. https://newsroom.t-mobile.com/news-and-blogs/t-mobile-unveils-the -t-mobile-g1-the-first-phone-powered-by-android.htm.

12. http://www.nytimes.com/2008/07/26/business/worldbusiness/26internet .html?mcubz=1.

13. http://en.c114.com.cn/w/?583-370327.

14. https://www.quora.com/Why-are-Audis-so-popular-in-China.

15. https://www.engadget.com/2008/12/04/iphone-triples-market-share-in -q3-2008/ ; http://macdailynews.com/2008/12/04/gartner_apple _overtakes_microsoft_as_worlds_3_smartphone_os_vendor/.

Chapter 3

1. http://www.zdnet.com/article/nokia-5800-the-quintessential-iphone -killer/.

2. Risto Siilasmaa interview with Olli-Pekka Kallasvuo.

3. https://www.statista.com/statistics/216459/global-market-share-of -apple-iphone/.

4. http://www.nytimes.com/2009/12/13/business/13nokia.html.

5. https://www.macworld.com/article/1141143/iphone3gs_faq.html.

Chapter 4

1. https://www.cnet.com/au/products/nokia-n900/review/.

2. https://www.cnet.com/products/nokia-n97/review/.

3. Ibid.

4. http://www.nytimes.com/2009/12/13/business/13nokia.html.

5. https://www.cnet.com/news/sony-ericsson-details-its-first-android -phone/.

6. https://www.eetimes.com/document.asp?doc_id=1172568.

Chapter 5

1. https://www.engadget.com/2010/02/15/
MeeGo-nokia-and-intel-merge-maemo-and-moblin/.
2. http://www.nytimes.com/2009/12/13/business/13nokia.html.
3. https://www.wired.com/2010/02/mwc-2010-the-year-of-the-android/.
4. Ibid.
5. Ibid.
6. http://www.macrotrends.net/stocks/charts/NOK/prices/nokia-cp-adr-a
-stock-price-history.
7. http://www.macrotrends.net/stocks/charts/NOK/market-cap/nokia-cp
-adr-a-market-cap-history.
8. http://www.macrotrends.net/stocks/charts/AAPL/market-cap/apple
-inc-market-cap-history.
9. https://www.crunchbase.com/person/kai-istm#section-overview.
10. The emergence of shared fear and its influence on communication between Nokia's middle and top management during 2006–2010 is described in detail in T.O. Vuori and Q.N. Huy, "Distributed Attention and Shared Emotions in the Innovation Process: How Nokia Lost the Smartphone Battle." *Administrative Science Quarterly*, 2016, Volume 61, Number 1, pp. 9–52. See also INSEAD Knowledge summaries: https://knowledge.insead.edu/strategy/what-could-have-saved-nokia-and-what-can-other-companies-learn-3220 and https://knowledge.insead.edu/strategy/who-killed-nokia-nokia-did-4268
11. https://www.wsj.com/articles/SB10001424052748703720504575377750449338786.

Chapter 6

1. https://www.nokia.com/sites/default/files/files/request-nokia-in-2010
-pdf.pdf.
2. http://www.bloomberg.com/news/articles/2011-06-02/stephen-elops
-nokia-adventure.
3. https://www.nokia.com/sites/default/files/files/request-nokia-in-2010
-pdf.pdf.
4. https://www.nokia.com/sites/default/files/files/request-nokia-in-2011
-pdf_0.pdf.
5. http://www.businessinsider.com/android-iphone-market-share-2010-8;
https://www.gartner.com/newsroom/id/1421013.
6. Ibid.

7. Ibid.

8. https://www.cnet.com/news/nokia-n8-review-hands-on-with
-symbian-3/.

9. https://www.bloomberg.com/news/articles/2011-06-02/stephen-elops
-nokia-adventure.

10. http://talk.maemo.org/showthread.php?t=67371.

11. http://www.bloomberg.com/news/articles/2011-06-02/stephen-elops
-nokia-adventure.

12. https://www.cnet.com/uk/products/nokia-n8/review/.

13. https://www.statista.com/statistics/268251/number-of-apps-in-the
-itunes-app-store-since-2008/; https://www.statista.com/statistics/
266210/number-of-available-applications-in-the-google-play-store/.

14. https://www.nokia.com/sites/default/files/nokia-sustainability-report
-2011-overview-pdf.pdf.

15. https://www.androidpit.com/It-s-getting-serious-Android-market
-hits-200-000-apps-mark.

16. https://www.bloomberg.com/news/articles/2011-06-02/stephen-elops
-nokia-adventure.

17. Ibid.; https://www.engadget.com/2011/02/08/nokia-ceo-stephen-elop
-rallies-troops-in-brutally-honest-burnin/.

Chapter 7

1. https://www.androidauthority.com/rise-androids-biggest-oem
-samsung-story-284808/.

Chapter 8

1. https://blogs.wsj.com/tech-europe/2011/02/09/full-text-nokia-ceo
-stephen-elops-burning-platform-memo/.

2. Risto Siilasmaa interview with Stephen Elop.

3. http://esr.ibiblio.org/?p=2921.

4. https://www.engadget.com/2011/02/08/nokia-ceo-stephen-elop-rallies
-troops-in-brutally-honest-burnin/.

5. http://www.bbc.co.uk/blogs/thereporters/rorycellanjones/2011/02/
nokias_burning_platform.html.

6. http://money.cnn.com/2011/02/11/technology/nokia_microsoft/.

7. https://www.youtube.com/watch?v=UY8lDQu4Ins.

8. http://money.cnn.com/2011/02/11/technology/nokia_microsoft/.

9. http://www.businessinsider.com/nokia-ceo-elop-denies-being-trojan -horse-for-microsoft-2011-2.

10. http://money.cnn.com/2011/02/11/technology/nokia_microsoft/.

11. Ibid.

12. http://www.silicon.co.uk/workspace/nokia-and-microsoft-two-turkeys -dont-make-an-eagle-20603?inf_by=5a299deb681db86e728b493a.

13. https://www.cbsnews.com/news/nokia-layoffs-the-result-of-weak -marketing/.

14. http://www.innoconnections.com/news/2011/nokia-started-negotiations -on-laying-off-1400-people-in-finland.html.

15. http://www.telegraph.co.uk/finance/newsbysector/mediatechnology andtelecoms/telecoms/8850842/Has-Finlands-Nokia-town-connected -with-the-modern-world.html.

16. https://www.wsj.com/articles/SB10001424052702304563104576359743926525676.

17. http://www.hbs.edu/faculty/Pages/item.aspx?num=48539.

18. http://allthingsd.com/20110406/htc-climbs-past-nokia-in-market-cap/.

19. https://www.wired.com/2011/01/android-os-leading-smartphone/.

20. https://www.theguardian.com/technology/2011/oct/26/nokia -launches-windows-phones-to-combat-apple-and-android.

21. https://www.reuters.com/article/us-nokia/nokia-proclaims-new-dawn -with-windows-phones-idUSTRE79P20T20111026.

22. Carolina Milanese, Gartner, quoted in https://www.theguardian.com/ technology/2011/oct/26/nokia-lumia-800-710.

23. https://techcrunch.com/2012/12/31/nokias-long-drawn-out-decline/.

24. Ibid.; https://www.nokia.com/sites/default/files/files/request-nokia-in -2011-pdf_0.pdf.

Chapter 9

1. http://www.zdnet.com/article/ best-phone-of-ces-2012-nokia-lumia-900/.

2. Ibid.

3. http://money.cnn.com/2012/04/27/technology/nokia-samsung/index .htm.

4. http://money.cnn.com/2012/04/11/technology/nokia/index.htm.

5. https://www.theguardian.com/technology/2012/apr/11/nokia-shares -slump-profit-warning.

6. http://www.businessinsider.com/apple-google-market-cap-chart-2013 -10.

7. http://money.cnn.com/2012/04/11/technology/nokia/index.htm; https://finance.yahoo.com/quote/NOK/history?period1=1325653200 &period2=1338523200&interval=1d&filter=history&frequency=1d.

8. https://www.reuters.com/article/us-nokia/nokia-suffers-second-cut-to -junk-as-sp-downgrades-idUSBRE83Q0W620120428.

9. https://www.tradingfloor.com/posts/analysts-revisions-nokia-punished -sandisk-trashed-amd-praised-1042215508.

10. https://finance.yahoo.com/quote/NOK/history?period1=1325653200 &period2=1338523200&interval=1d&filter=history&frequency=1d.

11. https://gigaom.com/2012/01/19/why-kodaks-bankruptcy-should -scare-nokia/.

12. http://www.businessinsider.com/nokia-bankrupt-2012-4.

13. https://www.theguardian.com/technology/2011/may/31/nokia-shares -dive-profit-warning.

14. https://www.wsj.com/articles/SB1000142405270230382220457746577 1376539532.

15. https://finance.yahoo.com/quote/NOK/history?period1=1325653200 &period2=1340078400&interval=1d&filter=history&frequency=1d.

16. https://www.wsj.com/articles/SB1000142405270230382220457746577 1376539532?mg=prod/accounts-wsj.

Chapter 11

1. https://www.microsoft.com/investor/reports/ar11/shareholder_letter/ index.html.

2. https://finance.yahoo.com/quote/NOK/history?period1=1339732800 &period2=1356930000&interval=1d&filter=history&frequency=1d.

3. https://techcrunch.com/2012/07/19/nokia-reports-q2-2012-results-e7 -5-billion-in-net-sales-negative-eps-of-0-09/.

4. http://www.techradar.com/news/software/operating-systems/windows -8-release-date-and-price-all-the-latest-details-1088425.

5. https://www.engadget.com/2012/11/02/nokia-lumia-920-review/.

6. http://www.independent.co.uk/life-style/gadgets-and-tech/features/ nokia-lumia-920-review-its-big-its-beautiful-and-probably-the-most -advanced-smartphone-on-the-market-8390384.html.

7. http://www.nytimes.com/2012/11/22/technology/personaltech/nokia -lumia-920-and-htc-windows-phone-8x-are-great-and-yet.html.

8. http://www.nytimes.com/2013/01/11/technology/nokia-sees-results -from-new-smartphone-line.html.

9. https://finance.yahoo.com/quote/NOK/history?period1=1355547600
&period2=1359608400&interval=1d&filter=history&frequency=1d.
10. https://gigaom.com/2013/01/10/youd-better-sit-down-nokia-is
-actually-doing-reasonably-well/.
11. http://www.nytimes.com/2013/01/11/technology/nokia-sees-results
-from-new-smartphone-line.html.

Chapter 12

1. https://www.cnet.com/news/
nokia-on-the-edge-inside-an-icons-fight-for-survival/.
2. https://www.statista.com/statistics/278305/daily-activations-of-android
-devices/.
3. http://www.techradar.com/news/computing/pc/big-brash-and-bullish
-how-ballmer-s-personality-kept-him-at-microsoft-s-helm-1176352.
4. http://fortune.com/2014/05/31/steve-ballmer-crazy/.
5. http://www.businessinsider.com/steve-ballmer-used-to-be-painfully
-shy-2014-3.
6. https://www.youtube.com/watch?v=XMrhoOHNOrI.
7. https://www.cnbc.com/2016/03/28/microsoft-yahoo-talks-now-versus
-last-time-around.html.

Chapter 13

1. https://www.theguardian.com/technology/2013/jul/14/nokia-elop
-lumia-windows-phone.
2. https://www.theverge.com/2013/7/11/4514064/nokia-lumia-1020
-hands-on.
3. https://www.cnet.com/products/nokia-lumia-1020/preview/.
4. T.O. Vuori and Q.N. Huy, "Board Influence on Top Managers' Strategy
Formulation Process: Cognitive and Emotional Dynamics," *Academy
of Management Annual Meeting*, 2017. See also T.O. Vuori and Q.N.
Huy, "Shaping Top Managers' Moods: Board Emotion Regulation in
the Strategy Formulation Process," *Academy of Management Annual
Meeting*, 2018.
5. Ibid.
6. Ibid.

Chapter 14

1. http://www.cellular-news.com/story/59313.php.

2. https://www.wsj.com/articles/SB10001424127887324436104578579173664529206.

3. http://community.comsoc.org/blogs/alanweissberger/infonetics-mobile-infrastructure-market-declines-while-mobile-m2m-spending-was.

4. http://www.wsj.com/articles/SB10001424127887324436104578579173664529206.

5. https://finance.yahoo.com/quote/NOK/history?period1=1372132800&period2=1373428800&interval=1d&filter=history&frequency=1d.

6. https://www.forbes.com/sites/rexsantus/2015/08/03/nokia-sells-here-to-german-automakers-for-3-billion/#6b45f6b66c47.

7. http://www.cnet.com/news/farewell-nokia-the-rise-and-fall-of-a-mobile-pioneer.

8. http://www.newyorker.com/business/currency/where-nokia-went-wrong.

9. http://www.nycareaweather.com/2013/07/july-19-2013-cooler-weather-returns-sunday/.

Chapter 15

1. https://www.pcworld.com/article/2455106/microsoft-lays-off-18000-including-a-third-of-nokia-in-largest-ever-job-cuts.html.

2. https://www.theverge.com/2013/7/18/4534124/nokia-q2-2013-financial-report.

3. https://news.microsoft.com/2013/08/23/microsoft-ceo-steve-ballmer-to-retire-within-12-months/.

4. https://www.youtube.com/watch?v=FU-a9uztdNw.

5. Nokia ADR closed on August 28 at $3.90 and on September 5 at $5.49, http://www.percent-change.com/index.php?y1=390&y2=549.

6. https://www.wsj.com/articles/nokias-stephen-elop-to-receive-about-255-million-1379601017.

7. http://www.bbc.com/news/business-31044810.

8. https://www.theregister.co.uk/2013/09/19/elop_exit_compensation_package/.

9. https://www.ft.com/content/f09bb478-237f-11e3-98a1-00144feab7de.

10. https://www.theguardian.com/technology/2013/sep/24/nokia-payoff-stephen-elop-microsoft; https://www.ft.com/content/f87caf30-250f-11e3-9b22-00144feab7de.

11. https://www.ft.com/content/f09bb478-237f-11e3-98a1-00144feab7de.

12. https://www.lowyat.net/2013/13430/could-the-nokia-board-have-been-behind-the-eventual-sale-of-nokias-devices-division-all-along/.

13. Ibid.
14. https://www.theguardian.com/business/2013/nov/19/nokia
    -shareholders-approve-sale-microsoft.
15. https://www.nokia.com/sites/default/files/files/minutes-egm-2013.pdf.

Chapter 16

1. "Nokia: Rebirth of the Phoenix," IESE *Insight*, January 2017, http://
   www.ieseinsight.com/fichaMaterial.aspx?pk=135634&idi=2&origen
   =3&idioma=2.
2. https://www.theguardian.com/technology/2012/may/14/nokia-falls
   -back-on-patents.
3. https://www.wired.com/2013/05/internet-of-things-2/.
4. https://www.nature.com/scientificamerican/journal/v311/n5/full/
   scientificamerican1114-60.html.
5. http://fortune.com/2013/10/22/businesses-must-embrace-the
   -programmable-world-or-die/.
6. https://www.strategos.com/innovation-principles-part-1/;
   https://hbr.org/2013/05/what-a-good-moonshot-is-really-2.

Chapter 17

1. https://www.cnet.com/news/
   south-korea-regulators-finally-ok-microsoft-nokia-deal/.
2. https://www.nokia.com/sites/default/files/files/nokia_uk_ar14_full_1
   .pdf.
3. Ibid.
4. https://www.hmdglobal.com/press/2017-01-08-nokia-6/.
5. http://nokiamob.net/2018/02/12/idc-hmd-shipped-59-2-million-feature
   -phones-in-2017/.

Chapter 18

1. https://www.reuters.com/article/us-nokia-alcatellucent/exclusive-nokia
   -weighs-alcatel-tie-up-after-microsoft-deal-sources-idUSBRE98O11G2
   0130926?feedType=RSS&feedName=technologyNews.
2. https://www.theguardian.com/world/2014/jan/06/french-workers
   -bosses-hostage-goodyear-amiens.
3. https://www.wsj.com/articles/alcatel-lucent-starts-sending-the-right
   -signals-heard-on-the-street-1414691875.

4. https://www.statista.com/statistics/199359/market-share-of-wireless -carriers-in-the-us-by-subscriptions/.

5. Ibid.

6. https://globenewswire.com/news-release/2017/08/09/1082529/0/en/ Nokia-Bell-Labs-leads-project-to-develop-next-generation-5G -platform-as-a-service-for-5G-era.html.

7. https://www.ft.com/content/af18dae8-e332-11e4-9a82-00144feab7de.

8. https://www.ft.com/content/93c0fbca-edb6-11e4-90d2-00144feab7de.

9. https://www.ft.com/content/7608e1a6-1b51-11e5-8201-cbdb03d71480.

10. https://www.nokia.com/en_int/news/releases/2016/11/02/nokia -finalizes-its-acquisition-of-alcatel-lucent-ready-to-seize-global -connectivity-opportunities.

INDEX

ABOUT THE AUTHORS

Risto Siilasmaa is the Chairman of the Board of Directors of Nokia Corporation. He joined the Nokia Board in 2008 and became Chairman of the Board in May 2012. As Chairman, he led Nokia through its transformation from an ailing devices company to a successful network infrastructure player through the divestiture of the Nokia device business to Microsoft and the acquisition of Nokia Siemens Networks and Alcatel-Lucent.

Siilasmaa is the founder of F-Secure Corporation, a Finnish cybersecurity company, and served as the President and CEO of the company between 1988 and 2006. Since then he has held the position of Chairman of the Board of Directors. Siilasmaa is a member of the Board of Directors of Futurice Corporation, Vice Chairman of the Board of Directors of the Confederation of Finnish Industries, Chairman of the Technology Industries of Finland, and a member of the European Round Table of Industrialists (ERT). He is also a member of Tsinghua SEM Advisory Board, International Business Leaders Advisory Council for the Mayor of Beijing, and High-Level Advisory Council of the World Internet Conference (Wuzhen Summit). In addition, Siilasmaa is the Finnish Chairman of the recently established China-Finland Committee for Innovative Business Cooperation.

Siilasmaa has received several awards including Nordic Chairman of the Year 2009, the Most Influential IT Leader 2007, the Leader of the Decade 2003, and Innovation Luminary Award 2015 granted by EU Open Innovation Strategy and Policy Group.

Siilasmaa holds a Master of Science degree from the Helsinki University of Technology, and he was awarded Honorary Doctorate in Technology by Aalto University schools of technology in 2018.

Catherine Fredman has collaborated on several bestselling business books, including *Only the Paranoid Survive* and *Swimming Across* with Andrew Grove and *Direct from Dell* with Michael Dell.